LEADING TEAMS
Mastering the New Role

John H. Zenger

Ed Musselwhite

Kathleen Hurson

Craig Perrin

Professional Publishing

Burr Ridge, Illinois

New York, New York

To our parents and spouses, who taught us the meaning of teamwork.

Editor-in-chief: Jeffrey A. Krames
Project editor: Lynne Basler
Production manager: Ann Cassady
Jacket designer: Image House
Designer: Heidi Baughman
Art coordinator: Heather Burbridge
Compositor: Precision Typographers
Typeface: 11/14 Palatino
Printer: Book Press, Inc.

Library of Congress Cataloging-in-Publication Data

Leading teams : mastering the new role / John H. Zenger — [et al.].
    p.   cm.
   ISBN 1-55623-894-0
   1. Work groups. 2. Leadership. 3. Work groups—North America-
-Case studies. 4. Leadership—Case studies. I. Zenger, John H.
HD66.L435 1994
658.4'036—dc20   93–12652

Printed in the United States of America
       4 5 6 7 8 9 0 BP 0 9 8 7 6 5

About the Authors

Dr. John H. Zenger has built a distinguished career as an executive, consultant, entrepreneur, and educator. After completing a doctorate in business management, he taught at the USC and Stanford Graduate Schools of Business. He was vice president of human resources at Syntex Corp. before cofounding Zenger-Miller, Inc., the internationally known training and strategic consulting firm that now serves over 3,000 organizational clients worldwide. As Zenger-Miller's CEO through 14 years of rapid growth, Jack's contributions to the field of management research, education, and training have made him one of the foremost experts on organizational effectiveness. He is now the corporate executive responsible for the three training/consulting companies owned by The Times Mirror Company—Learning International, Kaset International, and Zenger-Miller, Inc.

Ed Musselwhite is president and CEO of Zenger-Miller and is a respected speaker, researcher, and consultant on the issues of team effectiveness, leadership, and organizational change. He began his career as a highly successful account executive and marketing manager with IBM. He later became cofounder and executive vice president of DELTAK, Inc., a pioneering, high-growth training company in the data processing industry that became a prized acquisition of a major international publisher. Ed joined Zenger-Miller in 1982 and was responsible for building its noted research and product development capabilities. With his record of business success, Ed has consulted for over 20 years with companies in industries ranging from manufacturing to financial services to help improve their team effectiveness and management results. He is a trusted advisor to executives and managers dealing with organizational change and has coauthored numerous publications, including the best-selling "how-to" book, *Self-Directed Work Teams:*

The New American Challenge. Ed is a graduate of Northwestern University School of Business.

Kathleen Hurson's human resources career includes responsibilities as the employee relations manager and corporate training manager for Raychem Corporation, a Fortune 500 manufacturer. Joining Zenger-Miller in 1984 as a product developer, she is now vice president of research and product development and is a member of the company's executive committee. Kathleen and her Zenger-Miller staff have researched and produced training programs that serve organizational clients in more than 25 countries worldwide. She is an accomplished team leader in her own right and has contributed significantly to the research and understanding of that pivotal role in today's organizations. Kathleen is a graduate of the University of Maryland and did her graduate studies in organizational development at Pepperdine University.

Craig Perrin is a senior project manager with Zenger-Miller and has been a major contributor to the research and development of some of the company's most successful training systems. In his R&D role, Craig works either as a team leader or as a team member as the project requires, thus giving him the first-hand experience, as well as the research base, to speak insightfully on the topic of team effectiveness. Craig is an accomplished journalist, writer, instructional designer, video producer, and college instructor. At one time he was the curator of exhibits for the California Historical Society. Craig holds a B.A. and M.A. in humanities from San Francisco State University.

Zenger-Miller, Inc., with offices worldwide, is headquartered in San Jose, California.

Preface

WHAT YOU WILL GET FROM THIS BOOK

Are you thinking about forming teams? Or wondering how to help existing teams be more effective? If so, this book can help you understand how the quality of team leadership can make or break a team. Such vital information has been too rarely available in the past, and the lack of it has cost organizations dearly in time, money, and lost opportunities.

Are you leading a team now? Or thinking about leading a team? If so, this book is focused directly on how to do that vital leadership job well. You will receive the benefit of the consolidated real-world experience of team leaders from a wide range of organizations. You will find here many ways to make your road a great deal less uncertain and less risky than it otherwise might be.

Many team leaders succeed brilliantly in that tricky role, but many others fail. Leading teams is no snap, particularly under today's intense pressures for high performance. This book is designed to tip the odds dramatically in favor of success for the team leaders who choose to master the proven skills outlined here.

You will be provided with both the big picture and the detail in Part One: The Reason, the Role, The Reward. In Chapter 1, you will see today's world of seemingly constant organizational change through an illuminating wide-angle lens. Beginning with the chapter's title, Better, Faster, Cheaper, the significant contributions expected from employee involvement efforts, especially from teams, are put into bottom-line perspective. You'll see why teams aren't just "nice to do"; they are absolutely essential elements in many organizational change initiatives targeted at dramatically improving performance.

In Chapter 2, How to Be an Explosives Expert, the lens zooms in closely on the very special role of team leader. The major differences between this leadership job and more traditional roles are surfaced and examined. The necessary *un*-learning and the new learning required begin to take shape, and the concerns and anxieties involved in such transitions are openly explored.

Chapters 3 through 10 focus on the specific practices and demonstrable skills required to succeed as a team leader in high-performance mode. The observations presented here are from real people doing well at this very demanding job. Emulating these practices and mastering these skills can make major differences in team effectiveness.

Part Two: Profiles in Team Leadership is a very special vehicle for learning. Here, you will find advice from other team leaders in their own words. Excerpted from hours of interview tapes, these personal insights can be of immeasurable value to you.

Read what these team leaders have to say, benefit from their experience, and—equally important—feel their sense of challenge, growth, and accomplishment.

This book was designed to make the research findings and conclusions highly accessible, easily readable, and bottom-line practical. The future of many organizations hinges on the success of people in leadership roles such as these.

ACKNOWLEDGMENTS

This book resounds with the voices of real-world team leaders from all across North America. From all organization levels, these leaders participated actively in the research that made this book and its associated training programs possible. Space allowed for only a few of these men and women to be singled out by name in the book, but we are deeply indebted to each one who helped us with gifts of time, candor, experience, and insight.

The research itself was accomplished by many Zenger-Miller associates, with particularly major contributions being made by Amy Avergun, Caryl Berrey, Susan Muttart, Darlene Russ-Eft, and Lilanthi Ravishankar. These professionals collected data from questionnaires, interviews, focus groups, and/or pilot tests and also helped enormously with the analysis that made the outcomes hang together as a cohesive whole. They contributed not only their considerable brain power but also some extraordinarily long work days and nights. We are priviledged to have them as our team-mates, as we are to have Jim Clemmer as part of the Zenger-Miller/ Achieve International organization. Jim's recent book, *Firing on All Cylinders*, was very useful to our thinking.

Also of great help were our friends and colleagues from BFR, Inc., Bill Belgard, Kim Fisher, and Steve Rayner, who shared with us their years of experience and writings regarding team effectiveness and organizational improvement. Their contributions are greatly appreciated.

The materials organization, writing, and editorial help we received from Barry Schwenkmeyer, Jeffrey Davidson, Leah Gold, and John Harrison made a great difference. Jeffrey Krames, our publisher's editor-in-chief, won the awards for patience and turning things around on a dime. Becky Ririe, Lisa Benson, Randie Sahim, and Rosie Morales were willing and able to handle the mountains of administrative detail involved, and their responsiveness made our work go far more smoothly than we probably deserved.

We know that a book such as this could never have been completed with just the work of the four ''authors'' fortunate enough to be named on the cover. Our sincerest thanks go to each person who made this book possible for us.

John H. Zenger
Ed Musselwhite
Kathleen Hurson
Craig Perrin

Contents

P A R T

I

THE REASON, THE ROLE, THE REWARD

Chapter One

Better, Faster, Cheaper

In the 1990s you can go from market dominance to decay in a couple of years. Only the nimble can avoid that fate.

Annual Report on American Industry
Forbes, January 4, 1993[1]

LEADERSHIP ON A HOT TIN ROOF

In the trenches or in the boardroom, you're just as likely to be feeling the heat. Today, all over the continent, leaders in organizations are struggling—often unsuccessfully—with unparalleled challenges. The more obvious ones are fierce competition, new technologies, rising customer demands, global markets, government regulation, and employees no longer willing to check their brains at the door.

Such opportunities and intense pressures, for many companies, put organizational change on the short list of inescapable events that once included only death and taxes.

"Everybody has heard that this is the decade of change," says Dean Olmstead, a middle manager at the University of Alberta Hospitals. "Not everybody appreciates that it's not change once and then on to a new plateau. I don't believe there are any more plateaus. And that's unsettling."[2]

Especially unsettling for supervisors, managers, and executives is the quiet carnage behind the headlines. Companies everywhere—even blue chips once known for their full-employment policies—are delayering, downsizing, right sizing, early retiring, and/or outplacing their management ranks. "Managers are losing their jobs out of proportion to their place in the work force," says

Eric Greenberg of the American Management Association.[3] In fact, reports *Business Week* magazine, "Since the mid-1980s . . . some two million middle-management positions have been permanently eliminated."[4] And according to Alvin Toffler, prophetic author of *Future Shock* and *Powershift*, "The massacre of middle managers . . . is going to continue."[5]

What's going on here? Why do more and more companies think they can get by with fewer and fewer managers? It's certainly not that planning, organizing, and controlling have gone out of style. But organizations under pressure can no longer pay the heavy price, in resources and efficiency, of layer upon layer of management. Instead, many companies are reaping huge operational benefits by shifting traditional management duties to *teams,* frequently of nonmanagers. Close-to-the-action employees often know more about customers and work processes than more distant managers ever could. That's why these teams often perform certain "management work" better, faster, and cheaper than managers ever did.

So, if you're a supervisor, manager, or executive—or aspire to be one—how can you retain and reassert your value in such a rapidly changing workplace? A solid first step is to master the skills and muster the personal commitment to lead in a team environment.

JUST DO IT. ALL.

This book is for and about some of the most essential people in today's work force: team leaders—by *any* official title, at *every* organizational level. But to see that new role in its full perspective, you'll first need to look at the wider world of organizational change. What you'll see is what you may already feel: a landscape literally shifting under your feet.

In the early 1960s, North America stood at the summit of world economic power. In those days the path to the top was neatly summarized by a sign that hung over the desk of one Midwestern manufacturing manager:

GOOD.

FAST.

CHEAP.

Pick any two!

Glancing up at his sign, this very successful manager used to tell an occasional young visitor how North American business *really* worked. "If you want quality and you want it fast, it'll cost you big bucks," he'd say. "If you want it fast and cheap, no problem, but it won't be good enough to last through the winter. And if you want good quality at a good price, that's fine too, but don't hold your breath for delivery. It'll probably take forever." Then came the visitor's cue to nod in wide-eyed agreement: "You always have to trade off one to get the other two."

And right we were to nod in those days. Using this trade-off model in a mostly seller's market, North America built a world-dominating economic machine. Particularly after World War II, with productive capacity down everywhere else and a world hungry for mass-produced goods, the trade-off model was plenty good enough.

Then somebody figured out a way to beat it: Do all three at once!

Competitors figured out how to design and build a deluge of better products in less time and for less money: automobiles, televisions, cameras, watches, machine tools, high-tech components, fax machines—even *baseball gloves*. Similar stresses have hit service market segments, like discount retailing, mail and parcel delivery, credit cards, and telecommunications. Today any organization that can't produce high-quality work both quickly and economically is at serious risk. An organization might get away with being good, fast, and *expensive* for awhile. Or maybe even good, economical, and *slow to market*—for awhile. But to prevail long term in virtually any market, an organization now has to deliver on quality, speed to market, and price.

That in a nutshell, is why so many organizations are putting themselves through so many agonizing internal changes, including the paring away of traditionally skilled managers. For until an organization becomes good, fast, and cheap, it's easy prey for any competitor that figures out how to deliver on all three.

TIME TO ESTABLISH SOME NEW TRADITIONS

Phrased more formally, being the good, fast, cheap competitor means that you engage in activities that will:

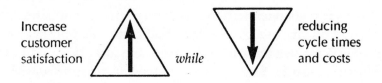

Increase customer satisfaction *while* reducing cycle times and costs

To accomplish that end, organizations can choose from an array of potential improvement activities. Here's a few of the more common labels: total quality management, strategic process management, self-directed work teams, reengineering, high-performance work systems, benchmarking, the learning organization, factory of the future, doing more with less, best practices, time-based competition. There is a variety of others, plus combinations and permutations galore.

Each of these activities, at one time or another, from somebody's point of view, can be a top priority. All have merit to the extent that they are intensely focused on, and successful at, increasing customer satisfaction while reducing cycle times and cost. The trick, of course, is to improve customer satisfaction, cycle times, and costs *at the same time*. If you address only one (say, cost reduction), you can make the others, and the whole situation, much worse.

Many, many organizations are having a very difficult time achieving these three improvements at the same time. Even when they attempt some of the improvement activities listed above, they get bogged down. They seem stuck, with failed implementations of potentially good improvement ideas. Why are they stuck? Often because they're laboring under the weight of three traditions that actually *prevent* serious organizational change from taking hold. Most of these stuck organizations remain:

1. Internally driven.
2. Functionally focused.
3. Management centered.

New Tradition 1: The Customer Is the Designated Driver

An organization is *internally driven* when it too often makes decisions based on narrow professional or departmental self-interest or habit, and not on constantly updated information about customers' changing needs. Like the auto makers that once redesigned cars every year with little or no buyer input, an internally driven organization can fall victim to any competitor that listens to customers and quickly gives them what they want at a good price.

In contrast, successfully changing organizations are becoming *customer-driven* instead of internally driven, so they can quickly and continuously understand, meet, and exceed their customers' changing expectations.

According to corporate strategist George Stalk and his colleagues, truly customer-driven companies "conceive of the organization as a giant feedback loop that begins with identifying the needs of the customer and ends with satisfying them."[6] What's more, according to Edward Lawler, director of the Center for Effective Organizations, "The life expectancy of many products has been shortened dramatically because of rapidly advancing technology and consumer demands."[7] In other words, the list is now expanding to better, faster, cheaper—and newer!

FIGURE 1–1
A Stuck Organization

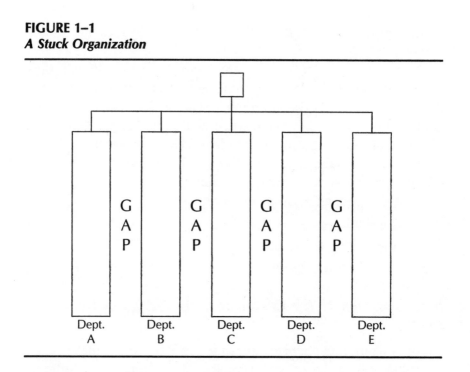

New Tradition 2: Let's Bridge the Gaps

Most of the stuck organizations are also too *functionally focused*. That means they see themselves primarily as a collection of separate departments—as "silos" of vertical power, which often waste time and energy competing with each other for resources and rewards (see Figure 1–1).

There's nothing wrong with this structure as a way of bringing together people who do related work. But when people behave as though their main allegiance is to a department or function, costly problems start cropping up:

- An "us-versus-them" relationship can limit communication between departments.
- One department, by focusing wholly on its own goals, can impede the performance of other departments.
- A department too concerned with its own needs can't or

won't always identify and meet the needs of external customers and suppliers.

- Unmanaged gaps between departments often disrupt the continuity of critical cross-functional work processes—creating redundant work, overlooked work, rework, sluggish systems, and cost expansions.

Overall, the common effect of a functional focus is to *reduce* quality while *increasing* cycle times and costs. That's the worst of all outcomes. "If a problem has been bothering your company and your customers for years," says Richard Palermo, a Xerox vice president for quality and transition, it's usually "the result of a cross-functional dispute, where nobody has total control of the whole process."[8]

Recognizing the severity of the problem, successfully changing companies are becoming more *process focused* instead of functionally focused. These organizations bridge the gaps between departments because they understand, track, improve, and speed up each work process moving horizontally, *across* the organization— as the customer experiences it (see Figure 1–2).

(For much more on the team leader's role in helping the organization become more customer driven and process focused, see Chapter 9.)

New Tradition 3: Lead, Follow, AND Get Out of the Way

Besides being internally driven and functionally focused, most stuck organizations are also *management centered*. In other words, managers see themselves as the central players in the organization and assume they need to control almost everything. As a result, managers (often inadvertently) can deny employees the information, skills, experience, and authority that employees must have in order to make meaningful improvements in their own areas.

In contrast, successfully changing organizations recognize that the world is moving too quickly for managers to:

1. know enough . . .
2. fast enough . . .
3. about enough things . . .
4. to be right enough . . .
5. enough of the time . . .
6. to control enough things correctly . . .
7. to keep the enterprise from being swamped.

What's their alternative to management centeredness? It's *employee involvement.*

Employee involvement is the systematic effort to build and benefit from the knowledge, skills, and commitment of nonmanagers. By their closeness to work processes and to the customer—and by their sheer numbers—nonmanagers *can* know enough fast enough to improve things on a grand scale. Further, today's reality is that there are fewer and fewer managers. That means the typical surviv-

FIGURE 1–2
A Moving Organization

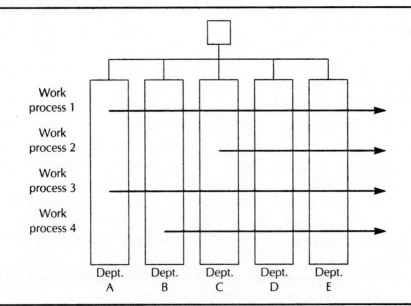

TABLE 1–1
Six Examples of Employee Involvement

Activities	Typical Type of Team
1. Managers decide, then inform employees.	***None required***
2. Employees provide information as requested and make suggestions to management.	***None required***
3. Employees as a group assume added responsibility for solving problems and making improvements within their own department or function.	***Intrafunctional team***
4. Managers assign a problem to a temporary group of selected employees.	***Problem-solving team***
5. People from different functions or departments meet regularly to address mutual problems.	***Cross-functional team***
6. An intact work group handles most daily operational issues with minimal supervision.	***Self-directed team***

ing manager now has a totally *un*manageable span of control without a huge increase in employee involvement.

Employee involvement is not an end in itself. It's just the best means to increase customer satisfaction and reduce cycle times and costs at the same time. Because of the enormous resources it brings to bear on the problem, employee involvement is the activating mechanism for all three kinds of improvement. And that's why few organizations have sustained major improvements in customer satisfaction, costs, and cycle times *without* a major increase in employee involvement.[9]

TEAMS: APPLYING THE POWER OF INVOLVEMENT

Employee involvement, often the bedrock for serious organizational change, takes many forms from light suggestion programs to full self-management. Table 1-1 arranges six examples of involvement in order from "hardly any" to "quite a lot." Notice that anything beyond the lightest forms of involvement usually requires some sort of team to be formed.

Teams are a predictable expression of employee involvement—for the simple reason that isolated nonmanagers usually lack the information and/or clout to improve cross-functional work processes and reduce cycle times and costs on a broad scale. These multifunctional issues involve numbers of people either in one department, in different departments, or in the gaps between departments. So teaming people up in various ways becomes essential as an organization makes serious moves to become more customer driven and process focused.

Here's a quick look at four basic kinds of teams that you may be involved with in your new leadership role.

Intrafunctional Teams

Some organizations expand the capabilities and responsibilities of both leaders and employees in the functional or departmental units of the organization. For example:

> An accounting manager works with her line supervisors on a complicated scheduling process until they're able to assume responsibility for it themselves. She is then freed to spend more time talking with customers and determining how to better meet their needs. Meanwhile, the supervisors gain a better understanding of the work flow and find ways to improve it. Supervisors also involve their teams in problem-solving efforts and so develop their abilities to assume a greater role in day-to-day decision making about their work.

Problem-Solving Teams

Some organizations use temporary *ad hoc* problem-solving teams and task forces in specific ways to deal with problems and opportunities. For example:

> When a manufacturing manager learns of plans to introduce a new product, he designates a team to study space and equipment requirements and propose shop-floor reconfiguration to accommodate manufacturing of the product.

Cross-Functional Teams

Some organizations establish permanent cross-functional teams to monitor, standardize, and improve work processes that cut across different parts of the organization. For example:

A wholesale distributing company determines that the single improvement most valuable to customers would be reduced turnaround time on their orders. Representatives from the order-entry, order-processing, invoicing, inventory-control, and shipping departments form a cross-functional team to determine how delays could be avoided and processes improved to save time.

Self-Directed Teams

A smaller number of organizations establish self-directed or self-managing teams. It's important to note that these aren't *unmanaged* teams. They're *differently* managed teams. For example:

A magazine publisher decides that the editorial staff—writers, copy editors, photographers, and production people—are capable of greater decision-making responsibility in their daily work. Trained and developed as a self-directed team, this group gradually takes over assigning projects, scheduling, allocating resources, and tracking progress toward deadlines. Their "deliverable" as a team is the stories, photographs, and page layouts for the nonadvertising portions of the magazine. The managing editor, who remains accountable for overall team performance, gradually backs off from many day-to-day decisions and activities as the team gains skill and confidence. Eventually he reaches a point where he keeps in touch with their activities mainly through weekly team meetings and occasional conversations with individuals. With his free time, the managing editor works with the publisher and editor-in-chief on strategic planning and provides the team with resources, information, and guidance.

180 DEGREES OF CHANGE

Using teams to become better, faster, and cheaper than the competition is a difficult, time-consuming, stressful, and risky undertaking for any traditional organization. How difficult? In each of several ways, the organization must make much more than a slight change of course. It must alter its course, in essence, by a full 180 degrees. Moving from *internally driven* to *customer driven* is a 180-degree change for the organization. Moving from *functionally focused* to *process focused* is a 180-degree change. Moving from *management centered* to *employee involved* is also a 180-degree change:

The Stuck Organization	The Moving Organization
• Internally driven • Functionally focused • Management centered	• Customer driven • Process focused • Employee involved

An organization and its people, like an ocean liner, can struggle to negotiate even a 20-degree change of course. But we're talking about bringing the ship to a full stop, turning it around, and heading it off at full speed in the opposite direction. Given this magnitude of effort, it's no wonder that so many organizations today are struggling so hard with change. But change they must to survive. And so must any supervisor, manager, or executive who wants to remain valuable now and in the future.

YOUR PIVOTAL ROLE

Teams are essential to the customer-driven, process-focused organization. Skilled team leaders are essential to effective teams.

So at the center of everything that's happening in such an organization is a role that, like an axle, must carry the load *and* move it forward. It's your *pivotal* role as team leader. Whether a team is temporary or permanent, functional or cross-functional, organized around an ongoing leader or moving toward self-management—that team needs your skilled leadership. You're at the very hub where strategy becomes reality.

Years of research and the practical experience of hundreds of companies moving to teams confirm the importance of your role as team leader. Specifically:

1. Without specially trained and skillful leaders, teams run a high risk of failing in their own eyes and the eyes of the organization.

2. Asked what they would have done differently, organizations implementing teams often report that they wish

they'd given much more attention, training, and support to their team leaders.

3. Within days of taking on their new role, team leaders usually realize they need a new set of team-leadership skills—quick! For supervisors or managers moving from a management-centered, nonteam, one-on-one role, that need is *urgent*.

4. Even where shared leadership within the team is the ultimate goal, the team as a whole still reports to someone who by definition needs advanced team-leadership skills. Plus, each team member of a shared-leadership team needs team-leadership skills. (These teams aren't leaderless. They're "leader-*full*.")

5. Formal team leaders who see themselves either as "top sergeants" or as "just team members with a few extra things to do" greatly increase the chance of total team failure.

Without skilled leadership, teams can easily flounder, get off course, go too far or not go far enough, lose sight of their mission and connection with other teams, lose confidence, get stymied by interpersonal conflict, and simply fall far short of their enormous potential—especially in the early months and years of their development.

These are the facts of life in hundreds of North American companies moving to teams. The team leader's role is pivotal, and performing that role requires the knowledge and skills outlined in upcoming chapters. But rest assured: Leading teams is decidedly *not* a matter of "You either got it, or you ain't." Being an outstanding team leader is no more a natural talent than being an effective team member. Both roles require new skills and lots of practice.

SO WHAT *IS* THIS ROLE?

Contemplating his changing role, Ron Deane of Spectra Physics in Eugene, Oregon, recalls his first thought the day it occurred to him that he might work himself out of a job by developing a team: What value do I have to the company if I'm not doing the daily traditional management work? What value do I have down the road?[10] That, or something like it, is a major concern for most supervisors and managers (and even some executives) when they hear about an organizational move to teams.

"You think, I'll be doing all this and my job will be going away once the team can take on more responsibility, maybe in a year or so," says manager Jean Conover of Amex Life Assurance in San Rafael, California. "But you never reach the end. There's always more to do. In fact, I've found that I have much more to do now as a team leader than I had before."[11]

The fact is, teams in no way devalue the need for skilled leaders. As former Citibank CEO Walter Wriston recently said, "The person that figures out how to harness the collective genius of his or her organization is going to blow the competition away."[12] How do you harness the genius of the people on your team? You have to:

- Trust team members and build their trust in you.
- Focus the team on its mission, goals, measurements, and boundaries.
- Keep the team energized and moving forward.
- Help team members bring their knowledge and experience to bear on solving stubborn problems.
- Expand the team's range of effectiveness.
- Encourage innovation and measured risk taking.
- Share key information with the team.
- Make team members genuine business partners.
- Help the team learn and grow from their mistakes.
- Build the commitment of the team to its own success and to the success of other teams and the whole organization.

Overall, you'll be helping team members gradually assume greater control of their own work—so they use not only their hands, so to speak, but also their intelligence, skills, and creativity to make the organization more competitive. Then, as the team takes on more responsibilities, you'll gain more time for more challenging, wider-impact, higher-payoff work.

"I certainly can't say that I have less to do," says manager Renee Roberti-Klemenck of Amex Life. "But the agenda is very different. Most of my time now is spent by being a guidance person, adding focus to the groups, acting as a facilitator and a coach. In a broader spectrum, I spend my time in senior management meetings, actually setting philosophies and procedures."[13]

Successful team-based organizations use teams not to pass the leadership role from one organizational level to another, but to create a breathtaking *expansion* of roles for everyone involved. As teams take increasing responsibility for daily operations, leaders at each level of the organization are able to share some of the duties of the level just above them. So with the coming of teams, says one experienced manager, "Everybody gets a better job."

Gradually, your role will tend to evolve toward leadership styles 3 and 4 in Figure 1–3.

FIGURE 1–3
Leadership Styles

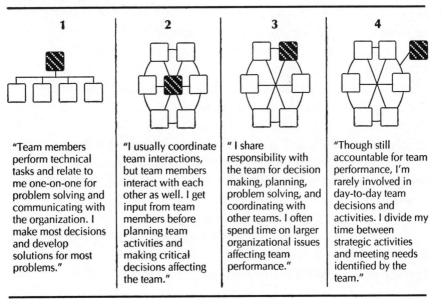

1	2	3	4
"Team members perform technical tasks and relate to me one-on-one for problem solving and communicating with the organization. I make most decisions and develop solutions for most problems."	"I usually coordinate team interactions, but team members interact with each other as well. I get input from team members before planning team activities and making critical decisions affecting the team."	" I share responsibility with the team for decision making, planning, problem solving, and coordinating with other teams. I often spend time on larger organizational issues affecting team performance."	"Though still accountable for team performance, I'm rarely involved in day-to-day team decisions and activities. I divide my time between strategic activities and meeting needs identified by the team."

You'll move along this continuum as you and your team gain experience with a more flexible way of leading and working. Eventually, if you learn to lead by *sharing* leadership, you'll make yourself far more valuable than you are now, not less, because you'll be making your organization far more competitive.

TAKING THE PLUNGE

New beliefs and new skills can open new doors for you. But becoming an effective team leader "takes some getting used to," says a middle manager who successfully made the transition in a multinational service company. "That is not how I was taught to be a supervisor or manager. So it does take some doing, it really does, and it takes practice and it takes learning."[14]

According to Alan Campbell, a production supervisor at the Kenworth truck assembly plant in Seattle, Washington, the skills of team leadership simply make you a better leader. "The job you were originally hired to do was to manage these groups and make them more efficient and to make the product better and to monitor safety and quality. And we weren't doing that," he says. "I know there's a better way."[15] Teams are that better way at Kenworth and for an increasing number of companies. And team leaders like Campbell are pivotal in making those teams successful.

Many are the reasons that so many companies see employee involvement via teams as a long-term solution to growing pressures. Technology and training allow for effective employee involvement, the rapid pace of business necessitates it, customers benefit from it, and staying competitive demands it. By unleashing the full talents of your work force, you too will uncover new ways to meet and exceed customer expectations, do things faster, and reduce costs. "I've been in the old way," says Campbell, "and I've tried the new way. It's not a new way, really. It's just that we've got off track somewhere, and we've got to get back to trusting the people to do it themselves."

As you master this expanding role, you'll expand your professional value to the company. Then, as a builder of teams, you'll help the company achieve what every organization vitally needs: increased customer satisfaction, faster cycle times, and lower costs for long-term success in the marketplace.

Teams are a big part of the future of North American business. But taking advantage of this opportunity requires your firm decision to master a challenging new role. "There is only one train," says Ron Deane after three highly successful years of teams at Spectra Physics. "You've got to make the commitment to be on that train."

NOTES

[1] "Annual Report on American Industry," *Forbes*, January 4, 1993.

[2] Zenger-Miller, Inc., research interview, 1992.

[3] John Huey, "Where Will Managers Go?" *Fortune*, January 27, 1992, p. 50.

[4] Bruce Nussbaum, Anne Therese Palmer, Alice Z. Cuneo, and Barbara Carlson, "Downward Mobility—Corporate Castoffs Are Struggling Just to Stay in the Middle-Class," *Business Week*, March 23, 1992, pp. 57–58.

[5] Greg Daugherty, "Powershift," *World* 25, no. 1 (1991), pp. 44–45.

[6] George Stalk, Philip Evans;, and Lawrence E. Shulman, "Competing on Capabilities: The New Rules of Corporate Strategy," *Harvard Business Review*, March-April, 1992, p. 62.

[7] Edward E. Lawler, III, *The Ultimate Advantage: Creating the High-Involvement Organization* (San Francisco: Jossey-Bass, 1992), pp. 19–20.

[8] Rahul Jacob, "The Search for the Organization of Tomorrow," *Fortune*, May 18, 1992, p. 95.

[9] Findings based on Zenger-Miller, Inc.'s extensive review of published reports and on research interviews with managers and change agents involving over 1,000 cases of attempted improvement of organizational quality and/or productivity.

[10] Zenger-Miller, Inc., research interview, 1992.

[11] Zenger-Miller, Inc., research interview, 1992.

[12] Quoted by Peter M. Senge in "The Leader's New Work: Building Learning Organizations," *Sloan Management Review* 32, no. 1 (Fall 1990), pp. 7–8.
[13] Zenger-Miller, Inc., research interview, 1992.
[14] Zenger-Miller, Inc., research interview, 1992.
[15] Zenger-Miller, Inc., research interview, 1992.

Chapter Two

How to Be an Explosives Expert

A new breed of managers is emerging in America. This new breed has discovered and applied a form of management [that] is responsive to the changing nature of the work force and to the pressures of competition. This is a social invention of such significance that it cannot be ignored by any organization interested in its own long-term survival and growth.[1]

From *New Roles for Managers*, a national study by the Work in America Institute

Under-used potential, poor morale, and just plain indifference continue to exact a heavy price in the North American work place. In some organizations, you can see the evidence every day. Managers complain that employees lack commitment. Employees complain that their jobs are unsatisfying and meaningless. And when morale goes sour, customer satisfaction, cycle times, and cost containment usually follow suit.

Why is job satisfaction and commitment so low among so many employees? It's a complex issue that can't be tied to a single cause. But what managers believe about leadership certainly plays a major role.

FROM THE GREAT PYRAMID TO THE GREAT PYRAMID COMPANIES

Many leaders, whether they realize it or not, share in beliefs some of which date back at least to ancient Egyptian times. In a more modern form called "scientific management," this top-down, or control-oriented approach gained wide influence in North American industry through the work of Australian theorist Frederick Winslow Taylor.

When Taylor published his views in the early 1900s, the average worker had only a third-grade education, so Taylor had a strong basis for one of his most important beliefs: Employees should be trained to perform limited tasks and be thought of more or less as interchangeable parts of the organization. According to Taylor's associate F. B. Gilberth, "It is the aim of . . . management to induce men to act as nearly like machines as possible."[2] Based on that belief, Taylor advised managers to make each task so simple and repetitive that anybody could perform it with minimal training. The manager's role, he said, is to control the activities of isolated workers by carefully defining the best way to perform each narrow task.[3]

Taylor's ideas worked well in the early days of industrial expansion, during an era of mass markets, huge production runs, and infrequent change. Managers boosted productivity and created millions of jobs for unskilled workers. Unfortunately, in mechanizing human activity, Taylor's ideas tended to discourage the creative contributions, so vital today, of rank-and-file employees. With the best of intentions, though not always the best of results, many organizations still operate according to Taylor's belief that each employee should perform a narrow task over and over. As a result, many employees with enormous capacity to contribute feel alienated by their jobs and perform only at the minimum required level. "I felt like I had all this wealth of knowledge," says team leader Nadine Lake about the days before teams at Amex Life Assurance. "But I wasn't doing anything with it. I felt like I was stuck in a little bowl because I couldn't share any of that."[4]

SAILING INTO THE WIND

Supervisors and managers in the tradition of Taylor tend to focus on controlling activities *within* the work place—and when the world changed slowly and predictably, that may have been just the right thing to do. Now the world is changing too quickly and unpredictably for leaders to spend most of their time developing control systems that stabilize the organization. "You can't run an organization with the same kind of vertical hierarchy that you ran Ford with in the 1920s," declares Tom Peters, the influential management authority. Comparing the competitive company to a sailboat taking advantage of the wind, Peters goes on: "If the market keeps dancing away from you—jibbing here and tacking there—you've got to have an institution that can jib and tack with it."[5]

For more and more companies, the sail that best catches the shifting winds of today's marketplace is employee involvement via teams.

In a team environment, managers focus not on making the organization more stable but on making it more *flexible*. The essential difference between the traditional, control-oriented perspective and the team perspective might be summarized like this:

Traditional Perspective	Team Perspective
Maintaining control is a leader's most important job.	Anticipating change is a leader's most important job.[6]

Once you begin to see *yourself* in the team perspective—as the person who helps your team foresee and prepare for continuous changes in the outside world—you can begin strengthening your organization and your own professional future.

If managers are supposed to make the organization more nimble and flexible, how does the workplace change when they do the job well? Table 2–1 lists some major differences between a work place in the tradition of Taylor (still quite common today) and a turn-of-the-21st-century team environment.

And how's all this working? What do *managers* say about the team environment?

TABLE 2-1

Traditional Environment	Team Environment
Managers determine and plan the work	Managers and team members jointly determine and plan the work
Jobs are narrowly defined	Jobs require broad skills and knowledge
Cross-training viewed as inefficient	Cross-training is the norm
Most information is "management property"	Most information is freely shared at all levels
Training for nonmanagers focuses on technical skills	Continuous learning requires interpersonal, administrative, and technical training for all
Risk taking is discouraged and punished	Measured risk taking is encouraged and supported
People work alone	People work together
Rewards are based on individual performance	Rewards are based on individual performance and contributions to team performance
Managers determine "best methods"	Everyone works to continuously improve methods and processes[7]

In a recent national survey of high-involvement organizations, 69 percent of managers say that moving to a team environment has markedly improved employee job satisfaction. An even higher percentage of managers say that team practices have improved several other key indicators of corporate health, summarized in Table 2-2.

Today most organizations retain some features of the traditional workplace. But forward-thinking managers see that traditional leadership is far too inflexible to keep their organizations competitive. In a team environment, the key leadership responsibility is no longer to *control* people. It's to build and sustain teams that bring the *best* out of people.

MORE OF A MANAGER, NOT LESS

Let's face it. With good preparation, training, management support, and leadership, teams have been known to work near-

TABLE 2–2

	Percentage of Managers Agreeing
Teams have improved **quality**	76
Teams have improved **productivity**	59
Teams have improved **profitability**	73
Teams have improved *my* **job satisfaction**	71[8]

Further, according to a different study, 85 percent of companies using teams have become more committed to the concept.[9]

miracles. That's why teams are more and more common—and also why you'll need to rethink your role as a leader if you're going to succeed in any organization moving to teams. Your new role, in a phrase, is to build a team with the vision, authority, accountability, information, skills, and commitment to assume more and better operational control of their own work.

By building such a team, you may gradually make some parts of your present role obsolete. To your advantage, though, as the team learns to perform some of your present duties, your role as a leader expands rather than shrinks. "You have more time to do things that you're not able to do right now," says Ray Lister, a manager and team leader at the University of Alberta Hospitals. "So you can become more productive as a manager."[10]

Typically, successful team leaders have the opportunity to explore other important aspects of the business, for example:

- Interacting more with customers, suppliers, and vendors.
- Looking at new technologies that could benefit the teams.
- Mapping out long-term strategies based on a thorough understanding of the organization's critical work processes and big-picture issues.

"The fact that a supervisor [or middle manager] delegates extensive authority makes him or her more of a manager, not less," according to a recent national study from the Work in America

Institute. "[You] may be given responsibility for a larger number of employees," the report continues, or "assigned to tasks that apply [your] experience to broader and more complex problems of the enterprise."[11]

DELEGATING YOURSELF INTO A *BIGGER* JOB

Even with that reassurance, many managers still feel threatened by the prospect of adapting to a team environment—mainly because they don't understand it well. They see management shrinking, and they think that fact spells trouble for them.

Such is the dark fantasy. Here's the far brighter reality.

Although organizations will be leaner in the coming years, they'll also be more efficient. If you take steps to ensure your success as a team leader, you'll find many organizations in big need of your services. On the other hand, anyone who thinks "I'll just ride out the storm" is in for a nasty surprise. What's occurring in North American business is no passing squall. It's a typhoon few will survive by boarding up the windows. Even if they do survive, they'll be too unprepared to excel in a radically transformed world.

If you're serious about embracing new principles and developing new skills—about moving beyond the role of boss—you're likely to find a valued place in a team environment. "You know what a good leader is?" asks Ray Lister, his eyes flashing. "A good leader is *not* somebody who says, 'Look at me, follow along.' It's somebody who helps an individual reach their potential. And by doing that, I fulfill my role and use my position of responsibility and authority."

You'll become a coach, a facilitator, an advocate, and a teacher in the best sense. You'll help your team acquire new knowledge, skills, and confidence. You'll guide the team through the changes you too are weathering. You'll prepare the team to take on some of the duties you now perform. And in the end, these changes will open new opportunities for you (in planning, coordinating, providing technical assistance, setting long-term strategies, gathering market intelligence, and in many other areas) and heighten your value as a leader.

So while moving to teams may seem risky at first, it's a high-potential step—for you, the team, and the organization. Gus Boetzkes, also a middle manager at the University of Alberta Hospitals, remembers his transition to teams: "I've had the same fears. I wondered, too, about my role." Eventually, though, "you see as I have that your value to the organization is increasing because your role is expanding. And likewise the people that are working on your team—their role is expanding, and their value is increasing. So everybody's in the same boat. They're all more valuable."[12]

PARENTING SKILLS

Leading teams can be confusing at first, especially when you seem to be getting contradictory advice. For example, somebody might tell you that you have to treat team members like growing children. "You have to develop your team much the same way you develop a child," says plant manager Dave Powell, a successful team leader with First Brands, Inc., in Rogers, Arkansas.[13] Then another voice of experience, like that of president Sarah Nolan of Amex Life Assurance, advises you to treat team members as *adults*: "If you took as a model of behavior how you would like to behave to your best friends, or to your peers, then you have a pretty good model for how to behave to associates."[14] So which is it?

In fact, there is no real contradiction here. A really good parent treats the child with basic human respect. And the long-term goal of both parent and leader is to build responsible, capable members of the larger community or organization.

"You have to develop the group to the point where they can handle the next responsibility," says Dave Powell of First Brands. So, like parenting, your new job never ends. It just changes. The growing independence of the team, like that of a maturing child, gives you more time for important matters you once were too busy to pursue because you were dealing with all the day-to-day problems.

"As they continue to grow, your role changes," says group leader Ramiro Mendoza of Subaru-Isuzu, Inc., in Lafayette, Indiana. "I'm sure you enjoyed your children growing up. It's no different than that. They went through the terrible two's, and you're going to go through the terrible two's. They went through being teenagers, and you're going to go through your teams being teenagers. That's what makes it interesting."[15]

Like parenting, leading teams requires the right skills. "I envy the younger managers," says section manager Stephen Merrill of Spectra Physics. "They come in without a lot of the out-dated ideas that I had in my early days. This is more a style that they see right up front, so they don't learn the bad habits before they learn the good habits."[16]

But what are these "good habits," and how do they contrast with the approaches you may be using now? Figure 2–1 summarizes the key differences between traditional supervisory skills and the more advanced participative skills—and contrasts both with the *team-leadership skills* you'll need to function effectively in a team environment.

While traditional *supervisory skills* are still useful from time to time, they do emphasize the top-down authority of the manager or supervisor. That's why they can be counterproductive if overused in a team environment. The *participative skills* help you to work *with* employees rather than dictating to them. As such, these skills remain important, especially early in your team's development. They preserve some of your traditional role, when appropriate, at the center of group activities. With the addition of *team-leadership* skills, however, you move well away from the "control" world of the past to build shared commitment and shared responsibility through shared leadership.

Your personal transition starts with a detailed understanding of team-leadership skills. That's what Chapters 3 through 8 are all about. With that foundation, you'll be far better prepared for the skills-building training required to learn how to actually do these things on the job. For now, a quick preview will help you see why acquiring and applying these skills is so crucial to your success.

FIGURE 2–1
Stepping up to Team Leadership

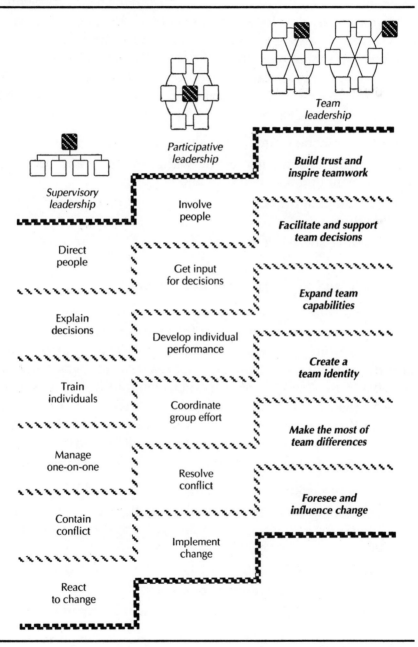

Build Trust and Inspire Teamwork

Trust, within the team and between you and the team, is essential
to teamwork. By developing trust over time, you help team members feel safe enough to take a chance, to give the best they have
to offer. When that happens, "the thing that just rips the covers
off your eyes," says Sarah Nolan of Amex Life, "is what enormous
creativity, what enormous contributions people at every level have
to give you." In Chapter 3, you'll begin to get a handle on:

- Being a living example of values that promote teamwork.
- Inspiring positive interaction within the team and between
  the team and its customers and suppliers.
- Encouraging the team to improve work processes and part-
  nerships.
- Building shared ownership of team activities and results.

Facilitate and Support Team Decisions

One of the trickiest parts of your new role will be getting team
members to make and implement the kinds of decisions you once
made mostly on your own. Many times, you'll be tempted to step
in and decide for them. But to involve team members as deeply as
possible in their work, you must help them to decide and carry
through their decisions. "Very seldom do I ever give my input or
my idea," says Ramiro Mendoza of Subaru-Isuzu. "I get them to
give me the idea that they have and try to mold it into the idea that
we *all* have." In Chapter 4, you'll become more familiar with:

- The various kinds of decisions your team will be making.
- Developing team decision-making skills, like establishing
  criteria for a sound decision and gathering key informa-
  tion.
- Clarifying the boundary conditions for team decisions.
- Helping the team reach a consensus.
- Actively supporting team decisions within stated bound-
  aries.
- Helping the team implement their decisions.

- Holding the team accountable for the results of their decisions.

Expand Team Capabilities

Helping your team take on new responsibilities will be taxing at first for both you and the team. In the long run, though, expanding the capabilities of your team will improve quality, productivity, and morale. "That's where the satisfaction has to come from—seeing the people grow and seeing them achieve and accomplish things that they never thought possible," says Joe Dulaney, a human resources manager with Levi Strauss & Co. But there's much more to expanding your team's capabilities than simply handing them a new task. "What we've had to do is really be in tune with our teams," says Dulaney, "and sense that frustration level of when you're trying to give them too much too quick. You have to back off and make sure you're not just throwing them into overload."[17] In Chapter 5, you'll gain insights into:

- Analyzing the team's readiness for a new task.
- Training the team to perform the task.
- Monitoring performance and coaching the team as they gradually master the task.
- Helping the team identify and remove barriers to performance.
- Building the team's confidence as you cultivate untapped potential.
- Helping the team find the necessary tools, information, and resources to get the job done.

Create a Team Identity

When a team forms or reforms, when it takes on new members, when it begins or completes a project, and at many other times, you must help the group to stop, reflect, and plan. By discussing key questions—for example, "What is our common purpose?" "What goals do we want to achieve as a team?" "What can we learn from what has just happened?"—the team develops a sense of itself and its potential contributions to the organization. In Chapter 6, you'll get lots of information about:

- Establishing ground rules for team interactions.
- Working with the team to develop a team mission statement.
- Helping the team recognize what they're doing well.
- Helping the team learn from their mistakes.
- Setting long-term and short-term goals.
- Planning a team celebration for reaching a shared goal.

Make the Most of Team Differences

Melding diverse individuals into a committed, productive team is a key challenge for you. And by helping team members to *leverage* their differences—professional and otherwise—you build interdependence and mutual respect. Sharon Chinn of Meridian Insurance clearly sees one of the main benefits of a team with diverse individuals: "Different perspectives can lead to a better solution."[18] Chapter 7 will help you think about:

- Building respect within the team for diverse points of view.
- Validating the different motives, values, and opinions within the team.
- Ensuring that all team members participate fully in team discussions.
- Integrating a range of individual perspectives during decision making, problem solving, conflict resolution, and other group processes.
- Rechanneling nonproductive conflict within the team.

Foresee and Influence Change

As your team takes on many of the tasks you once handled, you'll be expected to look beyond the day-to-day issues, to stay abreast of critical changes both within your organization and in the outside business environment. You'll identify key trends and emerging technologies, bring back vital information to your team, and champion ideas—both your own and those of the team. For Russell Francis of Spectra Physics, "My focus is much less on the day-to-day, and much more out a week, a month, a few months, and resolving those issues beforehand."[19] In Chapter 8, you'll discover the value of:

- Continuously scanning the business environment for key information.
- Translating changes in the business environment into practical opportunities for the organization.
- Helping teams decide how to be responsive to market information.
- Securing organizational cooperation for needed change.
- Maintaining close customer ties and keeping priorities connected with customer needs.
- Communicating information to the team about other areas of the company.
- Treating team members as valued business partners.

HOW TO LIGHT THE FUSE

These six skill categories—from building trust to influencing change—are the foundation of effective leadership in a team environment. Remember, though, it takes special skills,[20] and the effort and commitment to put them into practice. There'll be setbacks, mistakes, and obstacles to overcome. In particular, while greater autonomy and responsibility appeal to most employees, team members will need a lot of help to begin sharing in your vision of a new kind of workplace. So even if employees want to begin exercising more control over their own work, they'll need your direction, training, support, and encouragement, especially at first. That's why it's so vital to learn and use skills in all of the six team-leadership categories outlined above.

From the beginning, your consistency and commitment will greatly increase your chance for success. Team members will watch closely to see how serious you are about transforming your own leadership style. They'll be watching for visible answers to this question: "Is this teams business just the catch-phrase of the month, or is it something that's really going to stick?" If you lack commitment to the team concept, to building their capabilities, to sharing some of your authority, to really listening to team members' views—the team very likely will be apprehensive, suspicious, or resistant. You can restructure the systems. You can revamp the procedures. You can even rewrite your job description and theirs. But if you don't demonstrate your daily commitment by continuously honing and demonstrating your new leadership skills, both you and your team will most likely fail to realize the promise of a team environment.

In a phrase, you need to become "an explosives expert"—as Spectra Physics production supervisor Russell Francis describes himself. "I blow the doors," he says, "I blow away the obstacles. I blow away those things that are obstacles to the team."

With that kind of commitment, many leaders like you have already carved a niche for themselves as valued contributors in a team environment.

NOTES

[1] Jerome M. Rosow and Robert Zager, *New Roles for Managers, Part III* (New York: Work in America Institute, 1990), p. 1.

[2] F. B. Gilberth, *Primer of Scientific Management* (New York: Van Nostrand, 1914), p. 50.

[3] Frederick W. Taylor, *The Principles of Scientific Management* (New York: Harper, 1911), p. 43.

[4] Zenger-Miller, Inc., research interview, 1992.

[5] Tom Peters, *San Jose Mercury News*, November 8, 1992, 3E.

[6] Belgard, Fisher, Rayner, Inc., a respected firm with whom we collaborate from time to time, is the source of a similar distinction. Also see Richard E. Walton, "From Control to Commitment in the Work Place," *Harvard Business Review*, March-April 1985, pp. 77–84.

[7] Belgard, Fisher, Rayner, Inc., is the source of a similar list.

[8] Brian S. Moskal, "Is Industry Ready for Adult Relationships?" *Quality Digest*, February 1991, p. 50.

[9] *Market Report for Zenger-Miller, Inc.*, Lakewood Publications, Inc., 1992.

[10] Zenger-Miller, Inc., research interview, 1992.

[11] Jerome M. Rosow and Robert Zager, *New Roles for Managers, Part I* (New York: Work in America Institute, 1989), pp 37–38.

[12] Zenger-Miller, Inc., research interview, 1992.

[13] Zenger-Miller, Inc., research interview, 1992.

[14] Zenger-Miller, Inc., research interview, 1992.

[15] Zenger-Miller, Inc., research interview, 1992.

[16] Zenger-Miller, Inc., research interview, 1992.

[17] Zenger-Miller, Inc., research interview, 1992.

[18] Zenger-Miller, Inc., research interview, 1992.

[19] Zenger-Miller, Inc., research interview, 1992.

[20] *TeamLeadership*™ *Meeting the Challenge of Change with Teams* (Zenger-Miller, Inc., San Jose, Calif., 1992) is a skills-building training system designed specifically to develop the special skills required for team leaders to be successful day to day on the job.

Chapter Three

Trust—That's the Thing

Stepping up to team leadership

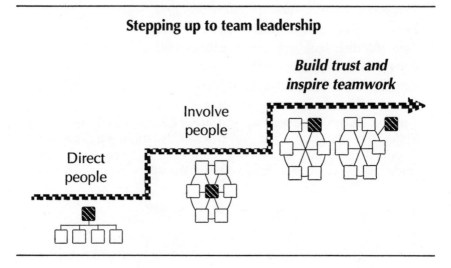

Trust your people, that's the thing. Trust your people until they let you down. And you'll be quite surprised that they don't let you down. . . . I haven't been let down yet.

Alan Campbell
Production Supervisor
Kenworth Trucks

When successful team leaders discuss their experiences, the common theme is trust. Only in an atmosphere of mutual trust and respect can a group of diverse individuals develop into a cohesive, fully functioning team.

In the traditional workplace, trust often occupies a lowly place on the scale of values. Managers who make decisions and issue directives have only to trust workers to do as they're told. In fact, many old-fashioned policies specifically compensate for lack of trust between managers and employees (such as policies requiring employees to punch in and out for breaks, submit to a search on leaving work, bring a doctor's note verifying treatment, etc.).

In the team-oriented workplace, by contrast, trust is fundamental. A team won't fulfill its promise unless you can trust the team to follow through on commitments. And you won't fulfill *your* promise unless the team can trust you to respect them and their ideas. Ron Deane describes how trust grows at Spectra Physics: "We set boundaries for the teams and let them know that they can make decisions within those boundaries. Then, as they grow and mature, we increase the boundaries so they can make larger decisions in a greater span of influence."

That kind of gradually expanding trust will allow the members of your team to achieve more of their potential as individuals—and to make greatly expanded contributions to the organization.

FORMING, STORMING, NORMING, AND PERFORMING[1]

Like a growing child, a growing team has different needs at different times. And trust, always vital, takes different forms to meet those changing needs.

You may not have worked with high-involvement teams, but you've probably experienced the strong emotions people feel during any major organizational change. Anticipation, anger, acceptance, and renewed self-confidence—in roughly that order—affect both the individual and the team as a whole. Researchers have found that those emotions correspond to four phases—ups and downs that every team must go through before it gels. Understanding those phases can help you and your team weather the confusion and suffering that always comes with serious change (see Table 2–1).

Just as every child finds a unique path through the phases of human growth, every team experiences these four phases in a somewhat different way. What's important is that your team will

TABLE 3–1
Four Phases of Team Development

Phase of Team Development	Typical Emotional State
1. Forming	Anxious anticipation
2. Storming	Anger, frustration
3. Norming	Acceptance, fear of conflict
4. Performing	Energetic self-confidence

go through some strong emotions, and each phase requires your special effort to strengthen mutual trust.

Forming. In this first phase, team members want to know "What's expected of me? How do I fit in? What are we supposed to do? What are the rules?" Anxiety quickly follows the initial excitement. But no one feels secure enough yet to be "real," so you probably won't see much open conflict. At this time, you'll plant the seeds of trust by helping the team develop operating guidelines, or "ground rules," that regulate how you and the team interact. It's critical that your early behavior clearly demonstrate teamwork and genuine concern for others.

Storming. During the second phase, enthusiasm usually gives way to frustration and anger. Team members struggle to find ways to work together, and everything seems awkward. You'll see mindless resistance, wrangling, hostile subgroups, jealousies, and general disgust with the whole transition to teams. Ground rules may splinter like trees in a cyclone. This phase is critical because, if you can all get through it, what emerges is something different from the sum of the parts: the team itself. "It takes everything you've got just to keep plugging," says an area manager at a South-western oil refinery. "You'll be player, coach, referee, fan, and weenie vendor all at once. The main thing is you can't do *anything* to violate their trust."

Norming. Gradually, the team gains its balance and enters the tranquil "norming" phase. People find standard ways to do routine things, they drop the power plays and grandstanding, and everyone makes a conscious effort to stay mellow. In fact, the main danger now is that team members hold back their good ideas for fear of further conflict. Your job is to help the team blow through their reticence—usually by increasing their responsibility and authority. Giving team members a new challenge demonstrates your trust in them. Meeting that challenge strengthens their trust in one another.

Performing. In this fourth and final phase, the team goes about its business with smooth self-confidence. By now, people have learned to disagree constructively, take measured risks, make adjustments and trade-offs, and apply their full energy to a variety of challenges. Given the high level of mutual trust, you can now step back and let the team demonstrate its considerable capabilities. Says support director Susan Mumme of the University of Alberta Hospitals, "I have to trust that they will take it in the right direction and not stick my nose in. It's a two-way street. They trust that I'll be there when they need me, but they also trust that I'm not going to step in and override them halfway through."[2]

It's important to note that reaching the *performing* phase doesn't mean smooth sailing forevermore. A team can experience a stormy period at any time—when it's under unusual pressure, for example, or when things aren't going as well as expected. The team can even return to the *forming* phase if it adds or loses members. If your team begins to recycle through earlier phases, you again may need to take an active role in helping the team find its balance and settle down to business.

EASING THE TRANSITION FOR EVERYONE

Trust is vital during every phase of your team's development from *forming* to *performing*. That's why your ability to build trust—both with and within your team—is fundamental to your transition from traditional leadership to team leadership:

Traditional leadership: Direct people. One of your main traditional functions, directing people, is something you'll do from time to time even after your team has reached the *performing* phase. Of course, directing people doesn't require an especially high degree of trust. A strictly traditional leader checks up on employees to make sure they're doing what they're supposed to.

Participative leadership: Involve people. To become a participative leader, you have to involve people in decisions that affect their work, usually by asking for their input before decisions are made. Here, mutual trust takes on much greater significance. Employees have to trust you enough to express their ideas without fear of attack, ridicule, or blame. And you have to trust that employees will live up to their commitments without your riding herd over them.

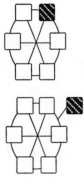

Team leadership: Build trust and inspire teamwork. Before you can be an effective team leader, building trust and inspiring teamwork must become a regular, conscious part of your daily job. Building substantial trust allows you to delegate substantial authority in the knowledge that the team will carry through without your direct supervision. Eventually, trust gives employees a stake in the organization and makes them genuine owners of what they do.

DOES YOUR BEHAVIOR ENCOURAGE TRUST?

Consider for a moment your current behavior with employees. How often do you make a conscious effort to do each of the following?

	Never	Seldom	Sometimes	Usually	Always
1. Build the self-esteem of employees by showing respect for their opinions.	☐	☐	☐	☐	☐
2. Help employees focus on the problem instead of blaming each other.	☐	☐	☐	☐	☐
3. Serve as a role model by demonstrating constructive team behaviors.	☐	☐	☐	☐	☐

If you can't answer Always to all three questions, you need to give more attention to how your actions as leader promote or prevent the growth of trust with your team.

Think about some effective leaders you know. What is it about their behaviors that inspires your trust in them? Do they keep their promises? Keep confidences? Respect your views, abilities, and feelings? Admit their own mistakes? Give you credit where it's due? Speak well of people not present? Trust you with significant responsibilities? The answer is probably "yes" to all of these questions.

To help you lay a foundation of trust with your team, you'll need to understand and apply the guiding principles that tend to inspire the trust—and the responsible actions—of your team. You must make a conscious, consistent effort to follow these principles with your team.

MANAGING BY PRINCIPLES, NOT BY RULES

A retired U.S. Army colonel tells a story that clearly illustrates the power and the danger of managing strictly by the book. Shortly after Pearl Harbor, this colonel, then a young lieutenant, stopped briefly at a certain stateside base on his way to the Pacific Theater. One afternoon after a brisk walk, he decided to relax on a bench near the base flagpole. "Sir, I wouldn't sit there if I were you," said a guard posted nearby. "That bench was painted this morning." The lieutenant thanked the guard, moved on, and shipped out the following week. Two and a half years later, now a captain, he returned home through the same base. One day after a walk he again approached the now weathered bench near the flagpole. "Sorry, sir," said a different fresh-faced guard, "that bench is off limits." "Why?" he asked. The guard didn't know, and presumably neither did the officer who ordered him to stand watch.

In the same way, many traditional organizations blindly follow rules, established for reasons long forgotten, that no longer serve their best interests. "Everyone knows you can't run an organization without regulations," says Ricardo Semler, a teams advocate and president of Brazil's largest manufacturer of marine food-processing machinery. "Everyone also knows that most regulations are poppycock. They rarely solve problems. On the contrary, there is usually some obscure corner of the rule book that justifies the worst silliness people can think up." For example, Semler continues, workers might "have to wear badges and name tags, arrive at a certain time, stand in line to punch a time clock, get permission to go to the bathroom, give lengthy explanations every time they're five minutes late, and follow instructions without asking a lot of questions."[3] Thousands of rules like these certainly give management the sense of "controlling" the work place. They also inhibit, if not *pro*hibit, the growth trust between employees and managers.

In sharp contrast, a high-involvement company like Semler's manages not by the rules, but by *principles*. Principles build trust if they encourage leaders and employees to treat one another as responsible adults. A clear set of principles—simply defined as "core beliefs that everyone accepts and tries to follow"—is the soul of a high-involvement workplace. To become an effective team leader, in fact, *you must learn to manage by principles*—and encourage their application by using them every day. You manage the principles, and the principles, in effect, manage the team. The resulting trust allows team members, with your coaching, to adapt or devise the most effective guidelines for day-to-day operations.

Of the many principles you might follow with your team, the following five Basic Principles summarize the bedrock values that help foster trust in most high-involvement companies:

THE BASIC PRINCIPLES[4]

1. Focus on the issue, behavior, or problem, not on the person.

2. Maintain the self-confidence and self-esteem of others.

3. Maintain constructive relationships.

4. Take initiative to make things better.

5. Lead by example.

Let's explore how each principle can help you build a foundation of trust with your team.

Basic Principle 1: Focus on the Issue, Behavior, or Problem, Not on the Person

To unite the team, and work effectively with the team, you must avoid the "who's-at-fault" syndrome that leads to finger-pointing and the slow death of team spirit. Even *implying* blame discourages team members from risking a new way of doing things—the essential ingredient in continuous improvement. Blaming people outside the team gives the team a reason to say, "We'd fix this problem, but it's out of our hands." By focusing on the work process, not on the person, you encourage the team to find a long-term solution rather than a quick fix. Further, during the transition to a team environment, focusing on the issues acts like a shock absorber to help you and your team ride out some major new speed bumps on the yellow brick road:

- Everything has to be better, faster, and cheaper—at the same time.
- Continuous improvement means you never really solve things once and for all.
- Lines of authority begin to blur, so you and your team have to redefine your roles as you go.

- Everyone is working toward multiple goals.
- Success is harder to measure or experience because it usually comes through small changes instead of big breakthroughs.
- The margin for error shrinks as the number of people that have to be satisfied grows.

These and other frustrations can have people at each other's throats. The coming of teams can also bring perceived threats—and whether or not the anxiety is justified, people can feel uncertain, vulnerable, defensive, hostile, frustrated, or stupid. If you consistently focus on the issue, not the person, says nursing manager Thelma Inkson of the University of Alberta Hospitals, "The people that work for you will recognize that you can be trusted, that you are not going to take advantage of them, that you support them."[5] As a result, they'll be much more willing to risk new ways of thinking and acting.

To focus on the issue you have to resist the very human urge to lay blame when a problem comes up. Instead, stop and ask yourself, "What's the underlying cause here? What data would help establish that cause?" If the issue seems to be someone's behavior, talk to the person privately whenever possible. Address what the person did or didn't do, not the person's character. For example, ask, "How could we improve the customer feedback we're getting?" instead of saying, "You're careless. That's why you're getting so many complaints." Refer to any formal team agreements, and if possible use the issue at hand to improve these agreements.

Help the team focus on issues whenever the group has to address team development problems. You might say, for example, "Some disagreement is normal for any team. Instead of talking about who's at fault, why don't we agree on some ground rules for these discussions?" You can also focus on the issue by highlighting process improvement or an alternative point of view—for example, "The other team is probably doing it the best way they know how. Why don't we look at the whole process, and see if we can give them some positive suggestions."

The clearest indicator that Basic Principle 1 has taken effect is that team members demonstrate they feel safe with the group. Instead of making themselves inconspicuous, trying to avoid blame or punishment, they step forward to work together on problems that come up.

Basic Principle 2: Maintain the Self-Confidence and Self-Esteem of Others

Self-confident people speak up, contribute their unique skills and perspective, take risks. People who feel beaten down often do as little as possible just to get by.

From John F. Welch, Jr., chairman and CEO at General Electric Company, "We defined *self-confidence* in our people as the catalyst that would release the ideas and energy we craved." Based on that belief, Welch initiated "a series of New England–style town meetings" as a forum for trading ideas and building self-confidence among "people of every conceivable rank and function." And "all that time," he says, "trust was building, confidence was growing, and teams were coming together."[6]

Like focusing on the issue, maintaining self-confidence and self-esteem helps you build trust by making it safe for people to contribute to the team. By airing their views in a supportive setting, team members can usually reach agreement on important matters affecting the whole team. If—having been attacked when they spoke up in the past—team members go along without voicing their real views, they rarely develop the commitment required to carry group ideas through to completion.

To build self-confidence and self-esteem, give the team tasks that stretch, without overextending, their abilities. Even then, says paint shop team leader Alvin Morgan of Subaru-Isuzu, make it very clear that everybody makes mistakes: "The first thing I tell 'em when they come into the booth, 'You gonna mess up. Flat out, you gonna mess up. If you do, don't go freak because you gonna do it. You gonna damage this body, you gonna burn this paint, you gonna mess up this car—until you learn what you're doin'.'"[7]

Beyond making it OK to fail, you can take many other steps to build self-confidence and self-esteem:

- Encourage the team to recognize and value different points of view.
- Be clear about your expectations, furnish resources, and be ready to coach when needed.
- Withhold your ideas to make it easier for team members to voice their own.
- Be clear about your intent as leader—to gradually increase the team's responsibility and authority in its assigned area.

During the *forming* and *storming* phases, when your team is gaining its balance, maintaining self-esteem is vital. "The difficult thing initially was to accept the fact that people tend to be so averse to change," says Brad West, production manager at Spectra Physics. You "have to allow them to work through that, spend the time with them to become comfortable with it, and give them enough information so that they'll eventually accept it."[8]

If, combined with their natural resistance to change, team members feel they can't try out new behaviors without being criticized or punished, they'll pull back, play it safe, and make very little progress. So be sure to acknowledge the difficulty of dealing with change, and check in frequently to help people keep the changes in perspective. With things up in the air, even long-time employees can feel unsure of themselves, and you'll need to avoid saying or doing anything that might be seen as a put-down.

Reaffirm the value of each person's opinion with your support of team decision-making. Build the team's confidence to participate in difficult decisions by sharing formerly management-only information—especially during times of change. Knowing what is happening will help people feel more confident about their ability to meet this new challenge.

And, finally, you can lift self-confidence and get some very good ideas by collaborating with the team on ground rules, operating guidelines, daily communication procedures, and the like. According to Russell Francis of Spectra Physics, "If you want to start on this road, start by talking to the group that you want to walk the road with because you are all in it together. It's not a team leader and a team. It really is just a team."

Basic Principle 3: Maintain Constructive Relationships

To become an integral part of the organization, your team must reach out to one another and to people outside the team. Old lines of authority and communication fade as an organization becomes more streamlined. People who once communicated only through their managers or supervisors have to find ways to work together directly. It's up to team members, with your help, to establish these new working relationships.

How difficult is it to encourage constructive relationships during a transition to teams? "I have talked to many people about employee involvement," says town manager Al Ilg, who implemented both white- and blue-collar teams in the governance of Windsor, Connecticut. "The people who are enthusiastic are HRD, psychologists, and group behaviorists. For them, relationships are easy. But for the average person in an organization, it's a tremendous hurdle, especially for department heads and very especially for technical department heads." Even so, town employees at all levels are developing new relationships with their customers—the citizens of Windsor. "In government, the word 'customer' is rarely used," says Ilg. "In our organization, we started using this term only three years ago, and we've been around since 1633. There is a much different perception of the customer, thus better customer service."[9]

Lacking strong outside relationships—with you and others— team members tend to focus on their own needs and blame others for self-induced problems. Meeting ambitious goals requires team members to stay in touch with others, to identify customer expectations, to form internal and external partnerships, to seek out and give constructive feedback, and to coordinate activities with other teams.

As leader, you can do a number of things to promote strong relationships. Create opportunities for interaction between the team and its internal and external customers and suppliers. Encourage clear agreements both within the team and between the team and outsiders. Help team members work through any apparent breach of agreement, and encourage those involved to revise agreements as necessary. Demonstrate and advise care in handing off work to other teams—one of the most error-prone activities in any organization. And help the team see that diversity within the team, and among teams, can often lead to better ideas and solutions.

Basic Principle 4: Take Initiative to Make Things Better

Today, fierce competition makes it imperative to continuously improve the way your organization operates. But the attitude implied in the old saying "If it ain't broke, don't fix it" can derail the positive efforts of your team before they ever get rolling. A safer motto these days is "It ain't broke, but that don't mean it's perfect!" Every work process, every work relationship, can be improved—and those who do the work and form the relationships are in the best position to make them better.

In the words of vice president Karen Gideon of Amex Life, getting team members to "stop, look, and listen" for ways to improve is central to your new role.[10] No longer is process improvement and meeting customer needs the exclusive concern of managers. As leader, you must teach and continually urge your team to make things better.

A big part of continuous improvement involves penetrating or removing the walls between parts of the organization. Critical work processes cut across functional boundaries to link people both inside and outside the organization (see Chapter 9). You must help your team see the importance of these newly understood relationships. Instead of focusing strictly on their own area, team members must now act in the interest of those they serve—other teams, other departments, and outside customers. Effective teams frequently ask, "What is it our customers really value in what we do? How could events in the outside business climate affect this company?

This team? How can I improve this product, this team, this organization?"—and so on.

Basic Principle 4 allows you as leader to *leverage* your ability to improve performance: You make things better by enabling your *team* to make things better. Specifically, you can:

- Help your team learn the skills, develop the relationships, and gain the confidence to play an active part in improving performance.
- Teach the team to look for cross-functional causes of functional problems, and to act on opportunities for cross-functional improvement.
- Show the team how to identify customer expectations, coordinate with suppliers, and gather data on emerging issues.
- Expand the team's responsibilities in step with their expanding abilities and confidence.

Basic Principle 5: Lead by Example

Whether you like it or not, team members will constantly analyze and judge your actions. In particular, they'll watch to make sure your actions match your words and carefully measure your commitment to teams. The fiery speech, the next sweeping program, this year's key objective, and all the rest mean nothing by themselves. To involve these people deeply in improving the performance of their team, you'll need to exceed their expectations of what a leader should be.

Basic Principle 5, lead by example, is your most powerful tool for teaching team members how to do what you say they should do. Your positive example can define how they respond to changes, how they handle new tasks and responsibilities, and how they relate to one another and the rest of the organization.

There's no easy way to lead by example. It requires personal conviction, knowledge of what team leadership actually is, and constant awareness of how your actions are perceived. Be clear about your commitment to teams. Keep dialogue open between you and your team. Praise and support any new behaviors, no matter how small, consistent with the goals of high-involvement teams.

As you get more comfortable with your changing role, you'll become more deliberate in your modeling of desired behaviors. But beginning immediately, plan out your work day so the priorities you emphasize, the agendas you set, and the way you spend your time are all consistent with a more participative, open environment.

Ask team members to tell you when your words do not match your actions—when, from their perspective, you don't "walk the talk." Work to change these inconsistencies until the people who gave you feedback tell you their perceptions have changed.

Admit your mistakes, share what you learn from them, and team members will begin doing the same. Look for decisions you don't need to make and prepare the team to make them. Ask qualified team members to facilitate team meetings. Keep the team focused on doing high-quality work—the one constant for the team regardless of other changes. And defer to the team's judgment, even if you have reservations.

These five Basic Principles can help you lay a foundation of trust. Even during the long *performing* phase, the Basic Principles must be a daily habit for you and your team. Otherwise, the foundation crumbles and teamwork fades. Karen Olson-Vermillion, a group leader at Subaru-Isuzu, knows how fragile trust can be. "It takes a long time to build up trust," she says. "And if you take a chance and don't tell your team something that they need to know, or forget to tell them, you destroy that."[11]

INSPIRING TEAMWORK

As you've seen, whether or not people pull together as a team depends on the mutual trust that you help to create. But teamwork also depends on how clearly people foresee an attractive future that they can create as a team.

So you have to ask yourself, "What exactly is the positive future that the team and I can achieve together?"

To inspire teamwork, you must plant the seeds of a well-defined vision of future greatness. Your thoughts about the future should be vivid enough to stimulate further ideas in the team and sketchy enough that their ideas will make it truly a shared vision. As it develops, this shared vision will portray a desired future state for you, team members, and the organization as a whole.

A vision in this sense is a collective dream that stretches the imagination by forcing people to rethink what is possible. Consider the vision of American settlers looking out over California's great Central Valley, of Martin Luther King, Jr., or of millions of people in the former Soviet Union longing for a free society. The shared vision you help your team develop need not be so lofty as these. It does need to be tangible, not abstract. And it needs to link with the current and projected needs of the organization.

JERRY'S VISION

Take the example of Jerry, a manufacturing manager in a large electronics company, whose clear vision of a possible future helped bring about fundamental change. When the company implemented teams and just-in-time manufacturing, Jerry saw a chance to eliminate many inefficiencies stemming from the functional organization of the plant. His initial vision had only one component: break workers into flexible product-focused teams directly involved in decision making.

Then Jerry transformed that shred of a possible future into a full-blown team vision. He "took the initiative" to talk up his thoughts all over the plant. He "focused on the issue"—inefficiencies due to functional teams—not on the people involved. He "led by example"—offering an idea, then asking others to offer theirs. As people at every level reacted to his thoughts and tossed out their own, Jerry's Vision, as they called it, started to sound plausible. They saw how this simple idea could bring more responsibility, involvement, and ownership to *their* jobs. Eventually, through their collective effort, their collective dream became highly successful reality. And top management later decided to implement product-focused teams in several other plants.[12]

Jerry did not have the power to bring about this change on his own. But his vision, when others made it *their* vision, did. You can inspire a similar kind of teamwork in your organization by focusing the energy of your team. As in Jerry's case, it's a good idea to tie your basic vision into other trends or developments—a product introduction, a plant opening, a new technology, new equipment or methodologies, or reorganization. Linking with such developments gives your vision a rolling start because people already have a concrete reason to change.

A VISION FOR ALL TEAMS

Some visions like Jerry's won't survive intact when transplanted from one place to another. The vision of the learning organization, on the other hand, is an integral part of every successful team environment.

The learning organization is a catch-phrase, yes, and eventually that phrase will fade. But the idea behind the phrase will be around for a long time. A learning organization is one that never stops growing and changing. It lives continuous improvement every day by responding to customer needs and carefully managing cross-functional work processes. It values knowledge and information, and freely disseminates both to every corner of the organization—through continuous training and communication at every level.

The high-involvement team—*your* team—is the basic building block of the learning organization, and your job as leader is to help·create the learning work force. For you, that translates into educating yourself and your team about service/quality, process management, customer focus, corporate responsibility, reducing cycle times, JIT, eliminating waste, shrinking bureaucracy, or any number of other topics that might be the watchword of change in your organization.

"At American Express," says Barb Anders, HR vice president with the Travel Services Group, "we're going to practice continuous learning. That's very important to us. Part of our process is saying it's OK to fail as long as we've learned from it. We've put into practice asking specific questions to help the manager generate a variety of ideas. We're also communicating our business results—financials, the direction the company needs to travel—to help teams build on their commitment. That's part of the way we motivate people."[13]

Helping your team members acquire new skills and knowledge is no longer a one-time thing. Beginning now, if you haven't already, you must keep finding new ways to help team members achieve the positive future that you and they foresee. To build trust and inspire teamwork, in other words, you must take initiative to make them smarter.

NOTES

[1] Bruce W. Tuckman, "Developmental Sequence in Small Groups," *Psychological Bulletin* 63, no. 6 (1965), pp. 334–99.

[2] Zenger-Miller, Inc., research interview, 1992.

[3] Ricardo Semler, "Managing Without Managers," *Harvard Business Review*, September-October 1989.

[4] The Basic Principles were formulated by Zenger-Miller, Inc., as the foundation of its values-based training programs for leaders and individual contributors.

[5] Zenger-Miller, Inc., research interview, 1992.

[6] John F. Welch, Jr., "Working Out of a Tough Year," *Executive Excellence*, April 1992.

[7] Zenger-Miller, Inc., research interview, 1992.

[8] Zenger-Miller, Inc., research interview, 1992.

[9] Zenger-Miller, Inc., research interview, 1992.

[10] Zenger-Miller, Inc., research interview, 1992.

[11] Zenger-Miller, Inc., research interview, 1992.

[12] For this example, thanks to Belgard, Fisher, and Rayner, Inc.

[13] Zenger-Miller, Inc., research interview, 1992.

Chapter Four

Where the Answers Live

Stepping up to team leadership

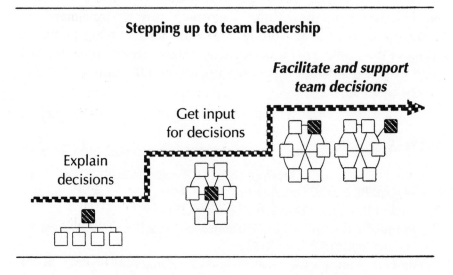

We're starting to understand who the experts really are.

Mark Kornhauser
Site Manager
Black & Decker[1]

Giving away decision-making power to a team is not something that most managers do naturally. "I'm supposed to have the smarts and experience to make the tough calls," they say. "Isn't that what I'm *paid* to do?"

In a traditional environment, maybe so. But outstanding team leaders know there's another way.

"The issue of who has the answers is really what this is all about," says president Sarah Nolan of Amex Life. "You want *them* to have the answers. And the only way they will is if they realize,

over time, that you don't think *you're* paid to have the answers."
According to Russell Francis of Spectra Physics, the essence of
your new role is to "help people make the decision themselves—
not by giving them the answer, but by asking questions of them
that will help *lead* them to the answer."

Experienced team leaders agree that effective group decision-
making is the heart of the team approach. Shared decisions help
make the team true owners of what they do. "The big payoff is
that you don't have to get people to buy in because they've already
bought in," says nursing manager Bertha Van Marum of the University of Alberta Hospitals. "They've made the decision. It's their
decision. They own it, and it's up to them to make sure that the
decisions come to pass, the work gets done."[2]

This doesn't mean that the team makes *all* decisions. As Thelma
Inkson, also of the University of Alberta Hospitals, points out, "In
a new team structure, a new environment, a new culture, there
still has to be decision making at different levels. That's where
we're all struggling right now, deciding what decisions should be
made at what levels."

So, as before, certain kinds of decisions still reside at different
organizational levels. But in a team environment, the team takes
on a much greater share of the kind of day-to-day operational
decisions you may now be making. Meanwhile, your role undergoes a remarkable transformation—from decision maker to decision *facilitator*. Specifically, you must be prepared to:

- Help the team identify the kinds of decisions they should
  make.
- Provide free access to information that the team needs in
  order to make sound decisions.
- Lead team decision-making sessions.
- Prepare team members to lead their own decision-making
  sessions.
- Secure the resources the team needs to implement their
  decisions.
- Slowly expand the boundaries of team decision-making authority.

- Allow the team to take calculated risks within the established arena of their decision-making authority.

As you do these things, as you increasingly defer to the collective smarts and experience of the *group*, the group gradually becomes a team. "As long as you're willing to try what they want to do, that's all they're really looking for," says group leader Ramiro Mendoza of Subaru-Isuzu. "Then, if they find out for themselves their idea doesn't work, that's better than you saying up front, 'No, I don't think that's a good idea.' When you let them learn by trying out their own ideas, that's when you become a facilitator."

DOING WHAT MAY NOT COME NATURALLY

Very, very few people can facilitate team decision-making sessions on native talent alone. So unless you're a natural, you'll have to work hard to master the facilitation skills that can help move you from traditional leadership to team leadership:

Traditional leadership: Explain decisions. Traditional leaders are decisive. They make firm decisions based on sound information, and they clearly explain to employees both the letter and rationale of their decisions. As you step up to the skills of team leadership, you can't abandon that tradition when conditions call for quick, decisive action.

Participative leadership: Get input for decisions. The more participative you become, the more often you'll delay decisions until you've discussed the issues with affected employees. Although you may end up making the decision and bearing complete responsibility for it, getting input beforehand tends to bring about better deci-

sions, higher morale, and more vigorous implementation.

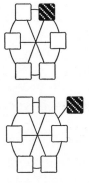

Team leadership: Facilitate and support team decisions. To succeed as a team leader, you'll need
to go beyond asking for input. You'll be leading
decision-making sessions—during which you'll
help team members to reach consensus and plan
how they will carry out their own decision.
Within the team's sphere of responsibility, your
views will carry no greater weight than those of
the team.

ARE YOU FACILITATING TEAM DECISION MAKING?

Consider for a moment your current efforts to develop your team's
decision-making capabilities. How often do you make a conscious
effort to do each of the following?

	Never	Seldom	Sometimes	Usually	Always
1. Show team members how and where to get good information for decisions.	☐	☐	☐	☐	☐
2. Help the team use a consensus approach to decision-making.	☐	☐	☐	☐	☐
3. Actively support appropriate team decisions.	☐	☐	☐	☐	☐

These three key behaviors may sound simple, but many managers and supervisors find them the most challenging part of becoming a team leader. For example, Stephen Merrill of Spectra Physics admits he was no natural. It was extremely difficult for him at first to give up some of his decision-making authority. Still, he says, "When I get other people involved, painful as it is, the result that I get is *so much better*. I'm not talking twice as good, quality-wise, or twice as fast. I'm talking *ten times* better—by getting people involved.''

THE POWER OF GIVING INFORMATION AWAY

Good decisions depend on good information, and that's why information is power in any organization, traditional or team-based. But where information lives and how it moves around is very different in those two worlds.

Traditional companies use the yo-yo approach to decision making: Information travels up the chain of command, decisions get made at the top, and decisions travel down to the people who implement them—up and down, over and over, like a yo-yo. A team environment, in contrast, uses the balloon approach to decision making: Information pumped into the organization in just the right amount spreads like compressed oxygen to every part of the organization. Then, because information and decision-making authority reside with the people who carry out the decision, team members can make informed decisions at the point where the work gets done.

For the balloon approach to work, you as leader must funnel appropriate information to your team. ''If we expect them to make decisions,'' says nursing manager Bertha Van Marum of the University of Alberta Hospitals, ''we have to make sure they have the information they need.'' You also must teach your team about the overall work process they're a part of so they can make decisions that help improve that process (see Chapter 9).

In Rogers, Arkansas, First Brands plant manager Dave Powell describes what tends to happen in a team environment: ''You'll find, as teams become more and more committed to a common goal, they ask more questions in terms of their own thought process and how to achieve the goal. And their questions might point toward areas typically you only cover with upper managers—be that cost information by product, machine efficiencies, standards, and a lot of whys. You can't brush those questions off. You've got to bring them definite answers.''

When information becomes a tool for every employee—instead of the property of a few managers—your power as a leader takes on an entirely different character. No longer the *source* of good decisions, you're now the *catalyst* for even better decisions, which team members are more likely to carry out. Vice president Karen Gideon of Amex Life talks of the central effect of that fundamental change in your behavior: "The more information you give away, the more information everyone has, the more powerful you are."

At this point, you may be thinking, "Isn't it risky to give away so much information and authority? What if employees blow it? I still take the heat, right?"

You'll still *share* the heat, yes, which is one reason why learning to facilitate is so challenging and so nerve-wracking. "If you look back in my past and say, 'What was the scariest thing?'—it was really learning how to give it away," says Karen Gideon. "How to let go of stuff. How to let it be out there and float out there."

Fortunately, in time, most team members will want to succeed as badly as you do. If you make it truly their decision, their decision makes it their piece of the business. And if it's truly their piece of the business, they'll work hard to help the organization succeed. That's why, three years after the coming of teams at Spectra Physics, production supervisor Russell Francis can say, "If they've got the right tools, if they've got the right information, 99 percent of the time they'll make the same decision that I would. And for the other 1 percent, it doesn't matter."

HOW DOES A TEAM DECIDE?

The right information gives your team the raw material for an effective decision. But what kind of decision should they make? To answer that question, both you and they will first need to understand the pros and cons of the following four basic kinds of decisions:

1. Minority decision. Here one or a few team members decide—either because there's no time to draw other people into the process or because they're the only people affected by the decision. In a crisis, the potential speed of a minority decision often makes it the best choice. If the decision-makers generally agree from the beginning, a decision can occur with very little discussion, though not necessarily so. If decision-makers disagree or if they want to consider a number of alternatives, a minority decision can take as long as any other kind. A major disadvantage of this method, especially if a minority makes a decision affecting everyone, is potentially weak team support. The people who have to carry out the decision may not feel like it really belongs to them. Further, as the complexity of the issue grows, the quality of a minority decision may decline if it doesn't reflect all relevant perspectives.

2. Majority decision. A simple majority vote allows the whole team to air their views and quickly reach a decision. For many issues, especially those in which few team members have a strong emotional stake, "majority rules" is often the best approach. But in cases where team members have an emotional or professional ax to grind, a majority decision may aggravate competing factions. One subgroup wins and everyone else loses, leading to what political scientists sometimes call the tyranny of the majority. As a result, a disgruntled minority, possibly one less than half the team, may resist the decision or resent those who supported it. In such cases, the consensus decision is usually a better way to go (see 4, below).

3. Unanimous decision. You have a unanimous decision when the whole team agrees on the best possible alternative. And it could well *be* the best alternative if the team spends a reasonable time reviewing information and other options. The main advantage of a unanimous decision is the strong commitment that usually comes with total agreement. The drawbacks occur in two different situations: when the team agrees immediately and when the team takes a long time to agree. If the team agrees quickly, there's always a danger of a poor decision due to group-think (a term coined to describe the failure of JFK's advisers to look at alternatives to invading Cuba at the Bay of Pigs). If the decision takes time, on the other hand, it often takes *a lot* of time, with no guarantee of real

TABLE 4–1
Four Kinds of Decisions

Type of Decision	Advantages	Disadvantages
1. **Minority** (as few as one person decides)	Quickest	Low commitment from non-participants
2. **Majority** (more than half of team decides)	Quick	Low commitment from "losers"
3. **Unanimous** (all agree on the decision)	High commitment, fast implementation	Can overlook other options
4. **Consensus** (all commit to carry out decision)	High creativity, high commitment	Takes time, patience, and facilitation skills

agreement, since some people may say they agree just to put an end to discussion and make it unanimous.

4. Consensus decision. You have a consensus when all team members openly express their commitment to implement the decision even if it's not their first choice. You do *not* have consensus if the decision in any way tends to compromise the ethics or values of any team member. The main advantages of consensus decision-making are (1) better, more comprehensive decisions through open discussion of alternative views and (2) a high level of team commitment, since everyone can at least say, "I can live with this decision even though it's not my first choice." The main disadvantages of consensus decision-making are (1) the time it takes, compared to, say, a minority decision and (2) the burden it places on your skills as leader to facilitate the process.

Table 4–1 summarizes the four main kinds of decision making.

Remember, not every situation calls for a consensus (type 4) decision. Suppose, for example, one team member happens to mention that a large piece of equipment gets in her way when she performs a certain operation. The two team members who use that equipment might make a minority (type 1) decision to remove it from the common work area. Or suppose two team members say they each want to represent the team on an interteam council. The best approach might be a majority (type 2) decision determined by secret ballot. Given the diversity of views found on most teams, a unanimous (type 3) decision is not only rare, it's usually inadvisable, since pushing for a total agreement can discourage some team members from expressing their legitimate concerns.

GETTING TO CONSENSUS

Consensus is the most usual kind of decision you'll be shooting for when you facilitate a team decision-making session. Again, consensus is general agreement by every member of the team to support a decision and actively participate in the related course of action. The decision won't be the first preference of every team member. (If it were, you'd have a *unanimous* decision.) At the same time, each person understands why the group hasn't adopted his or her first choice and can live with the decision of the group as a whole. You know you've got consensus when every team member can leave the meeting saying:

- "I've heard their positions."
- "I believe they've heard mine."
- "The decision doesn't compromise my values."
- "I can support the decision."

Your task as leader is to figure out when consensus is appropriate and to facilitate a meeting that allows all team members to lay their ideas and concerns on the table. Leading that kind of meeting requires (1) general facilitation skills and (2) a step-by-step process for reaching consensus—both topics you'll read about in this chapter.

When is consensus the right kind of decision? Any time you must gain the commitment of the whole team to a workable course of action. It's also useful when you want to focus an open discussion of differing needs, to generate a creative decision by people with hands-on experience, to coordinate people and resources, or to lay the groundwork for long-term teamwork.

Stay alert to other cues that signal it's time for you to reach consensus with your team. Does the team have little experience with consensus? Do some team members express their real views only outside of team meetings? Does the team often make hasty decisions or fail to identify the requirements for a sound decision? If so, consensus is probably the right way to go. On the other hand, consensus is usually unnecessary, undesirable, or impossible if the decision is a done deal, if it's outside the authority or expertise of the team, or if a crisis requires immediate action.

GENERAL FACILITATION SKILLS

When your team needs to make an important decision as a group, good general facilitation skills, or meeting-leading skills, are critical. Becoming an accomplished facilitator takes time and practice, of course, but a good first step is to review the following four component skills.

Prepare the Team for a Focused Meeting

Before any decision-making meeting, to prevent frustration for everyone, define for yourself the purpose of the meeting (for example, "to decide on ways to improve our shipping procedures") and the desired outcome ("two or three key improvements and a plan to implement them"). Then list the subtopics to be covered, think through how you'll handle them, and estimate the time for each topic. Decide whether to invite nonteam members, perhaps someone with special information or expertise. Finally, determine when and where the meeting will occur, and let participants know in advance—usually in a memo including the purpose, desired outcomes, and agenda. For an impromptu meeting, it's still important to let people know in advance about the purpose and desired outcomes.

At the start of the meeting, introduce any nonteam participants and restate the purpose and desired outcomes of the meeting. Review or revise the meeting agenda and respond to any questions. If this is an impromptu meeting, work with the team to create an agenda on the spot. Develop or review ground rules governing behavior ("no put-downs," for example, "no monopolizing air time," or "no interrupting each other"). Then define any special roles (say, that of a note taker), and describe any non-negotiables like discussion time limits or confidentiality. Be sure to get the team's agreement on these rules up front, so you can fairly invoke them later if you need to. Provide any information team members will need to make the decision—but present it neutrally without weaving in your own opinions.

Encourage Diverse Points of View

As team leader, you must see to it that everyone participates, no one dominates, and all opinions get a fair hearing. To begin discussion, ask everyone to contribute and clearly describe the type of participation you want—identifying decision criteria, brainstorming a list of options, or what have you. Let people know that you value what they say, and be careful whenever you toss out your own ideas—so team members don't think you're asking them to rubber stamp a foregone conclusion.

If not enough people are participating, you can call on team members by name or ask for a show of hands on a particular question. You can also ask the team to withhold any comments about ideas (so people feel free to contribute without being judged) and use one or more of these techniques:

- Ask questions that call for an extended response—for example, "What ideas do you have for reducing turnaround on special orders?"
- Ask for contributions from those with special knowledge or experience.
- Ask team members to think about an issue from a different point of view—the customer's or another team's, for example.
- Acknowledge and support the person who expresses an idea at odds with the majority.

- Encourage team members to express their partial ideas, which often contain the seed of a creative solution.
- Clarify and paraphrase ideas to help everyone understand them.
- Save your ideas and opinions until others have spoken.

At times, you may be so grateful for any participation that you overlook its irrelevance. Remember, though, your goal is to encourage constructive participation that helps achieve the purpose of the meeting.

Handle Disruptive Behavior

Even when team members' disruptive behavior is unintentional, it can undermine a decision-making session. Before that happens, you need to stop it—without making a scene and without embarrassing the people involved. Disruptive behaviors include getting seriously off the topic, nay-saying, dominating discussion, interrupting others, being an obstructionist, or holding a side conversation. These behaviors are no big deal once in a while. When they persist, they can reduce the value of the meeting and the decision.

How you respond to disruptive behavior should depend on how it's affecting the group, not on your own level of irritation. If the team doesn't seem to mind, let it pass and perhaps talk to the person privately. If the behavior begins to irritate the team or slows progress, use the following techniques, as appropriate:

- Stay calm and try a light approach—the least abrasive action that will correct the problem behavior.
- Reinforce any acceptable behavior in the disruptive person.
- Call attention to relevant ground rules established by the group.
- Wherever possible, allow the group to discourage the disruptive behavior.
- Return to the task at hand by summarizing what was going on before the disruptive behavior began.

If nothing else works, ask the person directly to refrain from the disruptive behavior. When you do, focus objectively and calmly on what the person is doing, not on the person's character. Sometimes it's helpful to acknowledge the reasons for any obvious emotion, usually anger or disappointment, that may be triggering the behavior. If your repeated efforts fail to stop the disruption, call for a break and talk with the person privately, or just let things cool down during the break and talk with the person after the session.

Keep the Team Focused and Moving

Decision-making sessions that drag or wander off the topic are worse than useless. They can actually reduce motivation to carry out any decision the team may reach. A primary part of your job as facilitator is to keep the team on track by managing both the meeting *content* and the step-by-step *process* you follow to reach consensus (see pages 67–70). This double-barreled task takes practice and concentration.

In general, let the group handle the subject matter of the meeting while you keep track of the flow of the meeting. Guide discussion toward consensus, give the team any information they need, and encourage joint ownership by limiting the number of ideas and opinions you contribute. If you must participate actively, consider asking someone else to facilitate the meeting.

Here are some other ways to keep the team focused and moving:

- Keep asking yourself if the discussion is on target: "Are we losing track of the criteria for a good decision?" "Are we talking about related but irrelevant issues?"—and so on.
- Refer to the agenda, purpose, desired outcomes, ground rules, nonnegotiables, etc., to help keep the meeting on track.
- Watch for cues that it's time to pick up the pace—for example, if the team looks bored or keeps saying the same thing in different ways.
- Watch for cues that discussion is moving too fast—for example, if certain team members are jumping to conclusions or can't seem to get a word in edge-wise.

- Summarize progress from time to time, or ask a team member to summarize and ask if the team agrees.

CONSENSUS: MASTERING THE PROCESS

The foregoing all-purpose facilitation skills will serve you in any team meeting regardless of its purpose or desired outcome. In a specialized meeting to reach a consensus decision, you'll also need to follow the step-by-step process outlined below.

Describe to the Team the Decision to Be Made

The purpose of the meeting is to reach a decision. Your description of the issue to be decided should draw a firm line between it and other issues. Cover the basics briefly and factually—what must be decided, why, by when, and any other useful background. "We need to decide how to allocate the new office space," you might say. Or "For the past two months, we've gone seriously over budget on travel expenses. We need to decide where to put our travel dollars next quarter." To promote an open discussion of everyone's ideas, avoid describing the decision in either/or terms. Point out the impact on the decision of any relevant policies, procedures, or priorities. And to make sure everyone's on the same page, you might want to ask someone to restate the main issue in his or her own words.

Explain Why Consensus Is Needed

Your explanation should boost enthusiasm and confidence by underscoring (1) the value of airing multiple views and (2) the power of consensus to improve team performance. With a new team, describe the main benefit of consensus—namely, a stronger decision that holds up because it meets everybody's baseline needs. With an experienced team, which may sometimes ask whether consensus is necessary in this case, stress that full discussion and agreement now can prevent later friction. Be sure to review your ground rules for discussion (see, "Agree on ground rules," page

94). Above all, make sure you're willing to abide by the team's decision. If you say, "make the decision" but really make it yourself, you can discredit yourself and sour the team on consensus.

Determine Guidelines for the Decision

Without solid guidelines for the decision (a.k.a. criteria for a good decision), the team can wander in pointless debate. Develop these guidelines by asking the group to brainstorm what's required in the decision, both the must-haves and the nice-to-haves. To help the team choose a vendor, for example, you might ask, "What are the most important things we're looking for in a vendor?" Ask if each guideline is essential or just desirable. Then rank them, as in the vendor example:

Essential	*Desirable*
1. Meet schedule	1. New equipment
2. Meet quality standards (1 and 2 tie)	2. Save money
3. Can't exceed in-house cost by more than 20%	3. Close by
4. Return calls within 24 hours	4. Electronic mail

Be careful not to confuse decision options with guidelines for the decision. One team working on incentives, for example, listed options like a half-day off, first pick of vacation schedule, and bowling bag. What they really needed were decision guidelines like "tangible items," "under $40 each," etc.

Lead an Evaluation of the Options

With the guidelines set, it's time to think through the options. Ask questions to help the team list a number of options—for example, "Who are the vendors we should consider?" Do your best to draw people out, get others to listen, and keep everyone on track. When you have a full list, ask the team to consider how each option satisfies the decision guidelines. Stay neutral, summarize the pros and cons, emphasize the important points, and prevent group-think by asking for alternative points of view. Remember, as facilitator, your job is to help the team keep track of what's been said, so you may need to downplay a desire to root for a favorite alternative. Let the team wrestle with the issues while you make sure they're looking at the options in terms of the guidelines they've already agreed to.

Help the Team Make Their Decision

As leader, you do not decide. Instead, you point the way and encourage the team to decide. Start by asking someone to propose a decision—an option already discussed, a variation, or a new option—and see how close the group is to agreement. You might say, for example, "OK, we've narrowed it down to three. Which one will it be?" Keep the team focused on their guidelines and other critical information. If they hesitate, reiterate the need to decide as a group. When you do sense an emerging consensus, summarize your understanding of the decision, or ask a team member to summarize. Then discuss any potential fallout, and if need be help the team revise their decision. If nerves get raw, retrace your steps and try to get more people on board. Explain that while there's no one best decision, the team has to be creative enough to find one that works for everyone.

Get Each Team Member's Commitment to the Decision

Until each team member can publicly support the decision, there's no guarantee of consensus. When you ask people if they can support the decision, you're really asking for a promise to help carry out the decision. And because you're also giving each person a chance to discuss any lingering doubts, you're also helping to ensure a real consensus. Call team members by name as you ask each person individually to commit to the decision: "Is everyone agreed on this? Andy?"—and so on. Wait for some sign of support, in word or gesture, from each person. If someone appears to have doubts, ask the person to say what modifications might make this decision work. Remain positive, for disagreement at this point can inspire some of the team's most creative thinking.

Plan Action Steps and Follow-up

The main benefits of consensus are better decisions and increased commitment to concerted action. But even with a strong consensus, you as leader must make sure that the whole team knows how to follow through on their decision. Help the team list and sequence action steps, decide who does what, and identify key dates and needed resources. If you have a true consensus, planning usually goes smoothly, and your part can be as simple as asking, "OK, who's going to contact the winning vendor?" After you make sure that someone is accountable for each step in a complete plan, distribute copies to anyone affected by the decision. Something in writing reminds team members of how they intend to carry out their agreement. Agree on ways to evaluate progress and, finally, thank the team for working hard to build a consensus.

TAKING TIME TO MAKE IT THEIRS

If team decision-making is starting to look a little daunting—and more than a little time-consuming—rest assured you're not the only one who finds it so. "The obstacle was the time and energy that goes into the process," says Bertha Van Marum of the University of Alberta Hospitals. "You have to wait for all the people to get all the information, assimilate it, discuss it, and arrive at their decision in whatever fashion it takes to get there."

But making the decision is only half the story. Your continuing role is to support the team's decision, to reinforce that team members really are in control, that it's their power for keeps. In part, that means standing back, even in times of crisis, says director Dean Olmstead, also of the University of Alberta Hospitals. "You're now seeing what you used to do happening in front of you, and you've agreed not to interfere. To maintain trust you must allow the staff to make these decisions."

On that point, Spectra Physics production supervisor Russell Francis could not be more emphatic: "I will support their decision, right or wrong, no matter what it is." How can he *say* such a thing? If you step in and override their decision, you destroy their self-confidence. You also render impotent any future effort on your part to build team ownership of team activities. "You need to keep them feeling good about themselves," says Karen Gideon of Amex Life. "Even if they're making mistakes or they're headed in a strange direction, you need to support people constantly."

"That's part of the team building," agrees manager Ray Lister of the University of Alberta Hospitals. "It might not be going the way I want it to, but as long as it's progressing, it's a good thing."

Neither of these drawbacks—the time it takes or the need to let the team fail—negates one irrefutable fact: People work much harder to implement a decision they have made as a team. "Sometimes people have a concept, and they will buy into that concept, and they will make it work," says Judy Pike, a production supervisor with Kenworth Trucks in Seattle. "Whether you think it could work or not, they will *make* it work."[3]

Some employees will like group decision-making from the very start. Others will feel at first like you've hung them out to dry. In either case, unless you're a natural—a Willie Mays of facilitators—learning to lead team decision-making sessions will take some special training and plenty of practice.

Eventually, though, both you and your team will recognize what Ryoko Marti, a long-time team member at Subaru-Isuzu, now knows: "Getting consensus takes time. But once we have reached that state, then everything goes very, very quickly."[4]

NOTES

[1] Zenger-Miller, Inc., research interview, 1992.

[2] Zenger-Miller, Inc., research interview, 1992.

[3] Zenger-Miller, Inc., research interview, 1992.

[4] Zenger-Miller, Inc., research interview, 1992.

Chapter Five

The Power of Letting Go

Stepping up to team leadership

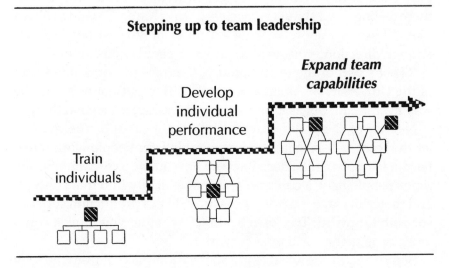

You really end up having more authority or more responsibility because now instead of just telling someone what to do, you've got to work with them so they learn how to do it, understand how to do it, and want to do it. And want to be a piece of the whole organization.

Karen Olson-Vermillion
Group Leader
Subaru-Isuzu Automotive, Inc.

As a manager or supervisor, you've always had two main functions: to make sure your team achieves its short-term goals and to improve long-term performance by developing individual employees. Now a changing world demands that you fulfill a third major function: to foresee and bring about changes that will help your company stay competitive.[1]

How do you find time for this third responsibility? Realistically, there's only one way. You must expand the capabilities of your team so the team can perform some of your traditional duties, such as budgeting, scheduling, setting performance goals, and technical cross-training. "You realize that you can't do everything," says area manager Ron Hubeck of Kenworth Trucks. "You have to have help from the floor."[2]

Under your guidance, your team will gradually assume increasing responsibility for day-to-day operations. When they do, you'll gain precious time to apply your experience in new ways—managing resources, ideas, technologies, and work processes. "Our workload is getting heavy enough that we really have no choice," says Dean Olmstead of the University of Alberta Hospitals. "If we want things to happen, we have to delegate."

To be a competent team leader, in other words, you must expand the capabilities of your entire team.

LEARNING TO LET GO

Learning to lead a high-involvement team is much more than "slapping a new program in place," says training specialist Ron Deane of Spectra Physics. "It's a cultural change. You have to change a lot of things you're personally doing. You have to give up some power."

For team leader Frank Moreno of Kenworth Trucks, "The biggest problem was letting go of some of my authority and giving it to someone else." And for area manager Stephen Merrill of Spectra Physics, "The very hardest thing is to give up power."[3]

Despite these fears, common early in the transition to team leadership, managers and supervisors find that expanding the role of the team does not shrink their own value to the organization. "If anything, I see myself as being more of a leader now than I was before," says Kenworth area manager Mike Boyle. "I have a role to play—to help people. I look at that as being more of a role instead of the daily 'You do this, you do this, you do this.' I don't need to do that anymore."[4]

"Once you let go, you find more and more things to do," says Ron Hubeck, also of Kenworth. "And it just keeps snowballing."

The key, then, is to let go of your traditional power—a scary thing to do because, in the old environment, that power is the source of your value to the company. Leaders who *won't* let go are like the old clerk who made himself "indispensable" by setting up a weird filing system nobody else could understand. In a similar way, traditional leaders sometimes refuse to share their knowledge or skills because they think "If anybody can do what I do, I lose my value, my job security."

Ironically, these managers doom themselves in a team environment, where the whole idea is to increase overall performance by sharing knowledge and skills with every employee. In that respect, leading teams boils down to letting go of your present role to make room for a much more valuable role: maximizing the contributions of other people.

President Sarah Nolan tells what happened when managers let go at Amex Life: "We set simple numbers for ourselves in the beginning that were 20 percent above a normal run rate. We blasted through those in about three months. Not by focusing on them. Not by beating on people to 'get the number, get the number.' But instead by asking, 'What is it you need to do this? How can we help you do this?'"

"That's the encouragement to let go," says Ron Hubeck of Kenworth. "It's not so much how much you'll lose, but how much you'll gain." For example:

- By giving up absolute power over your team, you gain the power to bring the best out of your team.
- By giving the team part of your present role, you gain time for a new, more strategic role.
- By respecting the abilities of your team, you gain the respect of your team.
- By learning to make others valuable, you gain value in the eyes of the company.

If this all still sounds a little odd, a little threatening, that's normal. When vice president Karen Gideon of Amex Life began her transition to team leader, she says , "I didn't really know whether I was setting off on the most fabulous adventure of my life or going out to Siberia. I did not know." Fortunately, she says, it turned out to be the former.

MAKING YOUR TEAM MORE VALUABLE

Every leader has a role in shaping the capabilities of employees. But your focus and methods will change as you transition from traditional leadership to team leadership:

 Traditional leadership: Train individuals. A traditional leader trains individual employees in the tasks that comprise their jobs. But since most traditional jobs require little independent thinking from employees, their potential contributions remain limited.

 Participative leadership: Develop individual performance. As you learn to encourage innovative thinking from employees, they gain the confidence to perform tasks requiring a wider range of skills. It's then possible for you to improve individual performance by training people in the higher level skills required to make more innovative individual contributions.

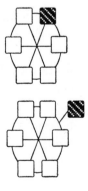 *Team leadership: Expand team capabilities.* To free your own time for your more strategic role (see Chapters 8, 9, and 10), you need to prepare your entire team to share leadership duties with you. In delegating activities like budgeting and scheduling, you in no way can dump your responsibilities on the team. Expanding team capabilities requires your long-term involvement with the team—training, coaching, monitoring performance, and assessing team readiness to take on new tasks.

HOW WELL ARE YOU EXPANDING YOUR TEAM'S CAPABILITIES?

It's part of your role as leader to provide team members with the challenges they need to keep growing, at the same time giving them the structure they need to succeed. How often do you make a conscious effort to do each of the following?

	Never	Seldom	Sometimes	Usually	Always
1. Assess the team's abilities and find ways to use untapped potential.	☐	☐	☐	☐	☐
2. Develop a detailed plan for handing off an important task to the entire team.	☐	☐	☐	☐	☐
3. Carefully weigh the pros and cons of stepping in when the team is having difficulty.	☐	☐	☐	☐	☐

As these three key behaviors indicate, expanding team capabilities involves much more than dropping tasks on your team and walking away. After all, you're still accountable for overall team performance. Preparing team members to share leadership involves:

- Assessing their strengths and weaknesses.
- Deciding what guidance they'll need in order to take on a new task or function.
- Giving guidance.
- Staying in touch as long as need be to make sure the team succeeds.

"A lot of managers just delegate everything, but all they do is dump their work on people," says production supervisor Alan Campbell of Kenworth Trucks. His advice? "Keep control of your group and delegate what needs to be delegated. Give people the authority to do what you know they're able to do better than you can."

THE TRANSFER OF RESPONSIBILITY: MASTERING THE PROCESS

To successfully expand the capabilities for your team, you'll need to monitor their changing needs and abilities , and work with them until they can successfully perform each new task. "You always have to be aware of how ready they are to take on new responsibilities, to take that next step," says production supervisor Linda King of Spectra Physics. In particular, be alert for the following cues that you may need to transfer specific activities that you now perform:

- You think that the team is ready to perform a task that you normally do.
- You need more time to address new responsibilities or priorities assigned by the organization.
- The team could do its work better if it had more decision-making responsibility in a particular area.
- The team needs to make direct contact with other people or teams in order to clarify and negotiate issues.
- Team members are asking you for more responsibility, decision-making authority, or challenges.

Once you've decided it's the right time to transfer a specific task to the team, use the following process to help ensure a positive outcome for both you and your team:

Assess the Team's Ability to Perform the Task

Successfully sharing leadership with your team depends in the first place on how accurately you judge the team's readiness to handle each new task. First, think through the task—what's involved and what will it demand of the team? Then analyze the team's ability to perform that particular task.

Develop a Plan to Enable Team Members to Perform the Task

If your assessment of the team's abilities has revealed areas of weakness, you'll need to work with team members to develop their skills. A good plan includes setting task boundaries and deciding on the right mix of training, coaching, and monitoring.

Describe the Task, Benefits, and Task Boundaries to the Team

It's important for team members to fully understand what the task involves and how they will benefit from taking it on. Meet with team members to go over the task, the limits on their decision-making authority, and any other key issues. Ask for the team's commitment to take on the task.

To build shared ownership, you need to involve team members in the decision to pass the responsibility or task to them. This is a two-way action in which you ask for team input and commitment, and you pledge your own in return.

Work with the Team until It Performs the Task

In expanding the team's capabilities, your ongoing responsibility is to maintain the right degree of involvement as the team gradually masters the task.

HOW TO WORK WITH YOUR TEAM AS THEY MASTER THE TASK

Once the team has agreed to take on the task, you'll perform the following four activities to help your team gradually master the task:

- *Set task boundaries.* You set task boundaries by specifically defining the limits or constraints (such as time, resources, or budget) that the team must adhere to in performing a task or making a decision.
- *Train.* You train by introducing team members to an entirely new skill or body of information useful in handling a task or type of problem. This new skill could be a technical, administrative, or interpersonal.
- *Coach.* You coach by offering tips, tactics, demonstrations,

and encouragement to improve existing skills in team members. Coaching is the critical skill that allows you to turn team performance issues into opportunities for building capabilities and self-confidence.

- *Monitor progress.* You monitor by closely observing the team's efforts to perform the task—without taking direct action. You remain alert and ready to act if necessary.

Setting Task Boundaries

As a traditional leader, you tell people what to do and how to do it. As a team leader, you set task boundaries that define the non-negotiable limits on the team's decision-making authority. Task boundaries establish the arena within which the team decides the specifics of performing a given task. Allowing this kind of leeway gives your team an increased sense of ownership and often leads to creative improvements in how the task is performed. When setting task boundaries, identify the minimal non-negotiable boundaries within which the team has to operate, for example:

- Organizational requirements
- Quality requirements
- Quantity requirements
- Customer or stakeholder needs
- Budgetary limitations
- Space limitations
- Technical limitations
- Availability of resources
- Key dates and deadlines
- Regulations

Avoid setting too many or overly restrictive task boundaries. They can cramp creativity and reduce the team's sense of owning the task. "I've been too tight with some people," admits section manager Stephen Merrill of Spectra Physics. "They come back and say, 'You're not giving me enough breathing room.' " On the other hand, you're setting the team up for failure if you fail to identify all of the critical limitations. According to production manager Brad West, also of Spectra Physics, "You've got to set the proper boundary conditions so they have a good chance of being successful. What you're really doing is defining all the constraints that you're aware of so the team will understand within what parameters they need to work."

Once you've set the task boundaries, don't change them without cause. Rather than undermining trust by rewriting the rules of the game, give careful thought to the minimal constraints *before* you announce them.

Training

When you need to train or prepare the team to perform an entirely new skill, keep in mind that team members, like anyone else, tend to worry about their ability to do something the first time through. So make a special effort to buoy their confidence and make sure they get off to a good start. Most of the training you'll conduct or farm out deals with three kinds of content:

- Technical skills (such as using a computer program)
- Administrative skills (such as scheduling, budgeting, or purchasing)
- Interpersonal skills (such as resolving conflicts or leading a meeting)

To prepare for a training session, begin by identifying the learning objectives—or what the team will be able to do as a result of the training. For example: "At the end of the session, team members will be able to prepare a six-month vacation schedule." For both you and the team, learning objectives clarify the what and why of training and help you explain how the training relates to the job. With clear learning objectives, you can reasonably decide who should conduct the training (you or a subject matter expert) and what training methods you'll use—presentation, discussion, demonstration, or practice. Incorporate as many methods as possible to accommodate a variety of learning styles.

Coaching

Coaching means helping team members refine a skill they already have. In contrast to training, in which the team learns an entirely new skill, coaching is a way to stretch and improve the team's developing skills. Even with advanced teams—who must address issues like shifting priorities and turnover—coaching allows you to turn a performance problem into a chance to build skills and confidence. According to Brad West of Spectra Physics, "You need the patience to coach people through the process, to really set it up so they can be successful." Coaching can involve:

- Pointing out a new way to use a skill.
- Putting the screws on the team to try out new skills.
- Providing information that improves the way team members use a skill.
- Helping the team look beyond "the way we've always done it."

Timing is critical in coaching—either at the beginning, middle, or end of the team's efforts to master a new task. At the beginning, you coach to make sure the team gets off on the right foot. In the middle, you should check in, coach, and make sure all is going well. At the end, coaching helps you evaluate how well the team has done and decide what further coaching is appropriate. Eventually, as the team becomes more self-reliant, says support director Susan Mumme of the University of Alberta Hospitals, "They identify when they need me to come in, when they need my help. Because I have links to other parts of the department and parts of the hospital, I can coach them."

Table 5-1 specifies coaching activities you might use at each general phase of handing off a task or responsibility to the team.

Monitoring

When you monitor, you actively listen, observe, and interpret information but refrain from direct action. Then, if the team gets bogged down or a full-blown crisis comes up, you're ready to decide what action, if any, to take.

TABLE 5–1
Coaching Activities as the Team Learns a Task

Coaching Activities	Beginning	Middle	End
1. Give words of support.	X	X	X
2. Explain how the task ties in with overall goals	X	X	X
3. Explain how the task links to something they've done before.	X	X	
4. Work with the team on the task for a short time.	X	X	
5. Hold a formal progress meeting.		X	X
6. Get an informal progress report.		X	X
7. Confirm the team's commitment to complete the task.	X	X	
8. Restate the desired outcome and task boundaries.	X	X	X
9. Help the team identify the expectations of key customers.	X	X	X
10. Help the team see things from a different point of view.	X	X	X
11. Help team obtain resources and information.	X	X	
12. Debrief the team on how well it performed the task.		X	X
13. Discuss what went well and what they'd change next time.		X	X
14. Identify follow-up action items.		X	X

You'll need to monitor even a very advanced team when it's taking on a new responsibility. "I got bit several times for stepping too far back and not giving the team enough guidance," says production supervisor Linda King of Spectra Physics. "I assumed they could handle the role, and they weren't ready yet." Your up-front assessment of the team's ability to take on a given task should help you decide how closely you'll need to monitor progress.

When you monitor the team's activities, you continue gathering information on two important matters: (1) any changes in the nature of the task itself and (2) the changing ability of the team to perform the task. The specifications, scope, complexity, and schedule of a task sometimes change, making it more difficult for the team to succeed. So do the dynamics within the team—growing skills and experience, frustration with a problem, or inability to perform a given task. Keep asking yourself questions like these:

- Has the task itself changed in any important way?
- Is there new information the team needs to know about?
- Have the boundaries changed in some way?
- Has the customer changed?
- Have the expectations changed?
- What are the indications that the team is doing well or struggling?
- Is it time for me to act? What will happen if I don't?

Often the best way to gather information is directly, through meetings or written reports. When you monitor progress informally, be sure to avoid giving the impression that you're spying, that you're excessively worried, or that you're bent on micromanaging the team. It's a fine line to walk. The best approach is to stay relaxed—or appear to be, anyway—and be honest with the team about the fact that you need to stay in touch.

TO INTERVENE, OR NOT TO INTERVENE

When a problem comes up, you've usually got a very tough call to make. Should you step in and help? If so, what exactly should you do? Here's the basic dilemma: You want the team to solve their own problems whenever possible, so it's sometimes better to let them struggle, figure things out, and gain experience and confidence as a result. On the other hand, you don't want the team to struggle so much that they lose all faith in themselves. Some failure is good—it's a learning experience for them—but you can't allow a real catastrophe to jeopardize the business or the long-term growth of the team. In short, deciding when and how to intervene is a recipe for major-league heartburn.

"I don't think it would be beneficial for me to jump right in and solve the problem," says Susan Mumme of the University of Alberta Hospitals. "They grow from solving the problem themselves. They see that they can resolve the conflict as a group. It gives them a sense of accomplishment."

But at Spectra Physics, production supervisor Russell Francis has seen the downside of a totally hands-off approach. "Sometimes, when a team is not as productive as I think they need to be," he says , "I will stay away too long. I assume that they will work their way out of it instead of stepping in and providing more direct leadership."

Spectra manager Stephen Merrill sees it this way: "I've been in the trenches doing these jobs, and I know the answers. Another guy comes along, and he certainly doesn't know the answers I know. How do I let that guy go out and find the answers without sinking?"

It's a cardinal rule for team leaders that sometimes it's preferable to let your team fail. Says production manager Brad West, also of Spectra: "You've got to accept the fact that one way people learn is through mistakes. They will fail and because you're responsible you also will fail. But the key is that they need to learn and grow from those experiences."

These points of views, obviously all over the map, highlight just how sticky this particular wicket can be. Deciding whether to help a struggling team can be as difficult as the initial decision to hand off the task. It *may* be time for you to intervene if the team has a serious technical, interpersonal, or performance issue; ignores a task boundary; looks like it will miss a deadline; seems unsure of how to proceed; asks for help or refuses to ask for help; forgets an essential work step; lacks critical information or resources; or runs into organizational barriers. Before intervening, carefully think through what your involvement will be. Ask yourself:

- Should I intervene to resolve the problem?
- What kind of involvement would be best?
- How can this problem be solved in a way that further develops the commitment and abilities of team members?

Your goal is to provide the team with exactly the help it needs to resolve the issue—without your reclaiming the task or making the team feel like they couldn't possibly handle the task without you. And remember, you're the coach, not the back-up quarterback.

LIFE AFTER THE BIG BANG

The main point of this chapter—of the whole book, really—runs something like this. When you hand off some of your present leadership functions, you free yourself to take on some of the leadership functions now performed at the level just above you. In effect, both you and your team *step up* to a higher level of leadership. Meanwhile, as the team gradually assumes control of their own day-to-day work, team members use their hands, their minds, and their collective experience to make the organization more competitive.

Obviously, it takes time for you and your team to get used to this more flexible way of working. Different organizations define the change in different ways depending on needs and conditions. But overall, the change is not simply the passing of power and responsibility from one group to another. Like the cosmic Big Bang scientists talk about as the origin of the universe, the coming of teams is a breathtaking *expansion* of power for everyone. The world of teams is an expanding universe for leaders and team members alike.

So contrary to what you might think, when the team takes over some of your old responsibilities, your value to the organization actually increases. Now you can *leverage* your time and experience by getting higher quality and greater productivity from people who truly own their own jobs.

"The best use of my time right now is getting support for these teams," says Stephen Merrill of Spectra Physics. "I'm there when they have an issue that needs to be elevated to management, to give them the support they need, in terms of people, money, whatever it is."

Likewise for Kenworth area manager Ron Hubeck: "I'm not as much involved in the actual production as I am a resource center now. People come to me and say 'Can I do this?' or 'Can you get a vendor to come in and talk to me?' Things like that."

"My title is still manager," says Abe Kossol of Spectra Physics, "but my job now is to lead people to participate, to coach, to manage by principles instead of policies."[5] Likewise for manager Ray Lister at the University of Alberta Hospitals, there *is* life after the Big Bang. "People's roles have expanded," he says. "And so has mine."

GRIEVING FOR THE SCRAMBLED EGGS

Like these managers and supervisors, you may already understand the important role you can play in restoring competitiveness, improving productivity, and boosting employee morale in your company. But even if you buy the basic idea of teams—that is, you *understand* the idea—it's easy to feel threatened by the change, to regret the perceived loss of power and control to employees. Right now in your company, a team environment might still be somebody else's pipe dream, perhaps the brain child of a high-level champion who's asked you to read this book. So at this point, it may seem easier to go through the motions than make a genuine effort to change.

"It took us a while to realize this," says one internal consultant in a high-tech firm outside Boston. "You can't assume managers will fall in line and support this just because their bosses do. They need to buy in to the new role and let go of the old one. Either you want it, really want it, or it really won't work."

Some managers, of course, never totally accept the new role. For them, teams are a loss, pure and simple: loss of status, loss of perks, loss of authority, loss of responsibility. They resent having to "give away the store" to their subordinates. In the words of one team leader, a former naval petty officer, "Managers work for years to get those scrambled eggs on their caps. They do it by dousing fires and playing the rules of the old system. So it's really hard for them to let go, to cash it in for something they don't even understand.''

One long-time manager in a Midwestern utilities company isn't afraid to say what he thinks: ''I can see why they want to do this, but that doesn't make it any easier. Most of these front-line people don't know their—well, you know what I'm saying. These people used to work *for* me. Now they're supposed to work *with* me, and I can't see the big improvement.''

These may be normal feelings, sure, but if *you* can't accept the new way of operating, you'll never convince your team that it's both necessary in the short term and more satisfying over the long haul. The unfortunate fact is that bitterness over a perceived loss of status or power can terminate your rebirth as a builder of high-involvement teams.

AN ALTERNATIVE FORM OF POWER

To make the transformation work, you must believe in the power of teams and live that belief every day. It may seem to fly in the face of common sense, but leader after leader has found that by giving up one form of power, you gain another, vastly superior, form of power. Letting go of your tight grip on employees gives you the freedom to explore many other important areas of the business crucial to the teams and to your own growth.

''It's made me a hell of a lot better manager,'' says Sarah Nolan, president of Amex Life Assurance. ''But better than that, it has made me a better person. Because when you think back about the things that you learn as you go up [the management ladder], they have to do with control and people being in their proper assigned spot.''

How do you undo that traditional mind-set, and move on to become a successful leader of teams? ''You can't make this cultural shift if you are not honest with people,'' says Nolan. ''It's taken me a long time to learn how critical that is. And some of it's hard because you're learning yourself, so you don't even know what to be honest about. The first thing is, 'We don't know where we're going, but it's to these objectives, and no, I don't know if this will work.' So that takes away the all-knowing, all-seeing, powerful leader and parent. And being honest about that sometimes is devastating. But in the end at least you have a foundation where everybody understands.''

Even though you'll no longer be "the all-knowing, all-seeing, powerful leader and parent," what you will gain is far more valuable in the expanding universe of teams. "I think that people in organizational settings are social beings," says vice president of human resources John Hofmeister, a pioneer in "teaming" previously at Northern Telecom and now at Allied Signal Aerospace. "It's only a matter of tapping into their wealth as individuals and reaching a shared understanding about how much wealth is present in a group of people." And what's the leader's role in tapping into the wealth of the team? "A leader or a facilitator with process skills is just invaluable. Identifying potential problems or issues is important, identifying the gaps between the players—different beliefs, different value sets, or different other factors. But the fact that we're all basically social beings makes the teaming process very natural."[6]

What you'll lose is the power and perquisites of a boss. What you'll gain is the power to mine the wealth of natural resources within your team.

NOTES

[1] For details on foreseeing and influencing change, see Chapter 8.
[2] Zenger-Miller, Inc., research interview, 1992.
[3] Zenger-Miller, Inc., research interview, 1992.
[4] Zenger-Miller, Inc., research interview, 1992.
[5] Zenger-Miller, Inc., research interview, 1992.
[6] Zenger-Miller, Inc., research interview, 1992.

Chapter Six

We Think Therefore We Are

Stepping up to team leadership

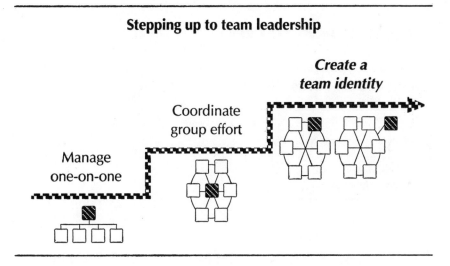

I had slogans like, "My door is always open." And that was my invitation for people to pass over problems to me. I don't use that slogan, necessarily. The door is always open, yes. But not for that.

Gus Boetzkes, Manager
University of Alberta Hospitals

No group will ever become a team without a clear sense that "this is who we are and this is what we do." The murkier their sense of themselves as a team, the more likely their energy will dissipate in pursuit of many "priorities." Cultivating a firm sense of team identity in many ways depends on your hard work and careful observation—not to mention your long-term dedication. As leader, you'll help the team figure out what is and what is not important to success. You'll help clarify a shared purpose, coach the team toward challenging goals, and celebrate success. Only that kind of leadership can transform a group of employees into a unified team.

But how do you get a group of individuals to agree on *lunch*—let alone on a shared purpose? And even if you do, how do you sustain the team's commitment over time?

ARE YOU HELPING TO CREATE A TEAM IDENTITY?

Think about your current behavior with your team. How often do you make a conscious effort to do each of the following?

	Never	Seldom	Sometimes	Usually	Always
1. Help clarify and reinforce the overall purpose of the team.	☐	☐	☐	☐	☐
2. Help the *team* set clear, achievable short-term goals.	☐	☐	☐	☐	☐
3. Recognize and celebrate the team's achievements.	☐	☐	☐	☐	☐

Even for an accomplished team leader, there's no minimum acceptable score for these questions. To create a team identity, you need to pay attention to desired results and encourage progress with regular praise and other recognition. The best kind of team identity derives from achieving ambitious goals the team has set for itself.

There's no mystery to creating and maintaining a team identity. It will be a routine part of your role for the life of the team. You begin by helping the group develop a mission statement that expresses their shared purpose. You get agreement on ground rules that regulate day-to-day teamwork, and you help set team goals that mesh with corporate goals. Then you maintain and refine the sense of shared purpose, give and receive feedback on progress toward goals, help the team learn from their mistakes, and recognize and celebrate success.

These and other leadership activities are the focus of this chapter. With them, you will build and sustain the deep conviction that you're all in this together.

TURN ON, TUNE IN, DROP OUT

To lead in a team environment, you must teach people to see you
as somebody other than the person with the answers. Your new
purpose as a leader is to *turn on* team members to what they can
be, *tune in* team members to what they must do to succeed, and
eventually *drop out* of day-to-day problem solving. When you do
those things, you begin to build a true team, capable of responsible,
independent action. Here's a quick summary of the evolution from
traditional leadership to team leadership.

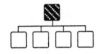

Traditional leadership: Manage one on one.
When you manage strictly one on one, you often
have to play the role of expert. Employees expect
you to make the tough decisions and solve the
tough problems. As a result, they feel part of a
team in name only: "We have the same boss,"
they might say to an outsider, or "We're in the
same department."

*Participatory leadership: Coordinate group ef-
fort.* At this point, employees get a taste of ownership. You ask for their input before deciding,
and they now communicate directly with each
other about some issues. But you still pack the
heavy guns. You make the tough calls, deal with
the trickiest problems, do most of the planning,
and take corrective action whenever things get
off track.

Team leadership: Create a team identity. The
identity you create and maintain is founded on
the team's belief that "We've got a brain in our
heads. We can do this ourselves." You're still
there—coaching, scouting resources, asking
questions, leading cheers. But even though you
may *be* a technical expert, you no longer *play the
role* of technical expert with the team.

"In the end, you stop answering the questions that they can answer," says Russell Francis, a stellar team leader with Spectra Physics in Eugene, Oregon. "You stop solving the little problems that they can solve themselves." Even so, you can never put yourself on automatic pilot. "That's probably the biggest problem, personally, that I have," he admits. "It's not that I still want to be the answer person. It's that I find myself falling into the trap."

GETTING IN SYNC WITH THE LIFE CYCLE OF YOUR TEAM

A team, like a living thing, changes over time. At birth, the team has no clear sense of itself as an independent unit. Then, over time, it undergoes four predictable phases of growth described in Chapter 3: Forming, Storming, Norming, and Performing.[1] You will need to facilitate appropriate team-building activities during each of these phases:

- *Forming.* Early on, team members get to know each other and begin sorting out their roles. They need to agree on their purpose as a team, set goals, and establish ground rules. Both you and the team may feel excited, enthusiastic, anxious—all at once—and you're all on your best behavior.

- *Storming.* The unsettling but inevitable second phase is marked by conflict among team members, between you and the team, and between the team and the organization. On the positive side, people are asking questions, negotiating trade-offs, and even challenging you (a good sign). It's a creative and productive time because team members are getting comfortable with new ideas. But conflicts breed resentment, and team members can become frustrated or disillusioned.

- *Norming.* Gradually, team members resolve many of their difficulties, learn to focus on the work, and enter a norming phase. The problem now is that team members may be so determined to avoid further conflict that they hold back controversial ideas and avoid dealing with delicate situations.

- *Performing.* Finally team members figure out how to maintain smooth relations and get the job done at the same time. They deal with conflicts as they arise, challenge ideas without getting personal, operate at peak performance, and take pride in their success. At times, the team hardly seems to need a full-time leader. Still, you need to maintain the team's momentum with new challenges.

Every team forms, storms, norms, and performs. In fact, it's not uncommon for a team to repeatedly return to an earlier phase as conditions change. You must stay alert to these changes so you can choose and administer team-building activities that meet the team's changing needs.

In the following pages, a number of activities that help you create a team identity are described under two headings: *launching activities* and *refueling activities.* Launching activities are most useful with a new team, refueling activities with an established one. But an established team can profit from certain launching activities, and a relatively new team can profit from some refueling activities. As you get comfortable with your new role, through training and experience, you'll gain skill in facilitating these activities—as well as increased sensitivity to the phases of your team's development. Then you'll be better able to choose activities from either category to meet changing needs of your team.

LAUNCHING ACTIVITIES

In the forming phase, team members are gathering impressions, forming relationships, and establishing patterns of behavior. Will team members pull together to achieve their goals or squander themselves in useless conflict? The following launching activities can help ensure a productive team from the very beginning.

Bring in a Senior Manager

A presentation by a senior manager is useful whenever the team needs to link into organizational goals—before working on a team mission statement, for example, or setting team goals. With an intact team, the senior manager might talk about the organization's mission and values, how the team can contribute to overall performance, the future for the organization and the team, and higher level support for the team. With a work-process improvement team, the manager might touch on the importance and scope of the process to be improved, on management expectations, and on available resources. Your job is to help the manager plan a presentation that encourages a sense of team purpose compatible with the rest of the company.

Agree on Ground Rules

Ground rules established by the team govern how team members work together during meetings, impromptu discussions, and at other times. Typical ground rules include "Begin meetings on time," or "Double-check all work before handing it off to another team." Establishing or reviewing ground rules is especially important when the team is forming, adding new members, coordinating activities, taking on a new task, reforming, and breaking in a new leader.

Develop a Mission Statement with Your Team

The first step in transforming a group of individuals into a team is to gain a shared understanding of the team's purpose. A team mission statement can generate enthusiasm and commitment by expressing that purpose. A mission statement also clarifies the team's part in achieving organizational goals and helps each person make stronger individual contributions.

To develop a mission statement with your team, explain the value of a mission statement, review or establish ground rules for the discussion, and provide key information—such as sample mission statements or the organization's expectations of the team. Then stimulate discussion by asking, "What has our team been formed to do?" "How can we add value to the organization?" "What would customers say our purpose should be?" and related questions.

Mission statements vary in length, but to be memorable, 200 words is probably an outside limit. Many statements, like the following example from a cross-functional order processing team in an insurance company, are quite short:

Team Mission Statement

We will continuously improve service
to the customer, reduce overall risk
to the company, and treat each other
as equal members of the team.

Post the statement in a prominent place and have the team refer to it frequently—when setting goals and priorities, making long- and short-term decisions, and coping with changes. Review your mission statement as a team from time to time and rewrite if necessary so it continues to reflect the thinking of the team and the organization.

Develop Performance Goals with Your Team

Goals are measurable performance targets that the team agrees to achieve. They divide the mission statement into manageable steps and help channel team efforts toward broad organizational goals. When team members set goals as a group, they feel a greater sense of ownership, see the scope of effort required to achieve the goals, and allocate resources more effectively. Group goal setting is useful at the beginning of any major effort—when the team is forming or starting a project, for example—or at regular intervals, such as quarterly. Every goal should be specific and measurable with a firm completion date. For example, ''By the end of the second quarter, we will process 95 percent of orders within three days of receiving them.''

REFUELING ACTIVITIES

No matter how committed to achieving its goals, any team can burn out. Fortunately, you can prevent or minimize the effects of burnout with the following activities for refueling your team.

Conduct a Progress Check

Conduct a progress check during either a regular or special meeting whenever the team needs to assess how well it's moving toward its goals. You'll discuss progress and obstacles, of course. You'll also coach, train, clarify authority, recognize success, share feedback, generate action items, revise schedules, and identify needed resources. A progress check is especially helpful when the team is having difficulty staying on schedule or appears stressed out for some other reason.

Conduct a Team Self-Evaluation

Like all living things, your team is constantly changing, and periodic self-evaluation can help it grow in a positive direction. Team members use a written assessment tool to decide how well they're working together. Then you meet with them to discuss their views and develop an improvement plan. A self-evaluation meeting is especially useful at the start or finish of a project or when the team is having some sort of difficulty.

Table 6-1, the assessment tool "How Well Are We Working Together?" can help you guide an objective discussion of sensitive team issues. Before the meeting, distribute and explain the tool to all team members and ask them to complete it before the meeting.

At the meeting, explain that this is a time to improve teamwork, not to lay blame. Then ask questions like, "Which items on the assessment do we need to pay the most attention to? Why?"—and help the team evaluate their own strengths and weaknesses as a team. Conclude discussion by asking, "How can we work together better as a team?" Make a list of constructive ideas, adding your own at this time.

TALBE 6–1"*How Well Are We Working Together?*"

Directions: This short assessment will help you evaluate how well your team is working together. Statements 1 through 10 are traits of effective teams—*as a group*. For each statement, circle the number indicating how little or how much you think the statement applies to your team.

	Stongly Disagree	Disagree	Neither Agree nor Disagree	Agree	Strongly Agree
1. The team knows exactly what it has to get done.	①	②	③	④	⑤
2. Team members get a lot of encouragement for new ideas.	①	②	③	④	⑤
3. Team members freely express their real views.	①	②	③	④	⑤
4. Every team member has a clear idea of the team's goals.	①	②	③	④	⑤
5. Everyone is involved in the decisions we have to make.	①	②	③	④	⑤
6. We tell each other how we are feeling.	①	②	③	④	⑤
7. All team members respect each other.	①	②	③	④	⑤
8. The feelings among team members tend to pull us together.	①	②	③	④	⑤
9. Everyone's opinion gets listened to.	①	②	③	④	⑤
10. There is very little bickering among team members.	①	②	③	④	⑤

Scoring and Interpretation

To find your total score add the numbers in the circles. To find your average score, divide the total score by 10. My total score: _____ My average score: _____

If your average score is 4 or higher, teamwork is strong. If your average is between 3 and 4, teamwork is healthy, but there's room for improvement. If your average was 2 or lower, something is getting in the way of teamwork. Whatever the score, discussing these issues together with an open mind is likely to improve teamwork.

During a team meeting, your leader may ask you to help compute a team average for each of the 10 items. To prepare for a discussion with your team, complete the following:

A. When I look at the average (not the total) score I gave my team, I am satisfied/dissatisfied (circle one) with the way the team is working together now.

B. The item on the assessment that we need to discuss most is number: _____ This item needs attention because: _____

C. Regardless of my answer in Question A, all teams need to have goals for improvement.
My best idea for helping my teammates work together more effectively is: _____

_____

Recognize Teamwork

Recent research on motivation has verified at least two important facts: Performance tends to rise to the expected level of performance, and praise produces better results than criticism does. That's why you help build confident teams when you recognize their efforts to achieve challenging goals.

Recognize your team frequently, not just when they reach a milestone, and recognize *behaviors* (such as agreeing on and using a standardized process) as well as *results*. Remember also that you can help create shared leadership by finding ways for team members to recognize one another.

Recognition may be offered publicly or privately, to individuals or the entire team. When recognizing a team effort, be sure to acknowledge hidden as well as obvious contributions so no one feels slighted. Formal rewards, like raises and promotions, are usually scarce, but other tangible and intangible forms of recognition can be equally motivating. In addition to spoken praise and thanks, consider a written note, a visit or call from upper management, an unexpected break with refreshments, an afternoon off, an outing, special souvenirs, a chance for the team to describe its efforts to other teams, a mention in the newsletter, a posted announcement, certificates, plaques, and so on. Use your imagination to find forms of recognition that work for your team.

Recognize What's Going Well

In the crush of day-to-day events, a team can lose sight of how much progress it's actually making. One remedy is "recognizing what's going well," a simple activity used during a team meeting that gives each person a chance to describe some good thing that the team, or a team member, has done. Use this exercise when energy drops, when the team has reached a milestone, or when you want to spotlight the growth of the team.

To recognize what's going well, simply explain the purpose of the exercise—to increase energy and teamwork—and ask the team to take turns briefly describing something that's going well. Begin with yourself if no one volunteers. Ask people to be specific—for example, "I think it's a major success that design and production got together on this data collection." When everyone has had a chance to speak, thank the group and move on.

This activity may feel awkward at first, but after a few times most teams get a charge out of it.

Learn from Your Mistakes

When team members sincerely try to improve, they will make a major mistake once in a while. When they do, they need to discuss why it happened and what they can do to avoid similar mistakes. If you treat a mistake by the team as an opportunity for improvement, not for blame, you teach the team that a setback can bring knowledge and that knowledge can bring success.

If possible, allow some time before debriefing a mistake. Before the meeting, announce the topic and hand out a list of questions for team members to consider ahead of time—for example, "What was the expected outcome?" "What was the actual outcome?" "What went wrong from your point of view?" "From the customer's point of view?" and "What lessons did we learn?"

At the meeting, review the questions you've sent out. You'll need your best coaching skills to give constructive feedback about what happened. Continue to ask questions that help the team clarify the lessons of their mistake. Offer your own views, but don't lecture or patronize the team. To conclude, list the main lessons, identify any actions necessary to minimize damage, and reaffirm your continuing support.

Celebrate

Achieving team goals is clearly cause for celebration, as is any positive event for the team. By giving team members a chance to enjoy both their success and one another, a celebration builds enthusiasm and teamwork. A celebration is also appropriate when the team finishes a project, seems to be losing enthusiasm, is working especially well together, or is having difficulty meeting its goals.

To plan a celebration with your team, review any non-negotiables—budget, time, space, policies, etc.—and brainstorm a list of activities on a flipchart: a lunch or dinner together, an outside activity like bowling, or whatever. Make sure everybody's ideas get a fair hearing. Then eliminate ideas that don't meet the non-negotiables, tally the team's top three, and reach consensus on one. Finally, celebrate! And continue looking for ways to celebrate on a regular basis.

Develop a Hand-off Plan

A hand-off plan outlines the transfer of tasks from you to your intact team as the team gains the ability to perform them. The plan details who will perform which of your present tasks and how the team will prepare to take them on. A plan increases the chance for successful hand-off by giving both you and the team a clear idea of the road ahead.

Use a hand-off plan when the team is ready for greater responsibility, when you assume leadership of a new team, when your changing role requires you to hand off some of your current activities, or when your team needs new skills for a new project.

Begin by keeping an activities log, briefly noting your daily duties, for a week. Then divide the tasks you perform into four categories:

1. Tasks the team should take on now.
2. Tasks the team should take on eventually.
3. Tasks I should keep or give to a specialist.
4. Unnecessary tasks that no one should perform.

Next, specify the training that will give team members the skills and knowledge to perform each task to be handed off. Set measurable standards for each task. Then decide what technical, administrative, or interpersonal training the team needs in order to meet those standards. Finally, identify the most suitable kind of training—usually classroom training or on-the-job cross-training. You may want to work with company trainers to choose an approach.

Remember, this hand-off plan is a tool, not a straightjacket. If the plan later appears unfeasible, negotiate revisions with your team.

Get Closure When a Team Reforms or Disbands

When a team reforms or disbands, a formal meeting for the purpose brings a sense of closure and satisfaction that carries over to the next team or project. It also ties up loose ends and highlights necessary follow-up. For example, if some people remain as a team, they need to know what duties are being handed off.

In a meeting or meetings with team members and others involved, decide whether the job is done. Has the team fulfilled its mission and achieved its goals? Spend time reflecting on the life cycle of the team. Ask questions that draw out discussion, such as "What did you gain from the experience?" "What advice would you give to others?" "What did the team accomplish?" "What problems did the team encounter?" "What follow-up do we need?" and "Who will do it?" Be sure someone keeps notes. Conclude the meeting with some sort of celebration.

Communicate key information from the meeting to appropriate people, especially anyone who needs to know that the team is disbanding. Later, it's a nice idea to update ex-team members about the results of their work.

CREATE A TEAM IDENTITY? LET'S GET REAL

No matter what kind of team you're leading, you need to be realistic with yourself and the team right from the start. No team-building activity, no matter how successful for other teams, can guarantee the commitment of every member of your team. Creating a team identity takes time, and mistakes will be made by all.

"A number of the experiments won't work," says Sarah Nolan of Amex Life. "They will just flop, and they will flop so publicly. Employees who are trying to learn what the new way is, as you are trying to learn what it is, can be quite doubtful. They can be very resistant. They know how to succeed in the old way. They don't even know what the new way is, and you can't even *articulate* it!''

The way you handle mistakes, both yours and theirs, is key. Your team will develop no positive sense of identity unless you make it clear that it's OK to make mistakes as long they learn from them. ''They have to know that when they make mistakes we managers aren't gonna take 'em out back and shoot 'em,'' says Randy Baldwin of Fite-Baldwin, Inc.[2]

Setting realistic goals with your team, and liberally praising whatever success they achieve, will tend to keep things on track. But remember, getting involved is a fundamental change for most employees, and some will have a steeper learning curve than others. ''You have to understand the reality around levels of awareness,'' says Sharon Chinn of Meridian Insurance. ''There are just different degrees in different people of how aware and committed they are. You can't get discouraged by it.''

Team members will waver. You will waver. But steel your resolve to create a firm and independent team identity.

''Don't back off,'' says Karen Gideon of Amex Life. ''If it gets ugly, and people decide they don't like it, hang in there. I look back at some of the team experiences, and some of our breakthroughs came right when we were about ready to throw in the towel. It's almost like they need to get to a certain critical state before they're ready to accept it.''

So whatever you do, don't give up. Things often get better sooner than you think if you keep saying to your team in word and deed, ''This is your baby. I'm here to help but not to do your thinking. You can make this work.''

For Abe Kossol, manufacturing manager with Spectra Physics, it took some trial and error to learn how to create a team identity. ''The first thing I did with this team-based environment was take the walls down around my office. I thought, I'll open the communication, people can come in and chat with me, and then it's safe because they really know what's going on.'' Later, Kossol realized he had perpetuated his old leadership style. So he put the walls back up. "I don't *want* people coming in and checking with me all the time, asking, 'Is everything OK?' Putting the walls back up is a sign that I want people to make broader decisions that have more impact on the business."

WHAT DOES A FIRM TEAM IDENTITY LOOK LIKE?

Many mature teams exercise complete authority over day-to-day operations. For example, teams that were forming five years ago in a Silicon Valley high-tech firm are now performing quite well. These teams oversee the total manufacturing process, redesign systems and processes, monitor quality, respond directly to customer complaints, conduct peer evaluations, select new team members, develop budgets, perform cost analyses, solve technical problems, and take disciplinary action as needed.

Managers of these teams no longer perform their traditional functions. Instead, they coach, advise, channel information, secure resources, arrange for requested training, champion innovations, run interference, and in general link the teams to the larger organization. In the five years since these teams formed, productivity, quality, morale, and profitability have gone through the roof.

That is what you're working towards. The needs of your organization, of course, dictate the specific form your team will eventually take. But all teams with a firm identity are essentially the same. They're confident. They respond to customer needs by becoming what the organization needs them to be. And they can turn on a paradigm.

"The biggest gain from our teams is the ability to make plants more competitive," says Joe Dulaney, a human resource manager with Levi Strauss & Co. "For the employees, teams add a lot to their life and their job because they're not locked into routine, repetitive motions. They're using their brains as well as their bodies."

A team that says with conviction "this is who we are and this is what we do" is a vital resource in any organization. When you can build teams like that, you will be too.

NOTES

1 Bruce W. Tuckman, "Developmental Sequence in Small Groups," *Psychological Bulletin* 63, no. 6 (1965), pp. 334–99.

2 Zenger-Miller, Inc., research interview, 1992.

Chapter Seven

From Many, One

Stepping up to team leadership

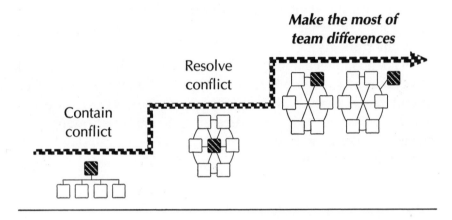

Contain
conflict

Resolve
conflict

*Make the most of
team differences*

*A team is similar to a battery, you know. If you let one cell go dead,
then it's much harder to get the car started.*

Ramiro Mendoza
Group Leader
Subaru-Isuzu, Inc.

By the year 2000, according to the U.S. Bureau of Labor Statistics,
women will make up 47 percent of the work force, and minorities
and immigrants will hold 26 percent of all jobs, up from 22 percent
in 1990. Clearly, it's no longer a man's world—and certainly not
a white man's world. White males will account for only 32 percent
of those entering the U.S. work force by the turn of the century.
What's more, these changes in gender and race are only the beginning. Growing diversity in the workplace reflects many other basic

human differences as well: age, country of origin, native language, socioeconomic background, education, literacy, religious beliefs, military experience, sexual orientation, work and life experience, and physical and mental capabilities.

Somebody might say that these differences really don't make much difference in the workplace because "a job is a job is a job."[1] But especially in a team environment, where you'll encourage people to bring more creativity to their work, different people perceive and perform the same job in very different ways. Differences in background, in other words, often go hand in hand with radically different work styles and points of view.

So it's no longer a question of when. The North American work force is already a vigorous mixture of peoples reflecting every permutation of humankind. The central question now is "How do we make the most of this ever-increasing diversity?" Among your challenges as a team leader is working out a practical, day-by-day answer to that question.

TWO FACES OF DIVERSITY

Differences among people make life interesting and exciting. They can also raise unwelcome issues. And when team members can't resolve these issues, differences can give rise to full-blown conflicts. In the worst case, if the team fails to protect self-esteem and preserve good working relationships, these conflicts destroy the possibility of real teamwork.

Like any other seasoned leader, you can probably reel off a list of diversity-related issues that you've either seen or experienced:

- Language differences make communication difficult.
- Teams break into subgroups based on cultural background, education, or other differences.
- Women in a male-dominated field, and vice versa, are discounted (or worse) by the other gender.
- Widely differing social or cultural assumptions (for example, what it means to be on time or polite) cause friction within the team.

- Poor math and verbal skills limit the contributions of otherwise eager employees.

These and other issues often crop up when unlike people begin to work together. Until you can help your team acknowledge their differences and resolve their issues openly and positively, it will never achieve the open-handed give-and-take of genuine teamwork.

People of different backgrounds bring different perspectives and abilities to any task. If you can focus those differences on a shared goal—and that's a very big if—then a diverse team is much more likely to generate and implement creative, workable ideas. Once you get a group of diverse people working harmoniously, team members will often piggyback on one another's ideas to build a shared plan, with each person's contribution reflecting his or her unique background and experiences.

"When you get people together in a team, the ideas seem to spring forth," says Bertha Van Marum, manager of pediatric nursing at the University of Alberta Hospitals. "One person will charge another person, and things that you've never thought of will come out. In our own environment, we are sort of locked in," she continues. "When we deal with other people outside our world, we begin to see things a little bit differently."

MYTH AND REALITY

The idea is not new that there is strength and creativity to be found in a unified group of diverse people. In fact, you'll find the basic notion stamped into any U.S. coin: "E pluribus unum" (a Latin motto literally meaning "From many, one"). But gone is the myth of the melting pot, in which gumbo, goulash, and gezpacho magically turn into canned tomato soup. Today people derive a sense of unique worth from whatever makes them different—gender, heritage, physical abilities, and so on. It's precisely those differences that add new perspectives to a shared team identity.

An obvious point bears mentioning here: You'll need to be especially sensitive to people who are in some fundamental way differ-ent from yourself. For reasons that may have nothing to do with you or them as individuals, these are the people you may have difficulty drawing into the give-and-take of healthy team dynam-ics. So to bring the best out of every member of your team, you must first look inward and work to eliminate any hint of bias from your values, words, and actions. Only then can you help your team to accept their differences and apply them constructively in striving for shared objectives.

As team leader, you'll be helping diverse people not only to generate creative ideas, but to select, implement, and track the impact of their ideas (see Chapter 4). According to GE chairman John F. Welch, Jr., by "facilitating, greasing, finding ways to make it all seamless," team leaders must focus a range of individual perspectives during complex group interactions like decision-making, problem-solving, and conflict resolution.[2] "This place couldn't run without [our] spending a lot of time facilitating the group process," says a veteran team manager at Cummins Engine, which implemented teams in 1973. "This is not done simply to improve communications or to make people feel good. It is done so that we can get at the guts of solving very practical problems right out there on the shop floor."[3]

In short, maximizing the performance of your team requires your ability to balance the needs and strengths of the diverse members of your team. When team members feel valued and secure, individual differences tend to promote team spirit, creativ-ity, commitment, quality, and productivity. But ignored, belittled, or otherwise denigrated, individual differences can create ten-sion, leading to burnout, isolation, confusion, and poor perfor-mance. One of the trickiest parts of your new role is to make the most of team differences, be they biological, cultural, or professional.

DEALING WITH CONFLICT

As a team forms and evolves, the demands of working as a close-knit group require changes in how you deal with conflicts resulting from team differences. Gradually, you'll replace your traditional leadership behaviors with those of the effective team leader:

Traditional leadership: Contain conflict. Traditional leaders tend to ignore differences among employees—in the hope that if you don't name it, it won't create problems. But if misunderstanding and resentment erupt into conflict, damage to work relationships can be irreversible despite the leader's earnest effort to smooth things over.

Participative leadership: Resolve conflict. Minimizing team differences won't work wherever team members must work together every day to solve problems and make decisions. Recognizing that fact, participative leaders coach the group to get conflicts out in the open and resolve them constructively.

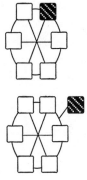

Team leadership: Make the most of team differences. Team leaders go beyond simply resolving conflict. They actively identify and acknowledge differences among team members. They help team members understand and accept their individual differences. Then they maximize the potential of the group by finding ways to capitalize on diverse backgrounds, viewpoints, and skills.

ARE YOU MAKING THE MOST OF TEAM DIFFERENCES?

Consider the things that you do as a leader to help make differences a positive force for the team. How often do you make a conscious effort to do each of the following?

	Never	Seldom	Sometimes	Usually	Always
1. Treat team members with respect while acknowledging their different motivations, values, work styles, and traditions.	☐	☐	☐	☐	☐
2. Encourage each team member to participate fully.	☐	☐	☐	☐	☐
3. Help the team get unstuck when differences lead to conflict.	☐	☐	☐	☐	☐

Behaviors like these help you demonstrate respect for individual differences, and ultimately apply these differences as a source of strength for your team. Says nursing manager Thelma Inkson of the University of Alberta Hospitals: "When I come in, I try to be positive and friendly to the staff and treat them very equally. It becomes a role model." It's important to note, however, that while treating people equally certainly means treating them all with respect, it doesn't necessarily mean treating them all the same. Because people are different, they don't relate to us, nor we to them, in exactly the same way. Still, even when you model these behaviors—accepting individual differences and treating everyone with respect—you won't necessarily turn your team into the Starship Enterprise, where beings from different planets live and work in total harmony. "What I see now," says Inkson, "are staff nurses that may or may not like each other very much. But they have a working relationship."

HOW TO MAKE THE MOST OF TEAM DIFFERENCES

Consider some of the many ways that the members of your team may differ from each other:

- Age
- Experience
- Gender
- Race
- Culture
- Way of expressing concerns
- Ability to work out problems
- Assertiveness
- Comfort with change
- Way of interpreting data

- Personal goals   • Job responsibilities
- Values   • Sense of humor

How similar or different are your team members in each of these areas? Do these similarities and differences promote teamwork or in some way prevent your team from achieving best results?

While both similarities and differences may promote teamwork, you can do a number of things as leader to minimize the drawbacks and maximize the advantages of diversity within your team. In general, the more you know about the members of your team, the better you can draw on their unique viewpoints, knowledge, and skills. "In a team we've got to know the people, their strengths, and their weaknesses," says group leader Basil Serra of Subaru-Isuzu. "Focus on each person's strength, not weakness. Use that strength."[4]

The five Basic Principles, outlined in Chapter 3, are a foundation for building trust in a group of diverse people. Unlike thinking and behavior patterns rooted in social background or other differences, the Basic Principles are rooted in human nature. They address issues vital to everyone, regardless of the differences that make each person unique:

- *Basic Principle 1: Focus on the issue, behavior, or problem, not on the person.* Focusing on the issue doesn't mean that people should ignore individual differences. It does mean that those differences cannot become the focus of ridicule, attack, or exclusion.

- *Basic Principle 2: Maintain the self-confidence and self-esteem of others.* Lacking self-confidence and self-esteem, people of any background often fail to contribute what only they can uniquely offer. That's why both you and the team will fan the fires of creative teamwork if you frequently recognize individual and group achievements.

- *Basic Principle 3: Maintain constructive relationships.* Everyone needs the acceptance of others and through it a positive connection to the workplace. By encouraging and modeling the acceptance of individual differences, team members can help each other make the most of those differences.

- *Basic Principle 4: Take initiative to make things better.* An organization that demands conformity can squelch individual initiative by disparaging the value of diversity. To realize the potential of a diverse work force, you must encourage employees' constructive ideas and actions outside of traditional patterns.
- *Basic Principle 5: Lead by example.* While good role models vary from culture to culture, effective leaders and team members the world over demonstrate certain key convictions: belief in the wisdom of the group, willingness to sacrifice for the group, and pride in the attainments of the group.

ENCOURAGE EVERY TEAM MEMBER TO PARTICIPATE FULLY

Think of diversity as an organizational asset. Make it a habit to point out the benefits of diversity when working with your team. Whenever possible, reinforce the value of the broad perspective and wealth of skill and experience that a diverse team can bring to bear in solving problems. "Treat people with respect and give them credit for having intelligent ideas," says Jean Conover, a director with Amex Life. "That will go a long way, I think, to making you an effective leader."

Remember that people outside the mainstream—culturally or professionally—can feel removed, self-conscious, or uncomfortable contributing to the team effort. Help these people by praising any contributions they make. Express your belief often, especially during full team meetings, that diversity can be a useful asset to any team effort. "It seems like once they start talking and the ground is broken or whatever, you can't shut 'em up," says area manager Mike Boyle of Kenworth Trucks. "But at first, it just doesn't seem to happen. It's quiet, and you better be ready for that."

So how do you break the ground? "I coach the people that aren't really interested in being involved," says Subaru-Isuzu group leader Ramiro Mendoza. "Those are the ones that you want to bring into the fold and say, 'I need your ideas.' And that's where the real challenge of coaching comes along. You already have people that know what they need to do. But you've got to bring this other one, who really isn't sure about anything, into the group. When that person melds in with the team, it's an accomplishment for me. That's when I'm standing there beaming. And I think I have a right to because our whole group is working the way it's supposed to."

THE IMPORTANCE OF BEING FRANK

Open communication is vital to helping diverse team members contribute to the common effort. When people bottle up what they really think, you lose important points of view, group decision-making bogs down, and team members can end up working at cross-purposes.

"The only way it's going to work in a team-based environment is to get things out on the table," says production supervisor Linda King of Spectra Physics. "If you have an issue with somebody, address it. Address it and move on." And at Kenworth Trucks, production supervisor Alan Campbell has emphatic advice for leaders and team members alike: "All you have to do is say the truth and talk the truth."

A noble ambition for sure, but very difficult for team members who, for reasons of personality or culture, will do anything to avoid a confrontation. If you notice a team member hesitating to speak out, it's your responsibility to make it safe for that person to contribute. You can't let your team lose a unique perspective just because someone is uncomfortable about entering in a lively exchange or about speaking up when the room is quiet. A typical device for good team leaders is to ask each person individually if he or she has something to add rather than allowing the active people to monopolize discussion. "The critical thing is inclusion," says Dean Olmstead of the University of Alberta Hospitals. "Bring everybody on board. Their opinion counts."

GETTING UNSTUCK WHEN DIFFERENCES LEAD TO CONFLICT

Insisting that team members adhere to the Basic Principles goes a long way toward minimizing the stress and possible damage of confrontation over team differences.

Sometimes, though, the team will find itself utterly stuck—unable to move forward because of serious conflict. When this happens, keep in mind that moving to teams causes enormous stress for everyone involved. Both you and your team must learn new roles, and many team members will be struggling with the heaviest work responsibilities they've ever had. Under these conditions, team differences can sometimes become the focus of caustic wrangling. A good way to help your team get at the root of the conflict and make positive use of their differences is to walk the team through the following step-by-step process.

Call a Time Out and Describe the Nonproductive Behaviors You See

Stay alert for destructive conflict within the team and be ready to call a time out when necessary, either on the job or during a meeting. If you can get the team to stop and look objectively at how they're interacting with each other, you've already taken the first step through even the most treacherous impasse. Your main focus now as leader should be the *interpersonal process*, not the content or topic of discussion. In this case, the part of the process to be addressed is the specific behaviors that seem to be preventing team members from working together effectively. Your goal now is to help the team look objectively at these behaviors.

Before you intervene, observe what the team is doing and saying. Are they attacking each other? Talking in circles? Interrupting each other? If so, politely invite them to take a break. You might say, for example, "Let's stop for a minute and take a look at what's going on here." When feelings are running high and you're unsure about whether or when to step in, remain quiet, give the team some time to vent their feelings, continue observing, and then call for the time out. Immediately after that—taking special care to focus on the issue, not the person—briefly describe the specific team behaviors you've observed. "I see people cutting each other off," you might say, or, "We don't seem to be listening to each other." Calmly describing the nonproductive behavior helps the team discuss what's happening without fear of attack. Avoid mentioning names or detailing who said what to whom.

Even after watching the group for a while, you may not be able to pinpoint the reasons for the conflict. That's normal because many conflicts have several or ambiguous causes. Call for the time out anyway and start the team moving in a more positive direction. Don't try to solve the problem yourself. Engage team members in developing a joint solution. If necessary, move discussion to a more appropriate setting or agree on another time and place to work on the issues involved.

Ask Team Members to Say What's Keeping Them from Moving Forward

When your team reaches an impasse, some members will have strong insights, and some will have strong emotions about what's happening. Unless you give people a chance to say what they think and feel—and assure everyone a fair hearing—emotions can explode later like a spray can in a bonfire. You can't deal with resentment and resistance unless you get them into the open.

Ask the team to describe what they've been observing and what they see as preventing them from moving forward. "Now, let's hear what each of you sees going on right now," you might say. Then, "Carl, what have you noticed that might be keeping us from working together more smoothly?" To give everyone a chance to speak, ask the team to keep their comments brief. If someone rambles, politely ask for the main point. If someone prefers not to respond, that's OK. The person may have no firm opinion or just may not want to speak right then. Avoid an exchange of comments at this time. Instead ask the team not to respond to each other until everyone has had a say. That usually prevents further wrangling— and encourages better listening.

Some team members will probably try to blame each other instead of stating their views objectively. If they do, calmly refer the team to the question at hand: "What (not *who*) is keeping the team from moving forward?" Remind team members to focus on issues and behaviors, not on personalities, and to follow all of the Basic Principles. Jotting down each person's main point will help you later to summarize and clarify what that person said.

This whole step should take no more than a few minutes. When everyone has had a say who wants to, move on.

Summarize and Clarify What Each Team Member Has Said

Now that their views are out in the open, team members could be feeling vulnerable. Let them know that everyone's heard and understood their views—even if not everyone agrees with them. Essentially you've now agreed to disagree.

Summarize each person's main point. By paraphrasing, you demonstrate good listening skills, acknowledge each view, and further objectify the discussion. Don't restate everything, just what each says about the source of the conflict. For very large teams, summarize what the whole group has said. Otherwise, address each person by name and summarize his or her main point—for example, "Maria, I hear you saying we should keep the customer's needs in mind even if it takes an extra day to finish the project. Is that right?" Then wait for the person to confirm or correct your summary. If, in summarizing, you need to describe how someone is feeling, do your best not to inflame emotions any further. "Yoshimi," you might say, "you feel frustrated because you think we've got a poor procedure for getting sign-offs." If you're unsure about what someone was saying, ask: "Wayne, are you saying you'd like more say about your role on the next project?"

At this point, especially, you may have to work to stay neutral. If you offer a critique of someone's views, you can aggravate people by appearing to take sides. Again, don't try to solve the problem. At most, you're gathering information about a possible problem so it's positively unwise to jump to a solution. Your job now is to summarize the various views so the *team* can begin thinking about a shared solution.

Ask Team Members to Identify Points of Agreement and Disagreement

With the various views now clearly and calmly expressed, team members often surprise themselves with how much they actually agree on. All you really have to do is ask them to identify main points of agreement so far. As before, give everybody a chance to speak. Then do the same for areas of disagreement. To make the transition to disagreements, you might say, "We all seem to be saying we want to make a contribution as a team. Now, without losing sight of that, let's list our points of disagreement. Any thoughts?"

If people seem uncomfortable itemizing their disagreements, remind them to think about specific actions and issues as opposed to personalities. Once they've identified the main areas of disagreement, summarize what they've said, emphasizing any comments that may help the team move forward.

Throughout this step, be positive. If the team just wants to rehash where they disagree, ask questions to help them see where they agree—but don't pretend, of course, that differences don't exist. Your purpose now is to lay the groundwork for future cooperation by clarifying the various points of view. You want everyone at least to understand the views of other team members. Remember, to successfully rechannel conflict, you as leader must withhold judgment. The team needs to get the sense that while you don't necessarily agree with everyone's view, you see the basis for everyone's view. As far as you're concerned, there should be no right or wrong answer. Allow team members to speak and don't challenge what they say. If other team members do challenge a speaker, repeat your initial question: "What are the points of agreement?"

Invite the Team to Suggest Ways to Proceed

Once the team gets a handle on why they're struggling, they must apply their knowledge to improve their working relationships. It's this knowledge—about what separates them and what brings them together—that allows them to make constructive use of their own diversity. The result can be a team eager to get on with a common task, not just a group of people trying to coexist.

Ask team members to suggest positive actions that address the points of agreement and disagreement they've just identified. How might they prevent this kind of conflict in future? What would they like to see happen? How are they willing to change? After you talk about some long-term changes, ask the team about what they can do in the short term. To move from the long term to the short term, you might say, ''Yes, we can definitely put this issue on the meeting agenda for next month. What else can we do right now to ease tension?''

Be practical about any suggestions. As team members propose actions, ask questions to help them clarify how their ideas might be carried out. Help them sort through ideas, look for workable suggestions, and segment any major course of action into small, practical steps. Useful suggestions might be as simple as deciding when to meet again. Before the team agrees to act on any suggestion, ask to make sure that everybody's had a chance to say their piece.

As the team considers possible actions, make it clear that they probably won't find a quick fix for any serious problem. The critical thing, you should say, is that everyone, in good faith, must bring their best thinking to bear on any remaining disagreements—which may require considerable time and effort to work through. Remember that you, as leader, are not the fixer. Your purpose is not to solve the problem or sugar-coat team differences but to help the team begin to solve the problem for themselves. What you're really doing is reducing their need for you by teaching them how to take a constructive, responsible approach to resolving their own issues.

Throughout the step-by-step process outlined above, it's probably impossible for you to show too much respect for individual points of view. You don't have to agree with every comment, of course. You do have to show that you understand every comment and that you respect the person who cared enough to offer it to the team.

WHAT'S IN A TREND?

People of all kinds—who inhabit the shop floors and increasingly the boardrooms of Main Street, North America—are an asset that leaders can no longer afford to squander. According to a recent national report, "The ability of American business to recover lost productivity, regain its competitive edge, and move into the 21st century [depends] on its ability to . . . manage the diverse talent [of] its new work force."[5]

But what's happening now is only the next phase of a trend (if you can call it that) that's been reshaping your world for at least a thousand years. Take a quick look at the millennium whose end we are now privileged to see:

- After the utter bondage of medieval serfs came the worldly power of Renaissance craftspeople.
- After bloody revolutions in France and America came mass production, mass education, and a vast new middle class.
- And now, in the midst of the civil rights and women's movements, comes the death of the communist state.

Through it all, the drift of history has made it possible in this Noah's Ark we call North America to build the team-based company. It's a trend, yes—like the Great Deluge was a trend. And it requires a transformation that most managers and supervisors have only begun to make.

You may be way out in front of this trend. If so, you already make it a daily habit to assess how your attitudes and behaviors are affecting people unlike yourself. Still, according to R. Roosevelt Thomas, Jr., executive director of the American Institute for Managing Diversity at Atlanta's Morehouse College, "An individual can appreciate difference, be free of bias, and still not know how to manage a diverse team."[6]

But why should you as team leader go through so much soul-searching and expend so much energy to capitalize on a diverse work force? "It is no longer simply a question of decency," says Thomas. "It's a question of business survival in an unstable environment. [Serving] a global consumer requires a multicultural business outlook. It only makes sense that [a global consumer should] be dealing with a multicultural, diverse work group."[7]

The fact is, the modern work team is one of the most effective tools yet devised for tapping the strengths of all employees, thereby promoting the survival and success of your organization.

For Anthony Carnevale, head of the Institute for Workplace Learning, "Diversity matters because new competitive standards are changing the way the work is done. Success will depend more and more on the ability of people to work in teams and to communicate with people who are different."[8]

And according to Ruben Simental of Pacific Bell, "The biggest push for diversity at my company came from the realization that survival depended on making it work. If we don't value our customers and our employees and take everyone's opinions into account, we're dead meat. For us," he continues, "diversity means valuing the individual and gaining the greatest potential from each person."[9]

Clearly, learning to leverage team differences is a key part of your action plan. Diversity is a business issue you can't ignore if you're trying to maximize your own value to the organization.

"A manager's job is to try to get the largest return out of their best asset," says Sarah Nolan, president of Amex Life Assurance. "That's optimizing your asset. And your best asset is the creativity of your people."

"We are individuals," says Mark Kornhauser of Black & Decker, "even though we keep talking about teams and team concepts. You not only have to accept that, you have to *leverage* it. That's what made us who we are. Other homogeneous societies lack some creativity because they don't have the diversity and perspectives we do. I think it's an advantage."

NOTES

[1] A paraphrase of Gertrude Stein's famous line. "A rose is a rose is a rose." Ms. Stein herself qualified as a walking lesson in diversity.

[2] Thomas A. Steward, "GE Keeps Those Ideas Coming," *Fortune,* August 12, 1991, p. 49.

[3] Robert H. Guest, "How Team Managers Look at Team Management: The Cummins Engine Experience," *New Roles for Managers, Part III* (New York: Work in America Institute, 1989), p. 67.

[4] Zenger-Miller, Inc., research interview, 1992.

[5] Audrey Edwards, "The Enlightened Manager: How to Treat Your Employees Fairly," *Working Woman,* January 1991, p. 45.

[6] R. Roosevelt Thomas, "Affirmative Action to Affirming Diversity," *Harvard Business Review,* March/April 1990.

[7] R. Roosevelt Thomas, "Affirmative Action to Affirming Diversity," *Harvard Business Review,* March/April 1990.

[8] Patricia A. Galagan, "Tapping the Power of a Diverse Workforce," *Training and Development Journal,* March 1991.

[9] Patricia A. Galagan, "Tapping the Power of a Diverse Workforce," *Training and Development Journal,* March 1991.

Chapter Eight

Class-A Fire Insurance

Stepping up to team leadership

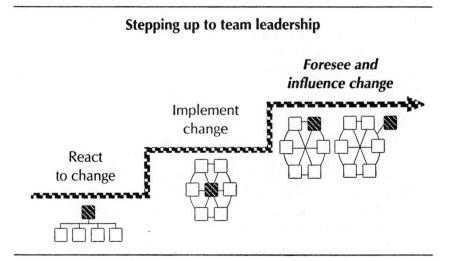

In the past as a manager you just put out fires. Now you have time to be proactive, to look into the future, to look at projects and processes that need to be analyzed and worked on.

Ray Lister, Manager
University of Alberta Hospitals

Because more and more organizations are using teams to cope with the furious rate of economic change, your future is bright if you can master the skills of leading teams. Strangely, though, you won't realize your greatest value as a leader if you focus solely on your team—or even on your department. You'll also have to monitor the whole company, follow industry trends, and bring about internal change to keep pace with a feverish world.

122

"I have a better understanding of the corporate vision now, the corporate values," says Gus Boetzkes of the University of Alberta Hospitals. "I monitor the whole organization more now than ever before."

The main characteristic of a forward-thinking organization is the same in every industry: Virtually every employee strives every day to identify and meet the most critical needs of the customer and the company. As team leader, you'll help build that kind of company. First, you'll scan the internal and external environment for new ideas and information. Then, with other key people, you'll champion internal improvements that anticipate changes in the external world.

"As managers, we've always been focused on seeing ourselves as a catalyst for change," says Barb Anders of American Express, "and that is expanding. We need to be very flexible, very proactive. It reduces stress to see that we are in charge of this change process. We are the change agents making it happen. We're not just being done to. This is something really being driven by the managers."

FORWARD THINKING

The question most commonly asked by managers moving to teams is "What will I be doing if I hand off many of my current duties to my team?" The long answer is the book you're now reading. The short answer is this: "You'll spend much of your time foreseeing and influencing changes that help keep your organization strong."

When your team begins to take on some of your traditional management duties, says Sharon Chinn of Meridian Insurance, "it gives you a chance to be much more forward thinking, much more the visionary, rather than putting out the daily fires and making decisions around daily fires."

To become "much more the visionary," you'll apply your new "forward-thinking" skills to:

- Big-picture planning and critical back-burner projects.
- Redesigning internal systems to support team development.
- Exploring new technologies that could improve performance.
- Devising ways to delight the customer and outpace the competition.
- Pinning down rapidly evolving customer needs.
- Giving your team, peers, and even higher-level colleagues a wider perspective on key business trends.
- Exerting far greater influence over organizational barriers to change.
- Helping the organization continuously reinvent the way it does business—so it can better respond to changing technologies, markets, and regulations.

To foresee and influence change is to be proactive, not *reactive*—to *prevent* fires so you don't have to fight them. And that's why, for both you and your company, the forward-thinking skills described in this chapter are class-A fire protection in a tinder-dry business environment.

CHANGING LEADERSHIP FOR CHANGING TIMES

They're quick, flexible, and committed: No wonder teams are ideally suited to a changing world. But before high-involvement teams can prove their real worth, your traditional leadership skills must evolve radically:

 Traditional leadership: React to change. Traditional leadership reinforces the *status quo* with ongoing small changes—mostly devised by managers and other experts—in well-established ways of doing things. When overwhelming outside forces make those methods obsolete, managers often have to scramble to adapt. As a result, a traditional organization can quickly fall behind more vigilant and active competitors.

 Participative leadership: Implement change. Here, while leaders don't necessarily embrace change, they do accept that regular internal change is a part of doing business. Participative leaders pride themselves on their ability to involve front-line people in generating improvement ideas. But improvements in a participative organization tend to be pre-fab changes devised and imposed by the executive eyes and ears of the company.

 Team leadership: Foresee and influence change. As your team gains confidence in performing some of your present duties, you gain time to function as another set of eyes and ears— and another brain—for the organization as a whole. You'll be anticipating outside change, formulating and proposing internal changes, and influencing others to bring about those changes, in part by seeking out and integrating the ideas of your team.

"Since we put a team together that worked as a team," says production supervisor Alan Campbell of Kenworth Trucks, "they've taken the day-to-day responsibilities on themselves. I sit back and do my job, which is the forward planning, or what helps them best."

ARE YOU A FORWARD THINKER?

Consider how you currently operate—whether your leadership style helps you foresee and influence change. How regularly do you do each of the following?

	Never	Seldom	Sometimes	Usually	Always
1. Keep an open mind about new ways of doing things.	□	□	□	□	□
2. Encourage and reward team members who promote innovation.	□	□	□	□	□
3. Tell the team about the latest technologies, markets, regulations, and events in the organization.	□	□	□	□	□

These and other forward-thinking activities described in this chapter will help you foresee and influence change, and develop a new relationship with your team. "They've got control of their daily life, I've got control of mine," says Kenworth supervisor Campbell. "Before, I had control of them, and they had control of me. Now, it's more relaxed. I've got more free time to help them more and give them what they want. And they've got more free time to make their environment better for themselves."

REQUIEM FOR A BUGGY WHIP

Foreseeing and influencing change is a big part of your new role because of a big shift in the way that companies see themselves. At one time, most organizations operated according to what's now called the closed-system view of their connection to the world outside. Many companies still do.

Organizations subscribe to the closed-system view if they think they can get by without paying too much attention to events in the world outside. These organizations focus mainly on their own internal operations and give little heed to fluctuations in the outside business environment. They view changes in customer needs, new competitive pressures, and sudden market changes as secondary to their main job: operating efficiently, productively, and profitably.

In the closed-system view of things, the manager's job is to focus *inward* and make darn sure that:

- Established processes are running as smoothly as possible.
- Employees use the "single best way" to perform any given job.

The closed-system view worked well when the world changed slowly. But even then, some companies got caught with their guard down. Take the once-thriving buggy-whip industry—or more recently, the typewriter industry. When computers and word-processing software began to appear, it didn't matter anymore who built the best typewriter because a new technology was about to overwhelm the entire market. What happened to all those typewriter companies that couldn't shake their closed-system thinking and learn to adapt to a changing world? May they rest in peace.

Today, organizations are moving to teams in part because of the failure of the traditional, closed-system approach to business.

OPEN FOR BUSINESS

The "*open*-system" view, as the name implies, is a completely different way to took at the organization. The open-system view says that, in a dynamic business environment, companies will prosper only if they continuously adapt to changes in that environment. Graphically, an open system looks something like Figure 8-1.

Every organization needs input, such as raw materials, component parts, or information. The organization then adds value for the customer by transforming input into output—finished products and services. The long-term success of an organization depends on how well it improves its products and services in response to feedback about ever-changing conditions in the outside environment.

The open-system view stresses that every organization is dependent on outside forces to survive and flourish. What nourishes an open system is the continuous flow of information into the organization about the changing demands and opportunities in the outside world—about customer buying habits, for example, or

FIGURE 8–1
The Open-System View

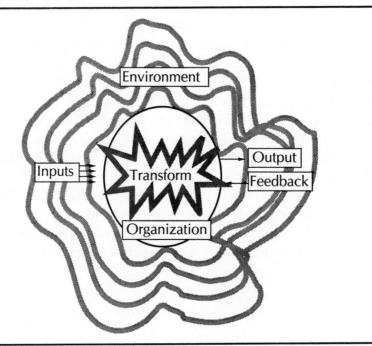

aggressive new competitors, or technical breakthroughs. It's the leader's job to continually gather and integrate this feedback into the way the organization functions internally. In that way, leaders assure that the input-transform-output cycle stays in sync with the ever-changing outside environment.

Barb Anders of American Express describes what this change in thinking means for her: "We're spending increasingly more time with customers and vendors. One new thing we see is management being able to understand customer needs and expectations and build them into the overall business plan. I'm also spending more time with vendors, with internal consultant colleagues outside the organization, as well as with the community and educational partners. Our collaborative approach outside the company is growing."

KEEPING YOUR BALANCE

According to the open-system view of things, a big part of your new job involves balancing internal technical systems and social systems with the changing external conditions that affect your organization. The better you can align and balance these three areas, the better the chance that your organization will succeed long term.

- Technical systems include equipment, materials, facilities, work flow, technologies, and anything else that aids in turning input (materials, information, feedback) into output (products and services).
- Social systems include anything affecting the work climate, or organizational culture—such as leadership style, decision-making practices, communication structures, training, and reward and recognition.
- Environmental factors include such outside influences as customers' needs and expectations, governmental regulations, growing or shrinking markets, surrounding communities, suppliers, raw materials, and the competition.

As part of your new role, you'll continually ask and answer questions about balance among technical, social, and environmental factors. Closed-system thinking focuses on getting optimal performance out of a particular work station or department, largely ignoring events outside the department. Open-system thinking takes a more global view. It focuses on adapting internal technical and social systems to the changing demands of the external environment.

To think about your organization as an open system, you'll need to ask three basic questions:

1. What major outside business conditions are we facing?
2. Given those conditions, how well do we transform input to output?
3. How can we improve the way we transform input to better respond to those conditions?

Answering these questions, not surprisingly, involves (1) analyzing the external environment and (2) looking at your organization's internal technical and social systems. Then you and your team can implement internal changes that better match what the team is doing with conditions outside the team.

In summary, a technical system consists of the work flow, processes, technologies, and equipment that turn input into output. A social system consists of the values, work styles, leadership practices, rewards, training, and whatever else governs human interactions at work. An open-system approach will succeed to the extent that you can match these systems with each other and with current business reality.

WHAT YOU'LL BE DOING

So much for theory. But how does theory translate into your day-to-day activities as a leader of teams? If your main focus has been controlling the work place itself (a smart approach when the world changed slowly and predictably), you must now spend much more time looking outward and helping the organization respond to a dynamic external environment. You can no longer simply channel employees' energy through a maze of set or incrementally changing procedures. Instead, you must help the organization adapt the way work is performed and the way jobs are defined in response to the shifting possibilities and demands of a volatile world.

At Black & Decker, for example, open-system thinking is now a way of life. According to site manager Mark Kornhauser, "We are getting suppliers involved earlier in the product development cycle, in corrective action, helping them understand our expectations relative to the product specs or services specs, understanding their expectations, getting them involved in continuous improvement activities that affect us. On the customer side, we're also much more involved. Our immediate external customer might be a distribution network, not the end user. We are trying to get much closer to both, to understand what customer satisfaction really is, right down to the end user. We constantly monitor that because that's really the bottom line."

On a very practical level, what can *you* do to become a more forward-thinking leader, to encourage your team to come up with

TABLE 8–1

Issues outside the organization	• Availability of qualified labor
• Customer needs and expectations • Business fortunes of key customers • Competitors' products or services • Prices for raw goods or supplies • Operational costs—rent, fuel, etc. • Government regulations • Changing markets • Mergers, restructuring • Joint ventures in your industry • Product safety testing • Interest rates, costs of capital • Stock prices	• Trends in contracts and orders • Labor negotiations • Employee compensation • The changing work force *Issues inside the organization:* • Fixed overhead expenses • Amount and kind of debt • Profit and breakeven points • Operational capacity • Budgeting • Progress toward financial goals

innovative adaptations to changing business conditions? The following four activities will help you foresee and influence change, and set the tone for your team.

Continuously Monitor the Environment

Because the open-system approach demands much closer attention to feedback from customers, suppliers, and the outside world as a whole, you'll be spending much more time scanning the business environment for useful information. In this way, your traditional planning activities will take on a new dimension. Now you'll be thinking more about long-term results and helping your team develop a sense of their role in the overall business—which in turn becomes the framework for developing and implementing their own ideas.

To scan the business environment (both outside and inside the organization), you'll have to decide (1) what information to gather and (2) where to look for it. Table 8–1 lists a few of many topics you might monitor.

Sources of information vary depending on your industry and organization. Table 8–2 shows some common channels you can start with:

TABLE 8-2

Outside sources
- General business publications
- Trade and industry publications
- Professional organizations
- Conferences
- Public workshops and seminars
- Customer/supplier forums
- Sales calls from suppliers
- Customer/supplier task forces

Formal inside sources
- Annual report
- In-house public relations
- In-house newsletters
- Employee orientation

- Design reviews
- Training sessions
- Staff meetings (all levels)
- Quality reports, updates
- Customer feedback surveys
- Budget meetings
- Bulletin boards
- Executive roundtables

Informal inside sources
- Your lunch buddies
- People on special task forces
- Office services
- People who update organization charts and operations manuals

Analyze the Information You Gather

Whether your focus is your team or the entire organization, you'll need to analyze the likely impact of trends on long-term performance. Information, by itself, won't necessarily point you in a useful direction. You'll need to analyze what you find in light of what you know about internal needs and priorities, and then decide on the next steps. As a rule, the more you can learn about your industry, the better. And the more you know about your organization—its core operations, how it's doing in the marketplace, hot issues, and so on—the better you can assess the importance of information you run across.

You'll be able to see an immediate link between some information and what's going on with your team or organization. With other information, the link won't be as obvious. But if anything *might* be useful at some point, file it (mentally or literally) for later reference. For example, a purchasing team leader might home in on developments in computerized inventory systems at the same time overlooking new findings about injuries to people who work at computers all day. But by noting and acting on such "unrelated" data, this leader conceivably could prevent much suffering and loss of productivity.

Make a Case for Needed Change

The ability to identify and apply key information faster than the competition is a baseline strategy for most organizations. When you offer your own suggestions for making best use of new ideas and information, you encourage forward thinking in others, help your organization stay competitive, and thereby make yourself a more valuable contributor.

Whatever your interests—safety practices, incentive programs, technical innovation, customer service, cash flow practices, or a thousand other vital topics—share them with others. Doing so stimulates the creative thinking and continuous improvement that mark an organization as a pacesetter. You might think that presenting your ideas is something you do at a formal meeting. It is, and you should, but making a case for needed change also means informally helping team members, peers, and higher level associates to see the value of new ideas.

To make your case, whatever the setting, simplify, simplify, simplify. As the person who explored an issue, you know more about it than anyone else . So you'll need to boil information down to the key elements, translate jargon into ordinary language, and help people relate complex information to the issues that concern them. If you've carefully monitored the environment and analyzed what you've learned, you should know enough about the issue to speak clearly and simply.

You'll also need to know something about whatever it is you'd like to see changed—the existing policy, work process, technology, or what have you. When you're planning to propose a major change, ask yourself questions like these:

- What was the original reason for the policy, procedure, or system I want to change?
- What will happen if it's changed or eliminated?

- How do I minimize the risks of doing away with the old and installing the new?
- What's the link between what I am proposing and the organization's mission?
- How can I address the concerns of people with some attachment to the old way of doing things?

Keep in mind that part of effectively influencing change is knowing who to bring on board early in a change effort and how to step lightly when there's a danger of trampling on sensitive toes.

Work with Others to Bring About Needed Change

Working for change, as described here, isn't necessarily about winning a crowd over to your side. It's about finding ways to work with others in creating a flexible, responsive organization.

These days, especially in a team environment, there's usually no shortage of workable ideas. The problem is finding somebody to shepherd a good idea to the point where it begins paying off for the company. In most organizations, bringing about needed change proceeds by influencing others. Here's a few proven techniques for working with your team members and others to bring about needed change:

- *Establish a positive focus:* If you present your idea as an intriguing possibility, not as an obvious improvement that nobody could object to—and if you keep emphasizing the opportunity involved—other people are much more likely to see the future through your eyes.
- *Build support among many groups:* Sometimes it feels good to play the Lone Ranger. Unfortunately, heroic individual effort rarely gains the necessary support to bring about lasting change in a team environment. Be a team player first. Build partnerships with the key groups touched by a potential change. These groups have people with the information, resources, expertise, and influence to further your cause.
- *Develop the potential of others.* Encourage other people—whether peers, team members, even people senior to

you—to get off the sidelines. If you've got a solid idea, all it usually takes is for you to take the first step, which others of course may see as taking the first risk. But if you do your homework and choose your cause carefully, you can take that step, leading by example, with a strong prospect for success.

- *Give recognition.* Recognizing the help of others, no matter how small their contribution, helps build alliances and encourage further contributions.

One of the most effective ways to bring about needed change is to help people see internal issues and events in a larger business context. Especially when working with your team, says Black & Decker site manager Mark Kornhauser, "It's important to give them as much of a perspective of what you're trying to do as possible—an overall picture, not just, 'Here's a slice of the problem. Go fix it.' You need to say, 'Here's the big picture. Let's understand what it really means to you, the business, the whole factory, the whole marketplace, the customers.' If you give them a human understanding, their reaction is much more genuine and more effective."

DRIVING CHANGE IN A TEAM ENVIRONMENT

As you expand the capabilities of your team, you will expand your *own* capabilities by becoming a bellwether and agent of change. "One of the big lessons we've learned is to arm managers with tools they need so they are driving and creating the change," says Barb Anders of American Express. "They're the ones carrying the banner and making it work."

At Spectra Physics, manufacturing manager Abe Kossol describes this new, more forward-thinking role: "I had no real vision at the beginning of how my job would be different. But after three years I am operating very differently. My focus is no longer on the factory and how it's running because [with teams handling day-to-day operations] the factory runs itself. My focus is now more on the customer, the marketing group, the sales group, the engineering group, and on R & D. What are they developing? What are they going to bring into the factory? Is it friendly to the machinery, to the robots, and to the people?"

The difficult thing for many traditional leaders to see is this: If you can master the skills of forward thinking, you acquire a new kind of value, very different from the control-oriented value of leaders in a closed-system organization. Says production supervisor Russell Francis, also of Spectra Physics, "My value is that I am taking on a portion of what my boss used to do. I'm also able to do more strategic planning, to pave the way to—to *greatness!* We could have gone along with the way we were doing business, and I think we would have survived. At least for awhile. Now we have an opportunity to make some new in-roads, to have a better product, a better organization, to be overall stronger and stronger in the marketplace. I have more than enough to fill my plate."

"I am a catalyst," says Mark Kornhauser of Black & Decker. "I enjoy this. It's not a task for me. It's my job to coordinate a strategy that makes us world class."

But let's not kid ourselves. Not everyone will slip easily into this new role—especially people who find it hard to let go of the old closed-system way of thinking. "The challenge is not just in helping the team to grow," says Russell Francis. "*You* have to change. You need to be willing to take on things that you are not familiar with. Which is the real reason most of us hang on to the old. It's familiar. It's comfortable."

So, if you want to be a forward thinker, what's the first step? According to production supervisor Francis: "Go break in a new pair of shoes."

Chapter Nine
_____

Let the Process Fit the Customer

> *The primary goal is to satisfy the customer. If you don't know what the customer needs, go and find out. As soon as you become customer-focused, all of the static in the teams just subsides. It's amazing, like magic.*

> Karen Gideon
> Vice president
> Amex Life Assurance

In your new role, you'll be getting out from under many of your daily administrative chores and exploring new forms of leadership. One of your most important new functions will be work-process improvement (or quality improvement), whose purpose is to give customers what they want by continuously improving the way the work is done. Whether these improvements are small or more radical, the goal always is to deliver ever-improving products and services to the customer.

A team environment gives you a unique opportunity to respond to customer needs because, as you know, you'll be helping your team, the people closest to the work, to think creatively and implement their ideas. To improve work processes, you'll work with your team to stay in touch with your customers' changing needs, analyze the processes your team is involved with, and revise those processes to meet and preferably exceed customer expectations.

Process improvement is not a one-time quick fix but a long-term, permanent change in on-the-job behaviors. The pay-off for you and your team is a continuously improving operation and increasing

137

freedom from the problems and inefficiencies that may be keeping team members from doing their best work. The pay-off for the organization is greater efficiency and customer satisfaction, leading to greater customer loyalty and improved bottom-line results.

PRACTICE MAKES PERFECT

What's so new about all that? Haven't managers always wanted to operate efficiently, improve service and quality, and meet customer needs?

The answer for most managers is, "Yes, of course we buy into the theory. The problem is putting theory into practice." For whatever reasons—an emphasis on short-term gains, the gradual buildup of uncoordinated procedures, or simply losing touch with the customer—many managers stray from these basics. Among the obstacles that can frustrate process-improvement efforts:

- *No place for customers.* Customer satisfaction is the ultimate measure of success. If there's no way to identify customer expectations and build them into your process-improvement efforts, the best intentions in the world can fail to satisfy your customers.

- *No link to strategic goals.* A team can be busy improving processes, but with no link between those efforts and the organization's strategic goals, the organizational pay-off is often minimal. As a result, top managers can begin to lose interest in process management as a strategic initiative.

- *Process gaps between departments or functions.* The greatest improvement opportunities often lie in the work-process gaps between one team, department, or function and the next (see pages 8–9). An organization that ignores these gaps will find it hard, if not impossible, to make significant work-process improvements.

- *Involvement gaps.* Uninvolved people obviously can't help with process improvement. They can even undermine that effort. Without mid-manager involvement, for example, an involvement gap can develop between strategic goals and the front-line activities of the teams.

- *No hard data.* Teams that think they already know what improvements to make may not bother to collect hard data about the work process. With no detailed knowledge of what they're trying to improve, team members can waste time and energy. Further, without baseline data, they have no way to measure the results of their efforts. Lack of data is a special problem in professional, service, and support types of work.

A FOUNDATION FOR PROCESS IMPROVEMENT

To avoid serious threats like those just listed, you'll need to help your team, peers, and senior managers make a daily habit of the following activities:

1. *Keep an unwavering focus on the customer.* A process-focused team continually strives to identify and meet the needs and expectations of its customers. The same approach carries over to working relationships within the organization, where teams must treat one another as valued internal customers.

2. *Pay close and constant attention to improving the way the work is done.* Because results improve when processes improve, you'll need to help your team continually improve the ways that work gets done. The team must prevent errors (rather than correcting them), reduce waste, and eliminate needless complexity. In this way, the team frees up time and resources to devote directly to meeting customer expectations.

3. *Promote long-term, top-to-bottom organizational commitment and support.* Process improvement is everyone's business: executives, managers, and team members. You may need to become a sort of a process-improvement cheerleader—for your team, peers, and senior managers.

By demonstrating these behaviors, you can do your part to make process improvement a permanent part of your organization—policies, procedures, and operating budgets, as well as daily life on the job.

FIGURE 9–1
Traditional Organization

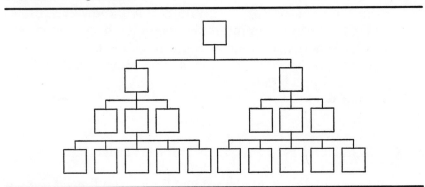

HOW DO PEOPLE WORK TOGETHER IN A PROCESS-FOCUSED ORGANIZATION?

In a team environment, process improvement becomes a way of life. What does such a workplace look like? What does it mean, for example, to focus on the customer? For one thing, it means that the question your team will have to answer every time they make a decision is, "How will this affect our customers?" In this way, your team will develop a new understanding of teamwork.

Every organization—process-focused or not—groups people into departments like manufacturing or finance, with subgroups in each department. A traditional organization chart like the one represented in Figure 9–1 shows the reporting relationships among these groups.

People in a process-focused organization still operate according to this traditional picture. They still maintain working relationships within their departments or functions. But they've also learned to see their working relationships in a new way. A process-focused organization encourages relationships based on processes that cut across departmental boundaries—relationships not represented on a traditional organization chart. Even a clear-cut process like billing, for example, might involve several departments: marketing, sales, customer service, data processing, accounts receivable. A

FIGURE 9–2
Processed-Focused Organization

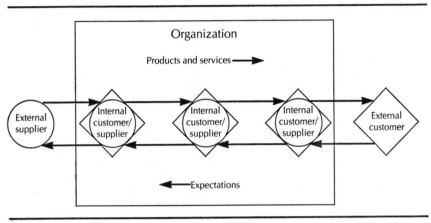

process-focused organization understands that strong relation-ships among departments or functions—not just within them—are vital for long-term improvement.

To visualize these *sideways* working relationships, you need a different chart—one that shows how departments involved in a work process act as internal suppliers and internal customers to one another.

Figure 9–2 represents any organization that receives materials or services from an external supplier and creates final products or services for an external customer. Inside the box, each figure represents a department—which is both an internal customer and an internal supplier to other departments. The arrows above indi-cate the flow of work from suppliers to customers. The arrows below indicate the flow of information about expectations from customers to suppliers. When people in an organization learn to see themselves this way, they can begin to improve their shared work processes, resulting in improved products and services for internal and external customers.

Process-focused organizations don't necessarily give up their traditional structure. They do loosen it enough so that people from different functions, departments, or teams can work together

FIGURE 9–3
A Cross-Functional Work Process

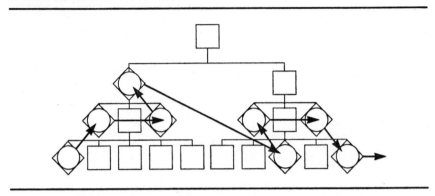

when they need to. That's why you see a lot of work in these organizations going on in cross-functional teams, as people get together to solve problems and improve operations. The members of a cross-functional team are internal customers and suppliers to one another. By figuring out how to better meet one another's needs and expectations, the team as a whole improves its ability to create products and services that meet the expectations of their shared customer.

To visualize how people approach their work in a process-focused organization, you need both the traditional organization chart and the sideways work-flow chart. If the path of single work process were illustrated graphically, it might look something like Figure 9–3—with work flowing from department to department, internal supplier to internal customer.

When people see themselves this way, it's not surprising that they pay close attention to work processes—analyzing them, measuring them, improving them. They develop charts showing variations in a given operation, for example, or comparing the impact of possible improvements in a work process. They take the time to ask questions and get the facts instead of relying on guesswork: "Exactly what does the customer expect?" "What would it take to make this change in this process?" "Will it pay off for the customer?" "Would another change be better?" and so on.

None of this happens quickly. Both you and your team will need time to learn new skills and put them into practice. But as these skills take hold, you'll be able to look back and see some profound changes in the way you do your job:

Before process improvement	*. . . and after it's in place*
Meet the assigned objective.	Meet the customer's expectations.
Focus on short-term results Inspection.	Focus on the process Prevention.
Follow procedures.	Improve procedures.
Best guesses.	Facts and figures.
Departments and functions.	Cross-functional teams.
Customers and suppliers = "them."	Customers and suppliers = valued partners.
Do only what's required.	Do your best.

As these lists imply, people involved in process improvement eventually adopt a new approach to their work—the inevitable outgrowth of new skills, new knowledge, and clear evidence that the organization values their work. At first, people may see "meeting customer needs" as one more catch-phrase, one more short-term priority. But given time, most people find themselves seeking out more and more ways to improve their products and services. And rather than feeling burdened, they now welcome each new opportunity to exercise creativity and exert a positive impact on work processes—and on their customers. Says Sharon Chinn of Meridian Insurance: "Process improvement has been one of the most exhilarating things I've been involved in. I could almost preach the gospel of continuous improvement and process management. For me, it's the second coming of corporate America. I just don't see any other way that we as a nation, and certainly we as an industry, are going to compete. So it has given me a charge that I haven't had in years. It has made me want to get out and learn more and more, so I can teach and coordinate and help people in the process."

A NEW WAY TO THINK ABOUT WORK

When your team "gets the gospel" of process improvement, they start thinking about work in new ways:

- They become more aware of how many separate work steps go into making a given product or service, and how they fit together to form a work process.
- They appreciate exactly how their work relates to the rest of the organization—not in a general sense, but in terms of knowing exactly what they need from others in order to do their work and what others expect from them in order to do theirs.
- They also learn how to quantify aspects of their work in ways that tell them if it's meeting customer expectations.
- They come to realize that most work-related problems are caused not by people but by flaws in the work process—and that to correct the problems they need to focus primarily on the process and not on the people involved.

With this new understanding, they're like travelers with a detailed map. Instead of having to find their way through trial and error—making false starts and perhaps never getting to their destination—they can set forth confidently, knowing they can choose among the best possible routes to get where they, and you, want to go.

The pay-off of this new way of thinking is an enhanced ability to make work improvements that benefit the customer, the organization, your team, and you. The goal of process improvement is customer satisfaction through products and services that better meet customer expectations. And, in the long run, efficient work processes and satisfied customers add up to a healthy and prosperous organization.

The long-term value of this customer-oriented approach is especially vivid when you compare it to short-term strategies like cutting back services, consolidating operations, or reducing staff. Such measures often produce immediate bottom-line results, but at the cost of long-term customer satisfaction, employee commitment, and organizational well-being.

Definitions

Before getting into the activities involved in process improvement, some formal definitions may help:

- A work process is a series of work steps that results in a particular product or service for the customer. (The customer can be a customer in the traditional sense or an internal customer—someone within your organization who uses the product or service turned out by your team.) People committed to process improvement see their organization made up of hundreds of related work processes; for example, *filling a customer's order.*

- A work step is a task or activity in a work process. Each work process consists of a number of work steps. Some work steps in *filling a customer's order* could be: *(1) complete the order form, (2) assemble the items in the order, and (3) pack the order.*

- A work system consists of several related work processes. A work system for this example might be: *Customer service system, in which filling a customer's order is one of several work processes.*

- An opportunity for improvement is either a problem preventing you from meeting a customer expectation or a chance to *exceed* customer expectations.

It's important to remember that analyzing a work process is not the same as solving a problem—although it's often a first step in that direction. When you analyze a work process, you step back to see how all the parts fit together and where the opportunities for improvement lie. These opportunities are sometimes problems or deficiencies in the process. When you solve a problem, you move in to take action: figuring out the cause, coming up with possible solutions, and carrying out the one that seems best. Taken together, analyzing a process and solving the problems you find add up to work-process improvement.

WHAT Process?

How do you decide which processes to analyze and improve? In organizations with an established process-improvement culture, all work processes are continually monitored—in the belief that, even without any obvious need for improvement, you can always build in greater efficiency and add safeguards to prevent errors. At Spectra Physics, for example, "What we set up is very much a continuous-improvement process," according to production manager Brad West. "You've got to constantly keep that working. If you back off, if you decide that you're there and you don't have to put as much effort and energy into it, it will eventually wither and die."

Initially, though, at the start of a process-improvement effort, a high-level steering committee often selects a particular work process in response to one or more of the following:

- *Warning signs*. Typical warning signs of a work process in trouble include increases in errors, scrap, customer complaints, overtime, and employee turnover.

- *Pressure to make a product or service more responsive to customer needs*. If your organization is losing ground in the marketplace, you might be able to turn things around by improving the work processes for a specific product or service.

- *Need to get people on the process-improvement bandwagon*. To get employees excited about process improvement, many organizations start out with a highly visible process for which improvements will make a big impact.

Two other important points: First, although you can analyze a work process by yourself, you'll find it easier to do as a team (often a cross-functional team) of those involved in the process itself. A team is more likely to give adequate attention to all aspects of the process. Second, a proper work process analysis takes time—

initially days and even weeks to collect information, analyze it, and summarize findings. If you'll be part of a team, you need to figure on extra time to get members together. What you get for all that time is an accurate and detailed map of your work process, which forms a solid basis for future improvements.

FINDING OPPORTUNITIES FOR IMPROVEMENT

Analyzing a work process involves the following steps.

Describe the Work Process to Be Improved

It's important to target exactly the work process you're going to analyze—where it begins, where it ends, and what the work steps are. Especially if more than one department is involved and if you plan to work with your intact team or as part of a cross-functional team, you need to make sure everyone agrees on exactly what work process is under consideration.

First, determine where the work process starts and where it ends. Define it broadly enough to include all the work steps that could affect the outcome of the process for the customer. For example, if you need to get orders to customers faster, you can't look only at the shipping process. You need to consider order-processing as well. But don't define it so broadly that you can't handle it. To cite another example, preparing monthly payroll might start with receiving payroll sheets from team leaders and end with distribution of checks to team members.

Next, lay out all the work steps in a detailed flow chart. Making a flow chart can take time, especially if team members disagree about the work steps, but it's worth the effort. The flow chart becomes the basis for all later steps, so it needs to conform as closely as possible to the process as it's currently performed. Just getting team members to agree on the work steps can be a valuable first step toward improving the process.

A flow chart for preparing the monthly payroll might look like Figure 9–4.

FIGURE 9–4
Preparing the Monthly Payroll

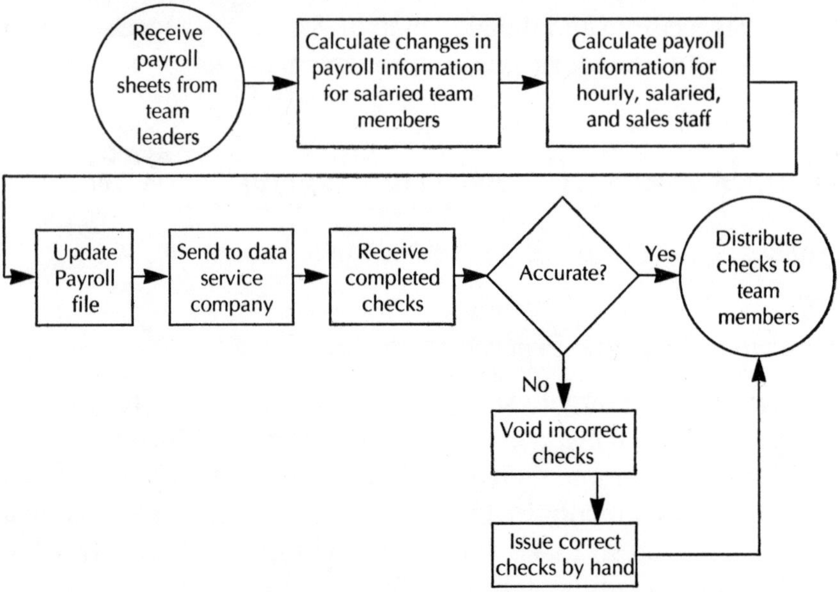

Determine the Key Expectations of Customers

Again, the purpose of improving a work process is to turn out a product or service that better meets your customers' expectations. That's why you need to find out what key expectations your customers (either internal or external) have of the process. Expectations may be general—for example, prices no higher than those of other companies. Or they may be specific: 24-hour service, for example, or a certain product feature.

Knowing your customers' key expectations helps you avoid wasting time on changes your customers don't care about or, worse, changes that leave customers less satisfied than they were before. The better you understand these expectations, the better you'll be able to adjust the work process to meet them.

Think about two sets of customers—external customers (for the final product or service of the work process) and internal customers (for interim steps along the way). A simple way to identify these customers is to look at your flow chart and list all the people involved in each work step. From this list, identify the customers for the end product or service. In the payroll example, a final customer is anybody who receives a paycheck.

Then identify the customers for each step in the work process. In the payroll example, this group might include the payroll administrator and the data service company representative. Including these people is important because each step in a work process can only be as good as the one before it. For example, the data service rep can't give the payroll administrator accurate paychecks without getting good information from the payroll administrator to begin with.

Talk directly to your customers (or a representative group of them) about their expectations. If possible, get them to quantify these expectations. If you can establish a numerical target, you'll have a reliable way to measure the success of your improvement efforts. Expectations will vary depending on the product or service, of course, but here are some common categories of customer expectations and a sample question for each category:

Category	Sample Question
Timeliness	How soon after you place your order do you expect to get it?
Reliability	Under what conditions do you expect to use this product?
Accuracy	How much detail do you want me to include in the report?
Ease of use	How much time are you willing to spend filling out this form?
Extra service	What extra services could we provide you?

When talking with customers about their key expectations, you'll need to make sure you and your team do each of the following:

- *Identify the product or service and explain why you want to discuss it.* Asking customers about their expectations can feel awkward because you're basically asking for feedback about your own work. To put the customer—and yourself—at ease, identify a specific product or service and explain your purpose in soliciting information. Once you establish this context for discussion, both of you will generally feel more focused and relaxed. Naming a specific product or service to be improved also helps prevent discussion from drifting into side issues.

- *Ask questions to clarify what the customer expects from your product or service.* Customers don't necessarily have their expectations very well thought through. As the supplier, you need to ask questions that encourage customers to think about their expectations in greater depth than they may have before. The more you know about what your customers need and expect, the easier it will be to identify needed work-process improvements.

- *Summarize your understanding of the customer's expectations.* By summarizing, you show customers you've taken their remarks seriously. You also give customers a chance to correct any misunderstanding and to change or expand on what they've said.

- *Agree on next steps and set a follow-up date.* Having encouraged customers to describe their expectations, you now shift the discussion to how you'll attempt to meet them. Agreeing on next steps and setting a follow-up date shows your customers that you're committed to their satisfaction.

Once you and your team have collected and summarized the information, prioritize the key expectations for your customer group. If you can't meet all customer expectations at once, you'll need to decide which ones to address first. And keep in mind that process improvement is *continuous*.

Monitor the Work Process and Compare Performance to the Key Expectations

The basis for any decision to change any work process must be hard performance data, not guesswork. So you'll need to find some quantifiable features of the process that relate to your customers' expectations. For example, if customers expect delivery within five days of placing an order, you'd look for time indicators: "How long does it take to receive an order? Process it? Mail it?"

Precise data about how the process is currently performed, compared with your customers' key expectations, tells you which key expectations the process is failing to meet. Look at each key expectation and determine ways to quantify how well the process is performing relative to that key expectation. If accuracy is a key expectation, how might you quantify the accuracy of the work process?

Here are some ways to quantify several common kinds of expectations:

Category	Possible Ways to Quantify
Timeliness	Number of days to complete task
Reliability	Number of service calls, returns, or replacement parts sold
Accuracy	Number of errors caught during inspection
Ease of use	Number of complaints or of partially completed forms
Extra service	Number of compliments

Decide how you'll actually collect data for each process-improvement indicator you select. If more than one person will be collecting the information, make sure they collect it in the same way. Otherwise, the final information may not paint an accurate picture of the work process. If possible, use existing sources of information. For example, if you were trying to find out how many days it takes to ship customer orders, you could check the dates on the order forms. When you collect the data, try to remain objective. If you look for only the data that supports a point you want to make, you won't gain a complete understanding of the work process, and you'll probably miss some important improvement opportunities.

Next, compare the information you've collected with your customers' key expectations and decide to what degree you're meeting those expectations. Say, for example, managers expect a new employee on the job within a month of submitting the request to human resources—yet the data shows an average elapsed time closer to six weeks. Obviously, you'll need to address the gap between expectations and actual performance.

List Opportunities for Improvement

You now know the current work process, your customers' key expectations, and where they are and are not being met. So you're ready to decide where to make improvements that will more closely align the output of a given work process with customers' key expectations.

First, list the situations you've uncovered in which key expectations are not being met. Write them as straightforward statements representing the facts you've learned. For example: "Each month an average of 5 percent of hourly employee computer-generated payroll checks are inaccurate and must be rewritten by hand." Or, "The service rate on the A-350 is 10 percent higher than the average of other products in the same line."

Review the data you've collected and identify redundancies, inconsistencies, needless complexities, and potential trouble spots. Like layers of paint on an old piece of furniture, rules and procedures can build up over the years in response to conditions that may no longer apply. Besides wasting time and money, they contribute to high error rates. Correcting errors adds to costs. If you can find ways to prevent errors from occurring in the first place, you can save significant amounts of money. For example: "Each requisition for a new support staff position must be approved twice by the department manager." Or, "Scrap rate has risen 15 percent in the last six months."

THEN WHAT?

Normally what follows from work-process analysis is a selection of improvement opportunities for your team to tackle using their problem-solving skills, tools, and techniques. The opportunities you select should coincide with the high-priority expectations of your customers. In other words, if customers want faster processing of purchasing requisitions, deal with that issue now and save the low-priority redesign of the requisition form for the next phase.

If formal process improvement is relatively new in your organization, you may want to select an improvement opportunity that will both pay off for the customer and generate excitement elsewhere in the organization. Such an opportunity would:

- Be highly visible.
- Have a high probability of success.
- Benefit a large number of people in the organization.
- Link with the organization's process-improvement goals.

Working with your team to analyze and improve work processes is one of the many ways your role as leader will expand. As you master this new responsibility, says site manager Mark Kornhauser of Black & Decker, keep in mind that "people need reaffirmation that they are the experts, that they know how to make their jobs better. They have day-to-day observations on what we do that's wasteful, how we do things wrong, how we can do things better every day, how we can be proactive."

In the old environment, meeting customer expectations was often the problem. In a team environment, it's the *solution*. According to Karen Gideon of Amex Life Assurance, "Any time we found that there were difficulties during our decision making, we just put the customer first. As soon as you do that, a lot of the parochial kind of barriers that are normally between people come down."

Chapter Ten

The Making of
a Team Environment
(A Primer)

I've been told that I'm sometimes too aggressive, that I move too quickly. But I believe that when people start to see the benefits, even the nonbelievers will come along.

Sharon Faltemier
Operations Manager
Raychem Corporation[1]

This is a book about your expanding role as team leader, at *whatever* level of the organization. You've already surveyed the principles and many of the skills you'll use to draw out and focus the energy, intelligence, and creativity of your team. Now you need to look at a final piece of your new role: helping to build an environment that allows those skills to achieve their fullest positive effect.

To help build your *own* team environment, you'll take part in many discussions about shaping the vision and reshaping the systems to match that vision. And you'll implement ideas that you, your team, your peers, and senior managers agree will maximize the pay-off of teams. In a phrase, you will become a co-architect of the substantial organizational changes necessary to support high-involvement teams. Leadership in this respect will demand your active involvement. According to Barb Anders of American Express: "A leader thinks in terms of renewal, causes change, affirms values, achieves unity, and understands customer needs, business economics, and what it takes to achieve success."

This final chapter won't give you everything you need to bake a team environment from scratch. No chapter or book ever could. But it will help you draw from your own experience, frame your thoughts, and contribute to the long-term dialogue about building and sustaining a healthy team culture. In short, it will help you to become a builder, instead of a victim, of the changing organization of the future.

A VISION FOUNDED ON FACTS

What has to happen to allow for the profound organizational change known as a team environment? One thing's for sure: Only a deep, long-term commitment of time and resources can bring about this magnitude of change. Without that commitment, teams are just another program destined to fade with the initial enthusiasm. A successful transition to teams involves every level, every system, and eventually every person in your organization. It requires intensive planning and dogged follow-through.

Because each organization is unique, there's no one right way to implement teams, no foolproof formula. At the same time, careful observation of literally thousands of client sites over many years reveals a relatively consistent big-picture strategy in many successful companies—and a corresponding lack of strategy in companies that stall out or fail.[2]

A team environment usually begins, to borrow an image, as a twinkle in some manager's eye. "The whole concept and the belief in this process has to come from the heart," says Norma Bermudez, a director with Amex Life Assurance. "You have to really believe in it."[3] Eventually, though, beliefs have to take shape in a clear vision of a team environment unique to your organization. With experience, discipline, study, and good advice, a founding group (usually of top executives) can define and steer toward a motivating vision of future successful teams. This group *can't* allow itself to drift indefinitely from one team experiment to another.

So the first stroke on the canvas is a vision of the future that the entire decision-making group can support. That collective vision is an explicit reply to these, among other, questions:

FIGURE 10–1

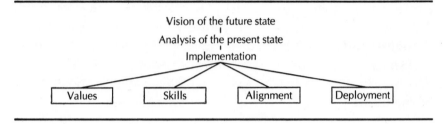

- What business are we in?
- What do we believe in?
- Where are we going?
- What will employee involvement look like?
- Why are we moving toward teams?

Armed with their answers, the visionaries will then need to assess the actual state of the organization at each level, typically using surveys and other data-collection tools. A thorough effort to collect and analyze information about the present state of the organization can dispel misconceptions, reveal hidden strength, and help senior managers gauge how far it is from here to there. Without accurate data, "the likelihood of wrong decisions and wasted resources is very great," say three researchers on the topic, since "individual biases, assumptions, and game-playing are likely to rule."[4] In other words, you can't build a desirable future until you really understand the present.

FOUR PILLARS OF IMPLEMENTATION

Committed to a vision of the future state that is based on detailed knowledge of the present state, the founding group can then develop a plan that details implementation activities under four headings—values, skills, alignment, and deployment.[5] See Figure 10–1.

To engage in the dialogue about your own team environment, and to make a practical contribution to building that environment, you'll need to understand these four pillars of a coherent implementation architecture. Team *values* (most of which you've already encountered in earlier chapters) are a foundation for the behaviors and partnerships that define a team environment. Those behaviors largely manifest themselves as *skills*, which allow leaders and team members to realize the promise of their new environment. *Alignment* (achieved when organizational systems and team activities support continuous improvement) applies team values and skills to the day-to-day business of customer satisfaction. And *deployment* organizes the substantial resources and long-term effort needed to ensure the success of a team environment.

Now let's take a closer look at some of the specifics under each major heading—values, skills, alignment, and deployment.

VALUES

You'd be very unwise to fling your body against a moored freighter in an effort to move it away from the pier. But place one finger against the hull and lean—and before long, it begins to move! In the same way, the steady pressure of new or renewed values can move great organizations.

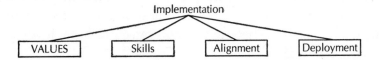

The term *values* here simply refers to the beliefs that give rise to the team-leadership role already described. According to Sharon Faltemier of Raychem Corporation, "Managers of the future need to understand who they are, what they stand for, what their beliefs are, what their values are, and how that impacts how they do their job." Among their core values, managers in team-based organizations often include the following:

- Everything depends on meeting and exceeding customers' changing expectations.

- You meet and exceed expectations by continuously improving work processes and partnerships.
- Every employee deserves respect as an actual and potential contributor to improved organizational performance.
- The leader's role is to build flexible, responsive, and responsible teams of capable, highly committed people.[6]

In particular, how you and your peers see your new role affects how team members see *their* roles. A common employee response to a move to teams, or any major initiative, is "*Now* what is management gonna do to us?" That's why it's so important that you and your peers model behaviors consistent with team values. You must do exactly what you ask employees to do: function as a team. Yes, values can move even great, sedentary organizations—*if* those values take consistent outward form in daily behaviors.

Signaling Your Commitment to Team Values

Signaling commitment to team values obviously involves much more than quoting team scripture. How do you send exactly the right signal? "Lead by example," says Sarah Nolan of Amex Life Assurance. "And the example we wanted was a belief that everyone at every level can contribute, everyone had to challenge everything, everyone had to take more risks, and everyone had to learn new things. You have to model that—an openness, an open-minded approach to what each person can contribute. If you don't do it, nobody will."

Since veteran employees are often too jaded to respond to the slogans and pep talks that come with each new program, the best signals are the day-to-day actions that make your commitment tangible:

- Prepare employees to make decisions that affect their work.
- Resist jumping in to solve problems when a team is struggling.
- Resist reclaiming responsibilities once transferred to a team.

- Make sure people get coaching and training to reach their potential.
- Seek out the coaching and training *you* need.
- Hold your opinions until others have expressed theirs.
- Pare away status symbols and privileges that set managers apart.
- Reinforce the organizational vision in word and deed.
- Reward and celebrate progress toward team and corporate goals.
- Make organizational systems consistent with team values.
- Reward innovation.
- Keep team members informed about the organization, industry, customers, and competitors.

One of the most important values in a team environment is quality improvement through careful attention to customers' changing needs and expectations (see Chapter 9). To signal your commitment to that value, you must encourage everyone to listen and respond to external and internal customers. As teams learn to act on their new values and become more self-sufficient, they'll also learn to make positive use of accurate, up-to-date information about customer needs. Help your team by arranging personal contacts with customers and by passing on pertinent information from surveys, market research, and focus groups, among many other sources (see Chapter 8). "I try to keep up on the news from a couple of different plants to see where we are competitively," says Karen Olson-Vermillion of Subaru-Isuzu, Inc. "Also, when we see articles in *Automotive News, Automotive Industry,* and some of the other trade journals, we pass that information on to our people." When necessary, remind the team that the needs of internal customers sometimes carry more immediate weight than those of external customers.

Educating People about Team Values

No matter how charismatic your top-level leaders or how deeply they believe in team values, they can't *will* a team environment into being. Instead, they'll need to allocate time and resources to build awareness and educate people about team values at every level of the organization. "Initially people tend to be averse to change," says production manager Brad West about the early days of teams at Spectra Physics. "If you have the patience to allow them to work through that and give them enough information, they'll eventually accept it."

In North America, strong cultural values exalt a form of individualism that may undermine teamwork. "I don't think individualism can succeed," says John Hofmeister of Allied Signal Aerospace. "That's not to say there isn't some room for autonomy and independence, but it's on the basis of greater *inter*dependence. Yes, there is more autonomy, but there's much more intimacy and sharing." So people who see team values as a threat to their personal autonomy need to understand that individual contributions take on even greater importance in the context of a team. According to University of Alberta Hospitals team leader Brenda Kuzyk: "It's really making everybody a manager of their own job. Just that autonomy makes your job much more rewarding because you have input into everything that's going on instead of being told what to do."[7]

Your organization has to share information and sustain the dialogue among organizational layers in order to clarify *all* team values as well as the overall corporate vision. You'll need to make sure everybody understands just how big this transformation will be. Explain that almost everything will change—systems, processes, skills, job responsibilities, even working relationships. "Sometimes it's saying the same thing over and over to the same people," says Emily Liggett of Raychem, "because they didn't hear it the first time or they want to make sure it's really true. It takes a lot of talking."

Hiring and Orienting People Likely to Support Team Values

You can stack the deck for successful teams by hiring and carefully orienting people likely to excel in a team environment. But who are those people? According to Dean Olmstead of the University of Alberta Hospitals, "People that are successful in this environ-

ment are excited about what they do. They like people, work well
with people, and appreciate the organization. They are open, willing, and able to change.''

Once the team values take hold, your reputation will draw some
potential employees and repel others. That's good. But even when
candidates seek you out, remember that every recruit at every
level eventually must ''own'' the organization's vision and values.
Don't hire anyone based on a single interview. Articulate your
values. Describe how things are done. Question applicants about
how they like to work, and make it very clear what it means to
work in a team. Do your best to find out if applicants are really
interested in becoming responsible team members or leaders. And
remember that a quick hiring process is very long indeed if you end
up having to replace someone who can't internalize your values.

Orientation for new hires should highlight team values, day-to-
day working norms, and the evolutionary character of a team environment. Depending on circumstances, orientation might be handled by human resources staff, line managers, team members, or
some combination of those groups. Executives often get involved
too since orientation is an excellent chance to sow the seeds of
organizational values.

SKILLS

Back on the bench after 27 at-bats without a hit, an aging baseball
player reflected on the difference between values and skills. ''My
mind is writing checks,'' he said, ''that my body can't cash.''
Something like that is also the fate of any organization that neglects
continuous skills training at all organizational levels.

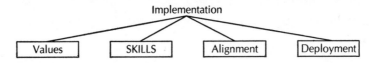

As critical as values are in teamwork, good intentions alone
won't build a team environment. What it takes is a new set of skills

for virtually everyone in the organization. In fact, the success of teams often grows in proportion to the investment in skill development.

Be sure you know the difference between *skills training*, on the one hand, and *education* and *awareness training*, on the other. Awareness training provides basic information about teams to people who have no experience with them at all. Education develops deeper understanding of team concepts, values, and practices. In contrast to both, skills training prepares people to use the practical tools and techniques that put concepts and values to work on the job.

An organization can get into serious trouble by mistaking awareness training or education for skills training. In the worst case, leaders think they're developing skills when in fact they're providing information or expanding knowledge (certainly good things to do in combination with skills development). Lacking formal skills development, some organizations never figure out why their teams and team leaders can't translate theory into practice or why a big training investment never quite pays off.

Team Leader Skills

By this point, you're on a first-name basis with the team-leadership skills required at every level of the organization. To be effective, all team leaders need training that enables them to:

- Build trust and inspire teamwork (see Chapter 3).
- Facilitate and support team decisions (see Chapter 4).
- Expand team capabilities (see Chapter 5).
- Create a team identity (see Chapter 6).
- Make the most of team differences (see Chapter 7).
- Foresee and influence change (see Chapter 8).
- Encourage customer focus and process improvement (see Chapter 9).

In addition, many developing leaders will need training in the skills elsewhere listed under the heading participative leadership (see page 29). This training, as a foundation for the more advanced team-leadership skills, helps supervisors and middle managers to:

- Involve people.
- Get input for decisions.
- Develop individual performance.
- Coordinate group effort.
- Resolve conflict.
- Implement change.

Especially important for all team leaders (and eventually for team members as well) is mastering an additional set of skills for facilitating successful meetings: preparing the team, encouraging diverse points of view, handling disruptive behavior, keeping the session focused and moving, developing an action plan, and following up. (See General Facilitation Skills, pages 63–67.)

Team Member Skills

Kenworth production supervisor Alan Campbell knows from experience that "you can't just say work as a team and they all work as a team. They have to be trained how to do it."

Teamwork and flexibility depend in part on technical cross-training for team members. But according to most successful organizations, nonmanagers have much greater difficulty mastering the nontechnical aspects of their role, such as participating in group decision-making or assessing whether a certain level of risk is warranted in the interest of innovation. Overall, team members' greatest challenge will be learning to become energetic, creative owners—instead of passive employees.

As leader, you'll play a major part in that transformation. But equally vital is nontechnical skill development for team members, most of whom have never had training in interpersonal or critical-thinking skills. Interpersonal skills allow team members to deal constructively with conflicts, unfulfilled expectations, and other communication issues that can undermine teamwork. Critical-thinking skills help team members track, measure, analyze, discuss, and resolve day-to-day technical issues.

Baseline nontechnical skills for team members include:

- Building trust and team-work.
- Active listening.
- Giving constructive feed-back.
- Learning a new technical skill.
- Getting your point across.
- Resolving issues with others.
- Dealing with changes.
- Keeping others informed.
- Finding needed help.
- Winning support from others.
- Using group interaction tools (to avoid group-think, handle differences of opinion, etc.).
- Planning.
- Securing resources.
- Addressing performance issues with other team members.
- Training and coaching other people.
- Orienting new team members.
- Making sound group decisions based on both big-picture and local nitty-gritty information.
- Analyzing processes and finding opportunities for improvement.
- Using a basic problem-solving process.
- Using problem-solving tools and techniques.
- Participating in problem-solving sessions.
- Leading problem-solving sessions.
- Identifying customer expectations.
- Handling customer dissatisfaction.
- Recognizing the efforts of others.

ALIGNMENT

Alignment refers to how well systems, standards and measures, and day-to-day team activities promote and reflect the values at the foundation of a team environment—values such as customer focus, employee involvement, and the dignity of the individual.

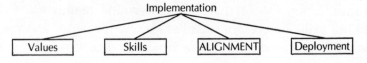

Aligning Systems to Support Team Values

The long-term momentum of a team environment depends on aligning such key systems as human resource management (like performance management, promotions, and job assignments), information systems, technology, organization structure, planning, control, reporting, and so on. The basic teams alignment question is: "Does this system promote or hinder team performance?" If it does, the system is in alignment. If it doesn't, it isn't.

It's the long-term responsibility of managers to monitor, analyze, and align all organizational systems to promote optimal team performance. In fact, aligning work systems with team values and behaviors will be one of your main activities once your team takes on increased operational responsibilities.

One core system, recognition and reward, will illustrate. Pavlov's dog proved long ago that what gets rewarded gets repeated—and that's why you'll eventually have to align all forms of recognition and reward to support team values. For example, "The sewing industry traditionally has an individual incentive pay system," says Joe Dulaney of Levi Strauss & Co. "It was all, 'I'm out for me and me alone, and everybody else better watch out for themselves.'" Obviously, individual incentive pay tends to undermine team values.[8]

Aligning work systems to support team values is a long-term process, prolonged in many cases by people who support the strategy but balk at overhauling a system they've come to know and love. To help managers and support people let go of an ineffectual system, you'll need diplomacy, a grounding in team values, hard facts, and time (see Chapter 8).

Aligning Team Activities to Support Continuous Improvement

Like organizational systems, day-to-day team activities need to align with core team values—in particular with the overarching value of continuous work-process improvement. Alignment here is essential to customer satisfaction and the long-term welfare of the organization.

How does work-process improvement occur in most organizations? Generally, managers think of ways to solicit improvement ideas from the group. Then the managers wade through scores of ideas for processes that they may not thoroughly understand and pick the best ones to carry out. One predictable result: "If I got an answer back to my idea, it might be five or six months down the road and things would have changed," says Nadine Lake, a senior customer service associate, about the era before teams at Amex Life. And because managers may be too distant from the front line to separate the wheat from the chaff, weak ideas may get the go-ahead as well as strong ones. In the end, says Kenworth production supervisor Alan Campbell, "You spend all day long motivating people to do what they should be doing on their own."

As you've seen, one of the big changes in a team environment is the gradual unification of thinking, planning, doing, and controlling—within the team itself. Team members, the people who know the process best, eventually assume substantial responsibility for improving it. At Raychem, says Sharon Faltemier, "All the teams need to be focused around a process that they own." And when they are, says Gus Boetzkes of the University of Alberta Hospitals, improvement ideas succeed far more often: "First of all, the information comes from the people who are closest to the action, and secondly, once they develop their own solution, they're more committed to implementing it."

Aligning Standards and Measures to Support Continuous Process Improvement

One of the main ways to encourage strong team performance is to align standards and measures to support continuous process improvement. Traditional measures tend to single out bottom-line productivity and profits—and that narrow focus, ironically, can lead to lower bottom-line results. Customer-focused measures apply to the *work processes* whose purpose is to meet and exceed the expectations of the customer. As a result, these measures give clarity and purpose to the day-to-day activities of teams and leaders. Karen Gideon of Amex Life: "Once you get a central focus like the customer and you're all focused on the same thing—which is what does that customer need—the teamness of that comes out naturally."

What are the pay-offs for making sure that day-to-day team activities align with the central team value of continuous work-process improvement? According to management theorist Richard Schonberger: "When focused teams take charge of their own resources, quality, and problem solving, overhead as a percentage of total cost plunges. Another result is sharp reductions in delays, wastes, customer returns, storages, and other hard-to-cost negative events."[9]

DEPLOYMENT

In military life, *deployment* refers to troops' strategic placement and call to action to support the overall battle plan. In corporate life, deployment has a similar meaning. It's the formidable task of managing the many components and people involved in building a team environment—which may involve revamping many systems and training thousands of people. That's why deployment, details of which vary widely in different organizations, is an enormous piece of overall implementation.

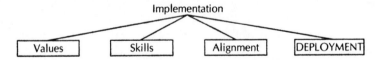

The volume and intensity of deployment depends on the kinds, the activities, and the number of teams to be implemented. A completely bottom-up approach to teams (sometimes growing out of a generalized employee-empowerment program) puts team formation, goal setting, and ongoing maintenance in the hands of the teams and their leaders. While this approach can encourage front-line involvement, it frequently brings some classic "bolt-on" problems often associated quality circles, since the teams operate outside of the management system and therefore detached from corporate imperatives. At the other extreme, a high-level corporate

team can charter and control a highly organized top-down implementation, which in turn cascades to local management steering
committees. Here the major danger is lack of local commitment.

If teams are initially a limited addition to a traditional command-
and-control, departmentalized organization, then deployment
may be a fairly straightforward. If the goal is a large number of
intrafunctional and cross-functional teams with high levels of responsibility and autonomy (see page 11), then much more extensive deployment work is appropriate.

The Basic Deployment Issues

Infrastructure simply refers to the array of people and groups that
guide the transition to teams. A strong infrastructure, as the name
implies, supports the whole deployment process. With a broad,
top-down implementation, the first successful team has to be the
one that works in the boardroom—a highly committed executive
group that plans and oversees the transition. The executive team
contributes to, modifies, and ultimately approves the implementation plan. It develops principles, policies, and guidelines for the
transition. And members of the team need to find or create opportunities to communicate and reinforce their vision.

Setting boundaries is a topic you've already heard a good deal
about (for example, see Setting Task Boundaries, pages 79–80).
Still, it's useful to look at boundaries again since the various steering committees and other guidance teams need boundaries every
bit as much as departmental or cross-functional teams. To extend
the deployment analogy, team boundaries are "the rules of en-
gagement" that define how the "troops" should conduct themselves under specific conditions. Without clear boundaries for all
teams, implementation "can be a very open-ended process that is
frustrating for the teams and in the end unsuccessful," according
to Brad West of Spectra Physics.

What are these boundaries and how do you make sure they're
a central part of deployment? "There may be cost constraints,
schedule constraints—whatever you want them to use in making
decisions," West continues. "You have to make sure that people

are aware of them. Particularly at first, the teams' role is not necessarily to decide what the goal is but to decide how to best execute that goal. What you do is frame the boundaries and ask the teams to come up with the best plan of execution. By doing this, you streamline the whole process."

And what happens to deployment in the absence of clear boundaries? "If you leave it wide open, just a blank canvas," says West, "the teams will have a great deal of difficulty in agreeing on what they need to do, how fast they need to do it, and under what constraints."

Without a strong *implementation plan*, your other pillars (values, skills, and alignment), no matter how well-conceived, can't bring about the required cultural change. This plan often includes background for the transition, a description of the vision of a preferred future, three or four guiding values, a policy statement linking values and practice, a rollout schedule, a training plan, roles and responsibilities of the various players, and a budget. Your plan may include other elements unique to your organization.

A strong plan arrays the resources necessary to sustain a team's implementation, which often lasts "much longer than these people who want to come right in and fix the world would like to believe," according to RoseAnn Stevenson of Boeing. For that reason, a plan is vital. But even so, says Joe Dulaney of Levi Strauss & Co., "You can't say what it's going to look like when you're finished because it's always going to be changing. Our idea now of what it's going to look like is totally different than when we started."

The Long Haul

Building a successful team environment requires resources, knowledge, sound advice, and commitment to a transformation that may take years to fully evolve. At Amex Life Assurance, for example, "It took a good half a year to a year for the teams to really start showing some success," says customer-service director Norma Bermudez, "not only working together as a team, but also in productivity." And at Kenworth Trucks, according to area manager Mike Boyle, "It was almost like nobody knew for awhile what their role was. If I was ever to guard against something from happening, it would be that."

How well the team concept takes hold in your organization— and how quickly you begin to reap the practical benefits—depends on how carefully you and your co-architects design and construct the four pillars of a team environment: values, skills, alignment, and deployment. But sooner or later, says plant manager Dave Powell of First Brands, team values and practices do begin to seep into even the most remote corners of the organization. "People-oriented managers fit into teams well," he says. "Yet in some departments, we have some very traditional managers, and even they have begun to see the successes of teams. They've been helped by teams through different situations. Then the barriers begin to come down, and they begin to support the team concept and utilize it—whether they really realize it or not."

The message is clear: With the right information, training, and skills, you can become a builder both of teams and of a workplace that permits those teams to thrive.

NOTES

[1] Zenger-Miller, Inc., research interview, 1992.

[2] Zenger-Miller, Inc., has been helping organizations to train leaders and nonmanagers and to implement teams in many forms since 1977. Zenger-Miller now serves about 3,000 sites worldwide including half of the Fortune 500.

[3] Zenger-Miller, Inc., research interview, 1992.

[4] Valarie A. Zeithaml, A. Parasuraman, and Leonard L. Berry, *Delivering Quality Service: Balancing Customer Perceptions and Expectations.* (New York: Free Press, 1990), p. 144.

[5] For this model and for much of the analysis in this chapter, the authors are grateful to Jim Clemmer and our other colleagues at Achieve International, a subsidiary and strategic partner of Zenger-Miller, Inc. For a book-length treatment of Achieve's "implementation architecture," see Jim Clemmer, *Firing on All Cylinders* (Homewood, Ill.: Business One Irwin, 1992).

[6] See also "The Basic Principles" (p. 43).

[7] Zenger-Miller, Inc., research interview, 1992.

[8] For an overview of realigning compensation systems with team values and behaviors, see Jack D. Orsburn, Linda Moran, Ed Musselwhite, and John H. Zenger, *Self-Directed Work Teams: The New American Challenge* (Homewood, Ill.: Business One Irwin, 1989), pp. 182–94.

[9] T. J. Rodgers, "No Excuses Management," *Harvard Business Review*, July-August 1990, p. 86.

Learning to Soar

By this point, you probably have a pretty good grasp of what this new team leadership role is all about. Still, you may also have some lingering doubts about the value or long-term security of becoming a team leader. You may not yet be convinced that team leaders aren't:

- Marshmallow managers who survive by doing whatever a team wants.
- Professionally suicidal since they're essentially giving their jobs away.
- Glorified gofers.
- Useless.
- Wimps.

What's more, if you harbor any such doubts, team leaders seem to incriminate themselves every time they open their mouths. Take Thelma Inkson, nurse manager with the University of Alberta Hospitals. In the old days, she says, she would answer questions, make decisions, solve problems, and generally rise to any occasion that arose. Now, she goes on, "I no longer do that. I give it back to them and say, 'OK, this is a problem. What do you think we should do about it?' "

Even Alan Campbell, the veteran supervisor who builds huge long-haul trucks—gleaming, rolling metaphors of North American manhood—sounds like he's gone soft: "They're really leading *me*," he says about his team. "They come to me with suggestions and ideas, and my job is to fulfill what they want."

Sure, some of these people leave themselves open for this kind of charge. But let's give them a chance to defend themselves. How do stellar team leaders respond to a direct accusation that they're passive, that they've abdicated their responsibility by handing over leadership to the team? What do they say about that?

"That is the exact *opposite* of the way it is," according to Brad West of Spectra Physics. "In reality, to be successful, you have to be a very good leader. It's just a whole lot different from a traditional role."

At Kenworth, Alan Campbell sneers. Then he bristles at the charge. "I have *never* been a marshmallow supervisor," he says. "My record in the past is as hard as they come, if you want. But that doesn't work. It doesn't work! All you do is drive yourself right into the ground and everybody else with you. If you command, command, command, they'll only do what they've got to do. You find that if you can do it a different way, which is this leadership thing, this guided thing, working as teams, it's completely different."

OK, OK—but could somebody be a little more specific? What is this different way? And please don't give us another lecture.

"You give the people the authority to do what you know they can do better than you can do," says Campbell. "That's not being a marshmallow. That's being savvy. That's being smart."

"I would say it a different way," says Amex president Sarah Nolan. "I want people to care about what they do. They don't have to bring everything into the workplace. They just have to care more than I do about what they do."

And that's it? But what if you're measured the way most managers are—on your bottom-line numbers? What then?

"If you treat people well, if you treat them as individuals that you care about," says Nolan, "they will treat your customers that way. If you treat them like a cog in a machine, one of many replaceable parts, they'll treat your customers *that* way. . . . You can achieve numbers wilder than you could ever imagine by focusing on the people and letting the ripples take care of the profits."

Sharon Faltemier, a line manager and high-powered teams advocate at Raychem Corporation, cut her teeth on teams at Procter & Gamble in the early 80s. She's heard plenty of "wimp" rhetoric over the years. "A lot of people, especially traditional managers, have this idea that these new managers are passive," says Faltemier. "In other words, that their job is *not* to do something as opposed to doing something positive or taking positive steps forward. That's a myth. That's a stereotype and a myth. It doesn't conform to the reality of who these people are. Because you've got to be aggressive," she goes on. "You are bringing about change, and you can't do that by standing in the wings and watching."

The plain truth is that the passive team leader is a convenient fiction. It's a straw man invented by someone with a rusty bayonet looking for an easy target—or by someone looking for an easy way to avoid facing the need to change.

Leading teams really does take the exact *opposite* of a passive nature. What it takes, according to Sarah Nolan, is patience and courage. But it also takes training. If she had it to do over, what would she do differently? "Well," says Nolan with an elbow to ribs of the authors, "the facetious answer is I would have read a book about teams, quality, learning environments. The more serious response is I would have spent a lot more money, time, and energy in training people in team interaction."

Ron Deane of Spectra Physics—the same Ron Deane who wondered, "What value do I have down the road if the tasks that I am doing today are being done by someone else?"—had a revelation about training and about his own ability to master a new role. "What I learned, and this was a big help for me, was it wasn't so much a natural thing. If I developed my skills, I could do it."

But what about the nagging thought that occurred to Deane and occurs to virtually every other traditional manager facing a transition to teams—that by being less of a boss and more of a coach, you'll delegate yourself out of a job? "Put aside all your worst fears of what might happen," says Ramiro Mendoza of Subaru-Isuzu. "Put aside all the feelings that you may have about where you're gonna end up. Because you'll always be a part of it. As long as you keep the teams growing, you'll always be a part of it."

Learning to lead teams is very much like learning to fly. In fact, the lesson for you is exactly what two brothers, bicycle makers, learned one morning long ago on the dunes of Kitty Hawk: If you believe, if you learn, if you practice, and if you let go, you too can soar with those who do it naturally.

II

PROFILES IN TEAM LEADERSHIP

INTRODUCTION TO PART II

As part of the research for this book (and for the *TeamLeadership*™ training system), associates of Zenger-Miller, Inc., conducted scores of interviews with leaders at all levels in organizations committed to teams and related practices. In a range of settings—public, private, service, and manufacturing—we heard a remarkably consistent story: Succeeding as a team leader depends in large part on living the values and mastering the skills summarized in the preceding pages. Some of the quotations illustrating key points in Part I of this book derive from those interviews.

We've also heard another very consistent message over the years while assisting thousands of people to transition to teams. People learning the team leadership role tell us that, in addition to nuts-and-bolts skills training, they want detailed information from others who have already mastered the role. "Give us more of those real-life examples," they might say. "We want to know what it's like in organizations with successful teams."

In the spirit of free access to vital information, the fresh air that quickens a team environment, Part II offers edited versions of some of the interviews we conducted. Here, in their own words, team leaders from every organizational level describe the paths they've walked and offer advice to those who will soon follow.

"What Do *You* Think We Should Do?"

Sarah Nolan
President
Amex Life Assurance

Zenger-Miller:

What were the issues and problems that you were trying to address by moving to teams?

Sarah Nolan:

When I came here in 1988, we began re-evaluating the strategy that we had then. The strategy was very repetitive—the same products delivered in the same way for 25 years. The company had been incredibly successful, made lots of money, and lots of people had risen up through the different hierarchies to become senior managers. But what you found when you really started talking to people is that they were stopped from doing anything new. There was a penalty for people who wanted to create new ways, and they soon learned to keep their heads down and be typical.

Zenger-Miller:

What steps did you take early on?

Sarah Nolan:

One of the things I did was to go around and educate myself—which seems like a simple thing but was quite revolutionary here. I asked each manager to set up an appointment so I could learn about what accounts payable people did, what did customer service people do, what did people in the systems area do, and so on. I had a day-long session in each

There was such waste of human creativity, such inefficiency—and it was everywhere!

area just sitting with the clerks watching what they did. And at the end of that, I was absolutely desperate. There was such waste of human creativity, such inefficiency—and it was everywhere! The people, with all goodwill, just kept doing the same things over and over. We said the file must move from place to place and different people must do very specialized functions—like stapling, stamping, sorting, filing. What you'd see is a file sitting on the shelf 90 percent of the time, and the actual work being a very small piece of all that motion and human effort.

Zenger-Miller:

What do you do about a situation like that?

Sarah Nolan:

You get the people to use their creativity to fix these things that are all around them. They sit amidst these processing chains, doing what they've been told, logging out when they come in the front door, and you have the best part of a human turned off. We were using them like arms and legs, the lowest common denominator, replaceable people who could staple. Instead, we wanted to build jobs for a higher common denominator. So the real issue became, how do you make it a requirement in a person's job that they become creative? And, also, how do you require that they be part of a larger team? Because you had to have a solution that went across a number of these functional silos.

> *We were using them like arms and legs, the lowest common denominator, replaceable people who could staple.*

Zenger-Miller:

Was the situation here unusual in your experience?

Sarah Nolan:

A lot of the 20th century model is built around piecing work into its smallest common denominator so you can have managerial control. But I do believe, and my philosophy is, that the thing that is your asset in your company is your people's creativity. And it's an amazing thing because it's nowhere on the balance sheet as an asset.

Zenger-Miller:

What do you mean by "creativity"?

Sarah Nolan:

You have people who you know on the outside of this corporate boundary. They're the heads of families. They're the heads of civic organizations. They're artists, writers, actors, singers, run their own businesses, are salesmen part-time. Huge creativity. And what do we teach them to do? Come in, hang up your creativity on the door post, do the same thing, don't question it, and make marginal incremental changes. What we do, basically, is pay too much for robots. What we *should* be doing is building jobs that make people stretch so that they give you the thing that they hold locked inside.

Zenger-Miller:

What about managers? What's their role in bringing out this creativity?

Sarah Nolan:

What you believe your job is as a manager really comes into question. If you believe your job is to produce profits and that people are just kind of cogs, then I think you will always miss the point. A manager's job is to get the largest return out of their best asset. That's optimizing your asset. And your best asset is the creativity of your people.

Zenger-Miller:

That seems like an easy thing to say. The question is, how do you do it? How do you get them to let go of what they have locked inside?

Sarah Nolan:

You use every method that you can think of. And some you can't think of—that only *they* can think of. It's quite daunting. The first thing is, you must believe they are your only asset. If you don't believe that, you will not act that way. Do you train people? If you don't, you're making no investment. So you don't believe people are your best asset. Do you reward people when they take the right kinds of actions?

Zenger-Miller:

OK, training and rewards. Anything else?

Sarah Nolan:

Let's say as a manager you wanted to double your sales. You would figure out many creative ways to do that—rewards, programs, products, whatever it was—if you really believed that's how you were measured as a manager. Well, suppose we say the sole measure I'm going to give to you is how creative your people are, and how well cared for do they feel? Do they feel that you believe in them? That's going to be the sole criterion for you by year-end. Do you think you can do that? The answer is yes, but you have to believe that's the way you're measured.

> *. . . suppose we say the sole measure I'm going to give to you is how creative your people are . . .*

Zenger-Miller:

So if I take care of them, invest in them, they'll be more creative. But the reality is, most managers are judged on their bottom-line numbers.

Is there a connection between caring for people, as you say, and overall business performance?

Sarah Nolan:

Yes. If you treat people well, if you treat them as individuals that you care about and take time and attention with, they will treat your customers that way. If you treat them like a cog in a machine, one of many replaceable parts, they'll treat your customers *that* way. Are profits a byproduct of managing your people well? I think they are. You can achieve numbers wilder than you could ever imagine by focusing on the people and letting the ripples take care of the profits. We set simple numbers for ourselves in the beginning that were 20 percent above a normal run rate. We blasted through those in about three months. Not by focusing on them. Not by beating on people to "get the number, get the number." But instead by asking, "What is it you need to do this? How can we help you do this?"

Zenger-Miller:

People around here do seem to have a sense of common purpose.

Sarah Nolan:

We believe we are a community of learners. And so, if you think about that as your responsibility, to teach people, to let them grow as far as they can grow, to give them honest feedback about their progress, and if you take that as an expression of caring and investing, then you have a better sense of what I mean. Most people in this company feel that they're part of an experiment where they have major contributions to make in terms of improving their own practices. They've been trained to do it, they've been rewarded for doing it, and they've failed and not been fired. Because if you're not failing enough, then it means you're not trying enough.

> *Most people in this company feel that they're part of an experiment where they have major contributions to make . . .*

Zenger-Miller:

I'd like to keep pushing on this question of how do you do it. That's what most managers will want to know.

Sarah Nolan:

You have to be committed to try many different techniques because no technique is perfect. And you have to have patience and courage because a number of those experiments won't work. They just will flop, and they will flop so publicly. Employees who are trying to learn what the new way is, as you are trying to learn what it is, can be quite doubtful. They can be very resistant. They know how to succeed in the old way. They don't even know what the new way is, and you can't even *articulate* it.

Zenger-Miller:

It sounds tricky. But maybe an example would help. Could you tell us about a time when something you tried actually worked?

Sarah Nolan:

Early on, it took 10 days to issue a simple policy. But what we couldn't figure out was, why couldn't it be issued the same day? So we took a group of clerks and asked them, "Why is it you can't do this the same day?" First they said, "We don't have enough people." So I wrote that on the board. "And we don't have enough systems." OK, we'll write that down, too. So what else is it you would need to do this the same day? They had to really think about it because those are the two answers you always give. So they went away, about six clerks, and worked and worked on it. In a week or two they said, "We can do it next day. No new people and no new systems." And all they'd really done was a flowchart. They figured out it sat on 50 shelves and took I don't remember how many checkers checking and monitors monitoring and stamping in and stamping out. All that wasted energy! They themselves had figured it out because they know the process better than any manager can ever know it.

> *. . . it took 10 days to issue a simple policy. But what we couldn't figure out was, why couldn't it be issued the same day?*

Zenger-Miller:

I see. And is that example fairly typical?

Sarah Nolan:

So many experiments were happening at the same time. We looked back over all the things we could remember from 1988, 89, 90, 91, and you see this huge list each year of about 15 cross-functional projects. Year after year, we built on what we had learned the year before. Some of the teams that started in 88 flowered in 89 and began to grow. Not because we said, "Here is a cookie-cutter thing." The whole point was creativity, acceptance, experimentation, but all driven toward the goals of new creative products and customer service. Now we have different formats for our teams in each department because each department's needs are different.

Zenger-Miller:

Let's come back to the leadership role. Was there any main leadership function, or behavior, or characteristic that seemed to carry through all of these experiments?

Sarah Nolan:

Lead by example. And the example we wanted was a belief that everyone at every level can contribute, everyone had to challenge everything, everyone had to take more risks, and everyone had to learn new things. You have to model that—an openness, an open-minded approach to what each person can contribute. If you don't do it, nobody will.

Zenger-Miller:

Again, how do you model that belief? What, specifically, can you do?

Sarah Nolan:

For a real simple example, you want people to be creative, and they come to you with a problem. Now in the old hierarchical way, you're supposed to give them the answer. You're this great fountain of all wisdom. And that is what you were paid for. But what I believe most is that Socrates had quite a good approach. He would guide them through their learning. So my favorite response when somebody comes and says, "Well, we've got this issue, bla, bla, bla"—my favorite answer is, "What do *you* think we should do?"

> *. . . what I believe most is that Socrates had quite a good approach.*

Zenger-Miller:

How do people usually react to that?

Sarah Nolan:

In the beginning, a lot of people thought this was a challenge. It was like, "OK, now I've got to put myself on the line about what I think. It must be a trap." It's amazing. But if people begin to think that you really care about what they think, the answer might be, they come prepared with an answer. They're willing to risk a little more. What you have to unlearn is that if you truly know the answer, you *might not*. So just that little bit of open-mindedness, even about your own expertise, is quite helpful in teaching them to be self-confident.

Zenger-Miller:

Did managers here find it hard to learn that lesson?

Sarah Nolan:

They truly did not know how to do a role which required them *not* to be the expert. They felt they were paid to be the expert, the housekeeper, to hand out work, know the answer, make sure people's habits were good, that they were in on time—all those kinds of things. As we continued to work together, we got much more used to a shepherding, coaching role. You're not paid to know the answer. You're paid to help them understand what the answer may be.

> *You're not paid to know the answer. You're paid to help them understand what the answer may be.*

Zenger-Miller:

How would you describe *your* role in all this?

Sarah Nolan:

People have said to me, "You created this, you have created this environment." In fact, I don't feel that I created it at all. It is larger than you as a leader. In the beginning what you think is, "I have to care more than most of the people in the company. They can only care from their perspective, but to knit the whole thing together and be the customer's advocate—that must be my role—I must try to find out answers for people." In the end you find you have people who are really working on making the customer's life better. They're trained. They have jobs that are worthy of their creativity. They know how to pull apart work processes, work on quality measurements, do business process improvement. They've been trained and rewarded for doing it and have a hell of a good time while they're doing it.

Zenger-Miller:

Could you explain a little more what you mean when you say, "It's larger than you as a leader"?

Sarah Nolan:

It's much bigger than anything you could have projected it would be. Even though you believed in this creativity of people, when it starts coming, it's like a flood. It's an organism that is above and beyond your own individual contribution or anybody's individual contribution. You'll be astonished. You'll think, "Well, you know, this is really a big issue. We must address it." And suddenly you find a whole group of

> *Even though you believed in this creativity of people, when it starts coming, it's like a flood.*

them has addressed it. They've gotten together. They've thought it is something to be worked on, and they're almost through. The point about management in this kind of environment is to be quite clear about the objectives but absolutely silent about the method—other than to train people to do problem solving.

Zenger-Miller:
What you're talking about is going to sound pretty radical, pretty risky, to many, many people brought up in a traditional world.

Sarah Nolan:
Suppose I say to you, "I want you tomorrow to put on your shirt first and then your pants," and every day you put on your pants first. Well now, you've got to have a reason to change that habit. And people in businesses, they have habits too about how they interact with people, how they make decisions, the whole thing. And it's all unwritten. The stuff that's really important isn't written down.

Zenger-Miller:
For example?

Sarah Nolan:
That the more powerful you are, the more people you manage. Now think how counter-productive this is because it means somebody is going to be compelled to pile up more and more people. But in fact, technology can now do amazing things, so you don't need hoards of people. Where's the reward system that says to people, "Flatten out this structure"?

Zenger-Miller:
Are you saying you can make do with fewer people?

Sarah Nolan:
The objective was to have better customer service and more innovation. So of course we have weeded out people at the associate level who wanted to do the same thing day after day after day. They had in effect logged out. And you have a lot of managers who only wanted to tell people what to do. They didn't want something where they had to coach people and guide them along and learn themselves and open up to different ways of thinking. As you shift any kind of culture to match a strategy, you're going to have people who are not going to adjust.

Zenger-Miller:
That sounds a little like Darwin. You know, "survival of the fittest."

Sarah Nolan:
If you have a culture and a strategy that calls for birds with blunt beaks, you get a lot of birds with blunt beaks that succeed in that environment.

Now let's say we shift our strategy, and now we need birds with sharp beaks. Well, lo and behold, in the old blunt-beak population you have a few that have sharper beaks, and they are suddenly quite dominant. The others either have to sharpen up their beaks, or you get new ones that come in. So you really have to be crystal clear about what your strategy is, what your priorities are, and what kind of cultural environment will support that. On the managerial level, people have understood what's required—

If you have a culture and a strategy that calls for birds with blunt beaks, you get a lot of birds with blunt beaks . . .

that they're supposed to be creative, they're supposed to be supportive. And if they can't, they get very direct feedback about it, it's reflected in their appraisal, and then they get the choice. But if they don't adjust, then we let them go.

Zenger-Miller:

So are you talking about a kind of "natural selection"? Are you saying people are successful leaders here only if they are *naturally suited* to a team environment?

Sarah Nolan:

You've already interviewed a number of our people today. It's a mixed group. Some of them are much happier in this environment because they were the people with the sharp beaks all along. Some of them think of this as a return to when they were a smaller company, when you really could care a lot more about the customer. Some had learned everything they knew in the old way, which is "I make the decisions, I discipline people"—the old parent role. For some of *them* it's been quite

I'd be interested to see if you could pick which ones it was more natural for and which ones it was harder for.

a hard adjustment. I'd be interested to see if you could pick which ones it was more natural for and which ones it was harder for.

Zenger-Miller:

As far as I could tell, they all had pretty sharp beaks. So to speak.

Sarah Nolan:

But the real thing is that people deserve a fair shot. They deserve a reward structure and honesty. That's the other thing. You can't make a cultural shift if you are not honest with people. It's taken me a long time to learn how critical that is. And some of it's hard because you're learning yourself so you don't even know what to be honest about. The first thing is, "We don't know where we're going, but it's to these objectives, and no, I don't know if this will work." So that takes away the all-knowing, all-seeing, powerful leader and parent. And being honest about that sometimes is devastating. But in the end at least you have a foundation where everybody understands.

Zenger-Miller:

Let's take a slightly different angle here. How do you know when it's all working, when this team environment thing has begun to take hold?

Sarah Nolan:

You can feel it. You walk down the hall, and regular associate-level people will come up and tell you something they're really proud of. They had a zero abandon rate—no customer hung up the phone before they answered it. They'll rush out to see you as you park your car and tell you. Or you walk down the halls and suddenly you notice they've had a luau, and they've got pictures of all these people in grass skirts. Now you say, "This sounds crazy." But the creativity is astonishing. Or you get a letter when you ask for feedback, and they say they hated change when I first came here. But they said they've had wonderful, tremendous personal growth over the last few years. That they truly feel that for the first time they've been treated like a person. Now think about how hard that is to say.

> *. . . suddenly you notice they've had a luau, and they've got pictures of all these people in grass skirts.*

Zenger-Miller:

Yes, I can see that.

Sarah Nolan:

Or they changed something and it's all taken care of. And you didn't order it. You could never have ordered them to do it as well as they do it because they are their own hardest taskmasters. It has more to do with this becoming a human environment and less of a business environment.

Zenger-Miller:

If you had it to do over, Sarah, what would you do differently.

Sarah Nolan:

Well, the facetious answer is I would have read a book about teams, quality, learning environments—all these things that now I've read. But the more serious response is I would have spent a lot more money, time, and energy in training people in team interaction. Because when you take away all the structure about handing out work and discipline, what happens is the people themselves, their personalities, get larger. So the whole issue of how they interact with one another, how they negotiate and get things done—like who's

. . . the people themselves,
their personalities, get larger.

going to cover the phones and who isn't—I wish I had invested tons more money in that. I just didn't know that's how critical it was.

Zenger-Miller:

Anything else you'd have done differently?

Sarah Nolan:

I would have learned how to build a process of communication and interaction between me and all different levels that was much more consistent. Because you really need a huge flow of communication all the time to learn what things are coming up, to be in a coaching role. Think about the first role of your secretary if you're a chief executive. What is it?

Zenger-Miller:

Uh . . . I'll never know unless you tell me.

Sarah Nolan:

Screen out people, preserve your time. And so you have to say to your secretary and to a host of people, "What I want you to do is create multiple opportunities for high access. A brown bag lunch every week. I want that. No, I'm not above it. I want it. It's necessary. Don't forget it."

Zenger-Miller:

It seems like what you're trying to do is to engage these people fully, to get everything from them that they can offer to the workplace.

Sarah Nolan:

I would say it a different way. I want people to care about what they do. They don't have to bring everything into the workplace. They just have to care more than I do about what they do. So you see in our situation here, we are in the process of selling the company. You'd think morale would be low because they don't know what is going to happen to their jobs. But the results that we have with our customers are 50 percent better than they were a year ago. They don't just turn this off because they are for sale.

Zenger-Miller:

It is strange. People don't seem down at all. But I wonder what's going through your mind now in this last few weeks of the company as you know it.

Sarah Nolan:

Someone asked me, "Don't you think that you should have not brought these people to this point? Because, ironically, your business is going to be sold and now the probability is that they will have to step back into more traditional environments." My answer to that is no! For all of us, living in this environment has been quite special. You're growing. You're challenging things. It's made me a hell of a lot better manager. But better than that, it has made me a better person. Because when you think back about the things that you learn as you go up, they have to do with control and people being in their proper assigned spot. And the thing that just rips the covers off your eyes is what enormous creativity, what enormous contributions people at every level have to give you.

Zenger-Miller:

Could you say more about some of the lessons you've learned here?

Sarah Nolan:

You learn to listen and be respectful of people even if you don't agree with what they are saying. What I have learned over time is you may not have enough facts to know the answer because you are so far removed from the front line and the customer. And so just the whole opening up of yourself to the fact that you probably don't know. Management is becoming who you will be, not doing what you have always done.

Management is becoming who you will be, not doing what you have always done.

Zenger-Miller:

That does sound challenging.

Sarah Nolan:

The other thing is this enormous sense of amazement that you get when you're in something that has no cause-and-effect. I mean when you give an order, it's easy to see cause-and-effect. I gave an order. It was done or wasn't done. But when you're part of an organism like this—where people see problems and begin to work on them, and you didn't give an order—this whole issue of where it starts and where it ends, that sense of causality, is not here. It's more like your brain where the networks just sort of flow back and forth.

. . . the irony of the organism dying and how I feel about that, in some ways, is beyond words.

Zenger-Miller:

I think I'm following. It does seem odd.

Sarah Nolan:

The other odd part is having created this organism which is now fated to die. It does not exist except in a community of people who have learned how to do this. It is a product of the people being together. So if the people aren't together, it doesn't exist anymore. There is nothing you can show to anybody. So the irony of the organism dying and how I feel about that, in some ways, is beyond words. The risk that we all fear is that we will never have anything this good again. But the good news about that is that it is created of people. So any place there are people you can do it.

Zenger-Miller:

The people I've interviewed today will take this with them. Like seeds on the wind.

Sarah Nolan:

The other good news, as you and I have talked about, is that this revolution is coming. It is borne and pushed by technology, by the diversity of organizations, by the increasing demands of customers who want to be treated like individuals. There is more and more over-capacity for every product you could name. So the whole issue is high-touch, highly individualized treatment, which technology is making possible but which people really have to execute. That's why a lot of these work groups are growing up.

Zenger-Miller:

I'd like to wind this up by returning to the theme. What advice would you have for a manager, or supervisor, or executive—a competent traditional manager—who wants to be effective in a team environment?

Sarah Nolan:

Your job is to figure out how to get people to really care about what they do. If you took as a model of behavior how you would like to behave to your best friends or to your peers, then you have a pretty good model for how to behave to associates. How is that? With respect. You don't order your best friends around. You listen to them. You joke with them. You don't always *agree* with them. But there is a whole sense of respect and mutual learning in those relationships. If you are able to open your mind enough, then you will be able to have the same thing happen with your team.

Authors' Note: Shortly after this interview, Amex Life Assurance of San Rafael, California, was sold. Much of the work force, including Sarah Nolan and most of the other managers, have since left the company.

"It's a Very Good Feeling"

Nadine Lake
Senior Customer Service Associate
Amex Life Assurance

Zenger-Miller:

When did you come here?

Nadine Lake:

I actually started working here in September of 1966. I began part-time. Then I was offered a permanent job, so I said, "Maybe I'll stay for a little while longer." Then I started going to school and got married, and here I am.

Zenger-Miller:

How long has it been since you started working in teams?

Nadine Lake:

Since June of 1989.

Zenger-Miller:

Are there any big differences?

Nadine Lake:

The differences are drastic. When I first started with the company, I was a file clerk. Then I was moved out onto the floor as a typist. Then I moved up to policy assembly and after that something else. But it seemed like my supervisors all planned my career for me. Now it's different. I have a lot of control over my own career.

. . . my supervisors all planned my career for me. Now it's different.

Zenger-Miller:

That seems like a major change.

Nadine Lake:

Another thing that's different is that we now have fewer levels of management. We used to have team leaders, supervisors, assistant supervisors, managers, assistant managers. So if I had an idea about how to improve the processing of a certain function, I had to go to my team leader and tell her about it. Then she'd pass it along to the supervisor. The supervisor would then take it to the manager, and the manager would have to take it to the director. If I got an answer back to my idea, it might be five or six months down the road and things would have changed. Now, if I

> *. . . before, it was, "Oh no, don't bother me with that. Just do your work."*

have an idea, I can test it myself and then say, "This is what I'm doing." I could present the reasons why I've suggested the change, the cost factor, and what it's going to save us or how much money it's going to bring in. Whereas before, it was, "Oh no, don't bother with that. Just do your work."

Zenger-Miller:

Do you like this better than the old days? Was it a good change?

Nadine Lake:

Yes, for me it was. I wouldn't say I always wanted to be in management, but I always wanted to be in control of my own career. If there's an area that I want to move into, I don't want to have to sit back and wait until my supervisor or manager feels that "Oh, well, Nadine is doing pretty well this year, let's see what else she can do." I want a chance to make my own choices about my career, and that's what I feel I now have the opportunity to do.

Zenger-Miller:

I understand that in your team you rotate leadership.

Nadine Lake:

Yes, and I really like it. Every month one of the team members has the opportunity of being the monthly coordinator. On our team it's only for a month, which we prefer, although on some other teams their coordinators go for two months. Being coordinator gives you the opportunity to sit in on coordinators' meetings and hear about what's going on in other teams, present problems, find solutions to problems, and come back and offer it to the team.

Zenger-Miller:

Could you tell me about a typical situation you might handle?

Nadine Lake:

OK, here's one scenario. We had a team member who was out on disability. She started at 6:00 A.M. and went until 2:15, and on phone days we really needed her to be ready to take those calls at 6. I normally get to work at 7:30, and it's impossible for me to be here before 6:30 using public transportation. I just can't do it. So what happened was the coordinator for that month brought the problem to the coordinators meeting and said, "Look, we need help with our 6 A.M. shift. Can you give us some suggestions?" And immediately all the other coordinators offered help. One of them said, "I'm a 6:00 person, so I'll take Maria's shift until someone comes in on your team to relieve me." And it worked out fine.

Zenger-Miller:

What's the best thing about being coordinator?

Nadine Lake:

When you're the coordinator, you have more of a handle about what type of work is coming into the team, how it's moving, and what techniques they're using to process it. At the end of the week they're supposed to turn in all the results to me, so I can start getting my figures together when I first come in Monday morning. It gives me an opportunity to make sure that everyone is doing what they need to do in order for our team to succeed.

Zenger-Miller:

Is there anything that's been a strain? Anything you'd rather not do?

Nadine Lake:

I have to personally take everyone's results and compile them onto one report for the department. I don't much like doing that.

Zenger-Miller:

Do you feel any more stress when you're the coordinator?

Nadine Lake:

Yeah, because there's so much that you have to make sure is going smoothly. You have to make sure that team member A understands what's going on so that they can process their work. You have to make sure that everyone is doing exactly what they're supposed to do to achieve the desired results. And then you have to do your own work too.

. . . it puts you in more of a leadership role when your team members rely on you . . .

It's not *that* much more stressful. But it's a real good experience because it puts you in more of a leadership role when your team members rely on you just a little bit more.

Zenger-Miller:

What about your teammates? What changes have you seen in them as a result of going to this team environment?

Nadine Lake:

More confidence in themselves. More self-esteem. Feeling good that they can make their own decisions. They don't get their hands slapped if they make a mistake. Everyone makes mistakes, but you learn from them. Processing their work with the confidence that it's going to be right. If they need answers to questions, they have someone to go to. They don't have to set up time with their supervisor to go over a problem with them, which would have taken two or three days before they even got to their supervisor.

Zenger-Miller:

Do people seem any more committed to their work?

Nadine Lake:

Yes. Before our work was very functionalized. A certain individual would only do address changes, beneficiary changes, and name changes, and that's all that person did from eight to five. Whereas now we have the opportunity to show that we can do more.

Zenger-Miller:

So now, after three years, how do people feel about working teams?

Nadine Lake:

When we first heard about it, it was very stressful because we didn't know exactly how it was going to affect us. I was very, very skeptical at first as to what was going to happen with me. I even had a talk with someone in personnel. But having management be very open with us and be telling us as much as they know makes it easier for us to take steps to

I was very, very skeptical at first as to what was going to happen with me.

make our own choices. I don't feel like they're hiding anything or there's something they know that they aren't telling us.

Zenger-Miller:

Do you feel that you've grown or improved your own skills by being on a team?

Nadine Lake:

It's strange that you mention that because I've just gotten a promotion about three months ago, and in our teams we evaluate each other. You see yourself differently than everyone else sees you, so when I got my performance appraisal, I actually cried. I know I do good work. But I didn't know my team members saw me the way they did to the point where my director immediately said, "Let's promote her." It made me feel so good.

Zenger-Miller:

Do you see yourself taking on more leadership responsibilities?

Nadine Lake:

Yes. Management has always felt that I was a leader, and I am to a certain extent. But I know I still like my technical projects. I love challenges.

Zenger-Miller:

How do you relate to people here? How would you characterize your style?

Nadine Lake:

My belief is, everyone deserves to be treated with respect. Just because Mary—and that's just a name that came up—just because Mary has never done the type of processing I've done doesn't mean her skills can't be developed. I feel that treating people with respect will take you a long way, and I try to do that. I try to be very, very pleasant with people and treat everybody the way I like to be treated.

I feel that treating people with respect will take you a long way . . .

Zenger-Miller:

That definitely comes through.

Nadine Lake:

It's also about being honest with people and getting them to be honest back. If they're having a problem with a worker or thinking, "I cannot process this work, I don't know how to do it," I find that I can draw it out of them. It's getting them to trust you, to be comfortable with you. I seem to just naturally do that.

Zenger-Miller:

Let's say your team has a tough decision to make and people have strong opinions on both sides. Maybe there's a little tension. How do you resolve that type of situation?

Nadine Lake:

You need to talk. Everyone needs a chance to say how they feel. Then we can start asking questions. "Is it something going on with the team that's bothering you? Or is it a problem at home that you're bringing to work? Is it something you think we're not doing? Or maybe it's that I get my work done, and you still feel like you have 30 or 40 items on your desk, and I only have 3?" We're workers, not psychologists. We can only work on a problem if you let us know what the problem is.

Zenger-Miller:

What would you say to somebody like yourself, but who's just getting started with teams, to help get them headed in the right direction?

Nadine Lake:

I'd tell them it's not going to be easy because it's a whole different perspective than what they were used to. I'd say, give it a chance to work, and I'm not talking about a month or two. It took us three years, and we're still making changes and finding things that can be different. I'd tell them to talk. Have meetings and talk. Don't just go, "Mmm-hmm, yeah, I understand." Make sure you *really* understand. Give input. You may have ideas on something that can really help the team. Just because you come to a team with few skills, it doesn't mean you can't fit into a team

> *Just because you come to a team with few skills, it doesn't mean you can't fit into a team environment.*

environment. We all learn from each other. It's not going to happen overnight. It's not going to happen next week or even next month. But one day you're going to sit back and say, "Hey, we've built a team environment!" And it's a very good feeling.

"That's Being Savvy"

Alan Campbell
Production Supervisor
Kenworth Trucks

Zenger-Miller:

Alan, since you've been working with teams, you've mentioned that your role has changed substantially. How would you describe this change?

Alan Campbell:

Oh, it's changed a lot for the better. I used to spend more time doing what I considered were other people's jobs—fighting fires, trying to get people to work together or relate to each other. Since we've switched over to teams, people have taken on all those day-to-day responsibilities themselves. They come up with the ideas now. In fact, they're really leading *me*. They come to me with suggestions and ideas, and my job is to fulfill what they want, whether it's helping them plan or getting the engineering and other support teams they need. It's made the job a lot more fun.

Zenger-Miller:

Think back. Is there anything you did in the old days that you regret having to give up?

Alan Campbell:

No, nothing. They've got control of their daily life, I've got control of mine. Before I had control of them, and they had control of me. Now it's more relaxed. I've got more free time to help them more and give them what they want. And they've got more free time to make their environment better for themselves. No, there's nothing from the past I'd want to go back to.

> *. . . there's nothing from the past I'd want to go back to.*

Zenger-Miller:

Was there a difficult transition period for you, a low point when things were just not going well at all?

Alan Campbell:

I can't really recall any particular low point. When I started in this job in the 60s, we were having a lot of labor problems. I was always asking, "Why do I have to be the motivator for every single little task?" As managers, we told everybody to do everything, and people got comfortable with that. So if Mike couldn't do his job because Bill wasn't cooperating, Mike wouldn't handle it himself. He'd run to me and say, "I can't do my job because Bill isn't cooperating. Would you talk to Bill?" I found myself constantly putting out fires and doing all the things I felt other people should be doing. Today I would just say, "Mike, go talk to Bill and sort that thing out, will ya?" When somebody comes to me with a problem, my standard response is "What do you suggest we do about it?"

Zenger-Miller:

Is this new approach more or less stressful?

Alan Campbell:

Oh, a lot less stressful.

Zenger-Miller:

How so?

Alan Campbell:

Because everyone is sharing responsibility. If anything, they've taken on more than I expected, and that's all because they started working as a team.

Zenger-Miller:

You mean they just started working as a team?

Alan Campbell:

Well you can't just say work as a team, and they all work as a team. They have to be trained how to do it. Once they do start working as a team, all the "it's-not-my-job-it's-his-job" starts going away. Also, because people have more time and are more resourceful, they involve me less. I used to be down on the floor every 15 minutes fighting one fire or another. Now I may go a week or even a month without a problem that needs me. A lot of times I only see them when we touch base. But when they do have a problem, I take it seriously, and I tell the engineers and managers to do the same.

> . . . all the "it's-not-my-job-it's-his-job" starts going away.

Zenger-Miller:

Suppose you don't agree with what they're telling you.

Alan Campbell:

Just because you can't see why
they want to do something, it
doesn't mean you don't do it. If   *If they want it, you make it*
they want it, you make it happen,   *happen, just as long as it*
just as long as it meets basic con- *meets basic considerations . . .*
siderations like cost and safety.

Zenger-Miller:

What kinds of leadership activities have you been able to transfer to
the groups?

Alan Campbell:

Depends on the group. In some groups everyone is capable of being
the leader, so if you've got eight people, you might spread the responsibility around. One might end up being the spokesman, another
might take on the role of technical advisor, and another might do the
housekeeping for the group. On the other hand, the group might be
more comfortable with a leader, so you have to find somebody who's
comfortable in that role and who has the ability to coalesce people. But
however it's set it up, instead of having to come up with all the ideas,
myself, the group's now coming up with them. All I do is help them
sift through. It's a bigger sense of achievement than telling them what
I want them to do all the time.

Zenger-Miller:

What would you say if somebody told you that you're kind of a marshmallow manager? That you're really abdicating your responsibilities
as a leader by delegating so much?

Alan Campbell:

I have *never* been a marshmallow supervisor. My record in the past is
as hard as they come, if you want. But that doesn't work. It doesn't
work! All you do is drive yourself right into the ground and everybody
else with you. If you command, command, command, they'll only do
what they've got to do. You find that if you can do it a different way,
which is this leadership thing, this guided thing, working as teams,
it's completely different. You give the people the authority to do what
you know they can do better than you can do, and a lot more efficiently.
That's not being marshmallow. That's being savvy. That's being smart.

Zenger-Miller:

How would you handle this situation? Let's say people were struggling
with a difficult problem you felt you had already had an answer for.

Alan Campbell:

When somebody has a problem like that, I always try and get them to think of the answer first. I might have to coach them a little bit, but I try not to come up with the answer for them.

Zenger-Miller:

How about the flip side. Say you have a gung-ho team with an idea you have serious reservations about.

Alan Campbell:

If you've got serious reservations, you tell them straightaway. Either it's too costly, or it's dangerous, or it's impractical, or we just don't have the time to do it. Whatever it is, we talk it out. If there's a genuine reason for your appre-hension, they'll see it. I've never yet had anybody, in this kind of a situation, who didn't come around. Sometimes, if they can't have exactly what they want, we'll look at what it is they're really after. And we may find another way to do it.

> *If there's a genuine reason for your apprehension, they'll see it.*

Zenger-Miller:

Could you give me an example of how you might give them more control over what they do?

Alan Campbell:

Right now I've got a big area with like 60 or 70 people. The tools in that area are all split between three lockers, and at the end of the shift everyone puts all their tools in one of these three lockers. So each locker has maybe 20 people's tools. Problem is, when they come in, sometimes a tool isn't there. Somebody else has taken it, so they've got to find another tool before they can start working. When we go to smaller work teams, I give each team their own locker so they can store their own tools and equipment. Now, instead of having 20, 30, or 60 tools to look after, they just have 5 or 6 tools. And they're *their* tools. They take personal responsibility for them. That's also five or six tools that *I* don't have to worry about. As we set up more and more small groups, we're finding we have greater control on a day-to-day basis. In fact, there's a bit of a snowball effect. The added efficiency creates more available time.

Zenger-Miller:

I wonder if you could put your role in a nutshell for us? What is the main thing that you're trying to achieve as a leader?

Alan Campbell:

I want a team that can come to work, start the job, and be the resident expert on what they do—more so than any engineer, any manager, any supervisor. I want them to be the last word on the subject. Right now, they buy their own equipment, monitor their process supplies, do their own budget, and do their own re-work and put it back into the system to eliminate waste. I see my role as not just a facilitator but as their link to all the other support groups they need to get these things done.

> *I want a team that can come to work, start the job, and be the resident expert on what they do . . .*

Zenger-Miller:

One of the things that traditional managers are afraid of is that they're going to delegate themselves out of a job by empowering the team to do the things that they do. Could you speak to this a little and maybe help the manager who is hesitant to move in the direction you've already moved in?

Alan Campbell:

If you want to live in the shoes that I've lived in for 20 years, trying to motivate people every minute of the day, you can have it because that's not how it needs to be. There's a better way. Not only is it a better way, it's a lot easier way. The job you were originally hired to do was to manage these groups and make them more efficient and to make the product better and to monitor safety and quality. And we weren't doing that. Without teams, you spend all day long motivating people to do what they should be doing on their own. I know there's a better way. I've been in the old way, and I've tried the new way, and believe me the new way is a lot better. It's not a new way really. It's just that we've got off track somewhere, and we've got to get back to trusting the people to do it themselves. And they can. And they do.

Zenger-Miller:

So, in a way, you're trying to build *self*-motivation.

Alan Campbell:

That's a big part of it. I give them control of the day-to-day environment. In the past, people would be told what to do and be constantly monitored by the manager. We now try to give them as much control during

> *What we do is monitor the output of the groups, rather than the individuals in the group.*

that eight hours as we possibly can, which is everything as far as I'm concerned. I see a real change of attitude when they're not worrying if they go to the bathroom that the supervisor's going to ask them where they've been. What we do is monitor the output of the groups, rather than the individuals in the group.

Zenger-Miller:

Any closing advice for somebody who's moving into a team environment?

Alan Campbell:

Trust your people, that's the thing. Trust your people until they let you down. And you'll be surprised that they don't let you down. As they take more and more responsibility and as they realize it's really their responsibility, they'll rise up to it and get the job done. I haven't been let down yet.

Interview Four

"You Need to Believe"

Joe Dulaney
Human Resources Manager
Levi Strauss & Co.

Zenger-Miller:

What's different about managing in a team environment?

Joe Dulaney:

For one thing, we've stripped away all indicators of status—visible things like special parking places and different break rooms. The other thing is, we keep turning more and more over to the teams. For example, our work teams have been trained in interviewing and EEO, so now they do their own interviewing when they have openings on their team. My job has become more of a trainer rather than a human resource or personnel person. In fact, we had so much training to do that I decided to get hourly people to also conduct this training. So we put out a letter and we asked people to volunteer. Only the hourly people got to vote on who was selected. Management people had no votes. Our job was just to train who they designated.

Zenger-Miller:

What other responsibilities have you turned over to the teams?

Joe Dulaney:

Teams are now involved in developing policies around absenteeism, tardiness, work hours, and line balance.

Zenger-Miller:

To what degree does management control the teams?

Joe Dulaney:

Very little. We don't nix it if they want to hire somebody. I mean, it's their person. They hire them. When we were looking for trainers, we let them pick a team of interviewers from different teams all over that production line, and they interviewed the candidates and made the selection. The plant manager and I didn't even talk to the person until the team had already chosen that person. And they select good people. One of the women they picked as a trainer has turned out to be exceptional. I was in a course here a week ago watching her, and at the end they all gave her a standing ovation.

> *We don't nix it if they want to hire somebody. I mean, it's their person.*

Zenger-Miller:

That's wonderful. But don't you have a lot more viewpoints now that need to be heard? How do you handle that?

Joe Dulaney:

We put them through a lot of training—leading meetings, participating in meetings, communication, problem solving, group problem solving, and so on. We teach them how to reach consensus. They go through all that training as part of preparing them to deal with being a team. Now, the plant manager and I still have to sit in occasionally. But what his job and my job have evolved into mostly is educating and doing work with those teams around accountability.

Zenger-Miller:

Do you have problems handling the diversity of the group—demographic differences or differences because you've got many people looking at the problem?

Joe Dulaney:

Yeah it is difficult at first, real difficult, for several reasons. First, people are resistant to change, at least a part of the group. The newer people aren't because they've never known it any other way, so for them it's great. But some of the people who have been here a long time felt comfortable in the old system because they never had to think. They never were held accountable for anything.

> *. . . dealing with personality conflicts in the teams is more difficult than dealing with ideas that come up.*

We've found that dealing with personality conflicts in the teams is more difficult than dealing with ideas that come up.

Zenger-Miller:

So how *do* you deal with personality issues?

Joe Dulaney:

In several cases we've had to sit in on meetings, you know, not trying to change their ideas but helping them deal with ways to leave personality out of it. If you can get them to do that, they can usually find the best solution and pretty well agree on it.

Zenger-Miller:

Would you say that most of the new ideas are coming from the teams themselves?

Joe Dulaney:

I would.

Zenger-Miller:

Is that where they came from before?

Joe Dulaney:

You've got to be kidding! They used to come from whoever the specialist supposedly was—the engineer or the manager or the supervisor.

Zenger-Miller:

How do you motivate people to get the work done compared with how you did it before?

Joe Dulaney:

That's something we're really having to deal with because the sewing industry traditionally has an individual incentive pay system. It was all, "I'm out for me and me alone, and everybody else better watch out for themselves." We've had to do lots of work and training around that—with all these training sessions and by assigning a coach. We're trying to experiment with different pay systems, but motivation does keep coming up.

Zenger-Miller:

You said that they can hire people. What else do they do differently?

Joe Dulaney:

Before, they couldn't do anything except what they were told: how to sit, how their machine was going to be set up, when to work, what their hours were going to be. And they couldn't deviate at all.

Before, they couldn't do anything except what they were told . . .

Zenger-Miller:

Very controlling.

Joe Dulaney:

It was, and not unlike most industries. Whereas now, they are involved in scheduling their daily overtime and line balance. They decide how it's going to be done based on how it affects their costs. They decide who they're going to hire. They keep up with their records.

Zenger-Miller:

Do they determine their own methods for doing the work?

Joe Dulaney:

Not totally. However, in our plant we've got an engineering person that believes in this concept, and he goes out and gets all of the input from a group before he even looks at methods or equipment. Then they pretty much decide what kind or brand of equipment we're going to purchase.

Zenger-Miller:

So they even have input about purchasing equipment?

Joe Dulaney:

That's right.

Zenger-Miller:

Is there any more latitude for mistakes?

Joe Dulaney:

If what they were doing involved closing the plant, we would probably sit down with them and say, "Have you thought of everything you can possibly think of?" But if they're not doing something that drastic, we let them make the mistake. Then they usually come back and say, "We tried this, and this is what happened. Do you have any input?" We try *not* to give our input because they usually know the answer. At least somebody in the group does. It's just getting them to express it. So you become much more of a facilitator in meetings rather than an order giver.

> *If what they were doing involved closing the plant, we would probably sit down with them and say, "Have you thought of everything . . .*

Zenger-Miller:

Have you changed the amount or type of information you provide the teams?

Joe Dulaney:

Oh yeah. In the old system, management carefully guarded information because that's what gave them the power. The top guy had all the information, and he doled out only what he wanted to the people under him so he maintained some degree of control. Then it just got doled out the same way down the line until, by the time you reached the workers at the bottom, there was nothing left. All they got was somebody telling them what to do. Now the teams have access to computer terminals where they can do their own parts utilization and cost studies. They do all of it. They can pull that information up at any time, and they have to maintain it.

Zenger-Miller:

I would assume that requires technical training on how to run the computers and how to use the cost system and so on.

Joe Dulaney:

Hours and hours of it. The one thing we never realized was how much in the dark we kept these people over the years. That's what we've really discovered. We didn't realize how much we had penalized them by keeping them in the dark.

> *The one thing we never realized was how much in the dark we kept these people over the years.*

Zenger-Miller:

Any other big differences you've noticed?

Joe Dulaney:

Yes, and it addresses one of the things we talked about before lunch— how I feel as a manager about the people. Before we went to teams, I knew their names, I knew their kids' names, and I thought that indicated I cared about them. But what I've discovered since going to this system is how for years I thought of people with problems as problem people. Now that we do a lot more work in counseling.

> *. . . we simply looked at them as problem people. We really didn't care about what their problems were.*

Zenger-Miller:

So now, as I understand it, you're treating people more as individuals, capable of handling information and responsibility. What about goals? Are people getting more involved there too?

Joe Dulaney:

Yep, they set their own. Initially we worked with them more on short-term goals because we first had to get them thinking in terms of goals. We'd ask them questions like, "What goals are you going to set?" and "What do you need to know to set these goals?" Then we moved into long-term goals—"If you're planning a product change, what will you need ask this merchandiser so you can meet their needs?'' This gets into things like budgets.

Zenger-Miller:

I guess long-term in your industry means six or eight months.

Joe Dulaney:

Right. But long-term also means setting goals that keep the plant open and keep their security.

Zenger-Miller:

Anything else you hope to rely on them for in the future?

Joe Dulaney:

Yes, because we keep finding new things. We've learned that you can't say what it's going to look like when you're finished because it's always going to be changing. Our idea now of what it's going to look like is totally different than when we started.

Zenger-Miller:

What do you see as the gains for going to teams?

Joe Dulaney:

The biggest gain for Levi Strauss & Co. is an ability to make plants more competitive. For employees, teams add a lot to their life and their job because they're not locked into routine, repetitious motions. They're using their brains as well as their bodies. Also, there's security for them in knowing that by making the plant competitive they'll increase the liklihood that they'll

. . . there's security for them in knowing that by making the plant competitive they'll have a place to go to work.

have a place to go to work. In a lot of towns we're in, there's not many other opportunities for work. So long-term job security is a big deal.

Zenger-Miller:

Are you more competitive now with overseas plants?

Joe Dulaney:

We'll never compete with them in wages because we're committed to paying our employees a fair wage. We try to focus on those areas where we can compete very well. In our industry, quality, timeliness, lead time, and so on are areas where we can compete if we get the people really involved.

Zenger-Miller:

What had to happen here before you could begin to hand over responsibilities to the teams?

Joe Dulaney:

Becoming convinced yourself that it was the thing to do. It's a scary thing. I've been with Levis 21 years, and I worked in some other businesses before that. All of that training from the time I was in college and graduate school taught me to manage in a certain way. You need to believe that there's a different and better way, that you can let go and be comfortable with it. Because if you can't do that, you'll never make it work. You'll still be manipulating.

> *You need to believe that there's a different and better way . . .*

Zenger-Miller:

Did this have to do with understanding that there's a different kind of power when you let go, that there's power in empowering other people?

Joe Dulaney:

That's where the satisfaction has to come from—seeing the people grow, seeing them achieve things they never thought possible.

Zenger-Miller:

Are there any issues about how much responsibility the teams will have?

Joe Dulaney:

Yes. In some cases we needed to slow down because we were giving too much responsibility too fast. Part of that came from a total lack of realization of how little information we've shared in the past. What we've had to do is really be in tune with our teams and sense that frustration level of when you're trying to give them too much too quick. You have to back off and make sure you're not just throwing them into overload.

Zenger-Miller:

So in those cases you might want to back up and do more training.

Joe Dulaney:

Exactly.

Zenger-Miller:

How are you managing the problems that can occur between the different teams? Is that an issue?

Joe Dulaney:

Yes. We've identified some people who are pretty effective at resolving issues. We call them coordinators, and they make sure that the teams get the right information on time. When information needs to be shared between teams or when two teams are having a problem, the coordinators facilitate the meeting so the two teams resolve it themselves. But they don't supervise. It's more like a head football coach.

Zenger-Miller:
Are there problems with competition between the teams?

Joe Dulaney:
There was initially when they started posting information on performance. We've had to work with them on the idea that—look, you may be on separate teams, but we're all still one plant, and the ultimate thing is the productivity of the plant. That seems to keep them focused on overall performance.

Zenger-Miller:
To explore this a little further, how do work processes go across team boundaries? How are you defining the boundaries for teams?

Joe Dulaney:
Well, the work comes through in little carts from station to station. Under the old system, nobody wanted to know anything but their job because the faster they got at that job the more they earned. But we're experimenting with a couple of pay systems that reward people for diverse knowledge and skills. Employees will basically decide which system seems to be working the best. As far as team boundaries, the teams are rotating jobs and cross-training. They're seeing that initially cross-training may hurt their short-term costs, but efficiency-wise they'll be much better off in the long-term if they do it all.

Zenger-Miller:
Are the boundaries becoming fuzzier for people as they learn more jobs?

Joe Dulaney:
They are. In fact, we've had a recommendation from some employees about our plans to switch over one line to jeans instead of jackets. We've never made pants at this plant, so this will be a big change. They're suggesting we go to bigger teams capable of making the whole product but with only 40 people instead of the 150 on a line now. There'd be a series of mini-lines where people would be cross-trained on several jobs. They'd be responsible for the whole production cycle—deadlines, the requirements, and so on. There could be a lot of cost advantages to doing it this way. I think we're going to experiment with that when we change over to jeans.

Zenger-Miller:
Sounds interesting. How about the managers here? How do they react to all this?

Joe Dulaney:

Some of the managers have been real accepting, and some have not.

Zenger-Miller:

How are you handling that?

Some of the managers have been real accepting, and some have not.

Joe Dulaney:

We do our homework and show them what we're doing and why we're doing it, so we have the numbers to show it's working.

Zenger-Miller:

Are employees spending more time talking with suppliers and customers?

Joe Dulaney:

Yes. When we have style changes, we have our merchandisers visit the plant now to speak with the employees about things we can and can't do. Before, they just designed the garment out in California and then sent it to us. If we said, "There's an easier, less expensive way to make it," they would say, "We want it made this way." Now they come out and visit with the people who are going to be making that garment to get their input.

Zenger-Miller:

Last question. How have you dealt with changes? Has it been difficult for you?

Joe Dulaney:

My stress level has been higher. A lot of it comes from the constant working with the teams and the pressure that you're under.

Zenger-Miller:

And is there pressure also from the teams? It sounds like it.

Joe Dulaney:

Oh yeah. They push you once they know they can do it. But that's what they *ought* to do. It's just been an interesting two and a half years. The reward for me is seeing people accomplishing things that others told them all their lives they couldn't do. Realizing I was a part of the old system for so long makes it rewarding for me to be a part of the change. Like the woman who became such a good trainer. I was sitting there proud as could be hoping I had a little to do with the fact that she was

*They push you once they know they can do it. But that's what they **ought** to do.*

up there. But the tough part was admitting to myself that she's going to be better at this than I could ever be.

Zenger-Miller:

You sound very proud, though. You really do.

Joe Dulaney:

I guess I am about a lot of them. This has made a big difference in people's lives.

"A New Pair of Shoes"

Russell Francis
Production Supervisor
Spectra Physics

Zenger-Miller:

Russell, you've been working here for some time so you've seen tremendous changes. What's the difference, in general terms, between what you used to do and what you do now?

Russell Francis:

I used to be focused on the product, the end result. Now my focus is on helping the team be successful. It's really come to where they're now telling *me* what they need. You might say I've become an explosives expert. I blow the doors, I blow away the obstacles. I blow away those things that are obstacles to the team. Another difference is that my focus is much less on the day-to-day and much more out a week, a month, a few months, and resolving those issues beforehand. I work with the team to establish goals and objectives and try to provide them with whatever tools they need to get there.

Zenger-Miller:

Could you tell me about some of the lows and highs over the last three years since you established the teams?

Russell Francis:

I'd say the low points happen two ways. When I'm faced with a difficult situation, I'm prone to step back into an active leadership role, and that ends up being a low point. When that happens, the team will take me aside and thrash me about the head and shoulders and suggest that I not do that anymore. I recognize I have this tendency so now I ask them to monitor me when the pressure starts to build. The other low

. . . the team will take me aside and thrash me about the head and shoulders . . .

point comes from not being *enough* involved with a particular group. The makeup of our teams is always changing, and sometimes, when a team is not as productive as I think they need to be, I will stay away too long. I assume that they will work their way out of it instead of stepping in and providing more direct leadership.

Zenger-Miller:

So it's a fine line between jumping in and solving problems with the team and leaving a team struggling too long. In either case the team can reach a low point.

Russell Francis:

Correct.

Zenger-Miller:

How do you decide when to step in and when to let them work it out?

Russell Francis:

As I get more experience in a team environment, what I find works best is when I address these things up front with a team. So every two weeks or every month, I ask them to tell me if I'm doing too much or not enough. I want to put the burden on them. *They* need to say when they want help. I've come to realize that I don't need to make that assumption for them. If I leave the decision up to them, they'll make the right one and come to me only when they have to.

> *I want to put the burden on them.* **They** *need to say when they want help.*

Zenger-Miller:

How would you respond to a traditional manager who questioned the wisdom of giving people so much responsibility?

Russell Francis:

I'd ask them how much responsibility their own supervisor was giving them? I'd say something like, "Do they treat *you* as someone who has a brain, or do they relate to you like you need to be force-fed every little bite?" And then I'd ask, "If that's how your boss is treating *you*, wouldn't you like the freedom to come up with your own ideas?" If you believe that people have a reasonable amount of intelligence, then you should treat them that way. What I find is some people shaking their heads and not understanding how it works or how it can work. They've been stuck in their own boots so long they can't see it another way.

Zenger-Miller:

I wonder if you could describe how you see your changing value as a leader in a team environment.

Russell Francis:

My value is that I am taking on a portion of what my boss used to do. I'm also able to do more strategic planning, to pave the way to—to *greatness!* We could have gone along with the way we were doing business and I think we would have survived. At least for awhile. Now we have an opportunity to make some new in-roads, to have a better product, a better organization, to be overall stronger, and stronger in the marketplace. I have more than enough to fill my plate.

Zenger-Miller:

What about the traditional manager who's afraid of becoming obsolete in this new environment?

Russell Francis:

I also understand the risk that people feel. The challenge is not just in helping the team to grow. *You* have to change. You need to be willing to take on things that you are not familiar with—which is the real reason most of us hang on to the old. It's familiar. It's comfortable. You need to go break in a new pair of shoes, so to speak.

Zenger-Miller:

How would you compare the stress you feel now with what you felt in the old environment? Is it more or less?

Russell Francis:

I find it a little more stressful but not a great deal. The additional stress is because part of what I am doing is not familiar to me. I'm having to do more work that has no established pattern. The other part is the stress comes with having the team make decisions but still being responsible for what the team decides. I feel, and I know other managers do too, a great deal of risk in not having my hand in there. But it's your choice to worry about it or not.

> *I feel, and I know other managers do too, a great deal of risk in not having my hand in there.*

Zenger-Miller:

So what *is* your role in decision-making?

Russell Francis:

Much of what I do in the New Product Division has me pulling off new people and forming a brand new team. When I do, the first thing I tell people is that I will support their decision, right or wrong, no matter what it is. I'll support it even if it means I go out the door. Their decision is the right decision to them, and therefore it is the right decision. I hold the option to give them more information, to question them about their decision-making process, to see if I can help them enhance it, or to provide them some other information they didn't have at the time they made the decision. I'll give them the opportunity to change the decision. But *I* won't change it. I don't have any problem taking that responsibility for the decisions they make because I believe if they've got the right

Their decision is the right decision to them, and therefore it is the right decision.

tools, if they've got the right information, 99 percent of the time they'll make the same decision that I would. And for the other 1 percent, it doesn't matter.

Zenger-Miller:

That makes sense, and it takes courage. Like you said, you need to recognize people as having the intelligence to make decisions.

Russell Francis:

But what *is* important is to let them know right from the beginning who you are and what you stand for and how you would react in given situations. I had to explain myself to the people who work for me. I needed to set the expectations they should have of me. Now, as long as I hold to those expectations, there should be no gripes. Of course, they do expect me to come back and ask questions. But I won't question the decision itself. I question the *process*. What process did you go through? What information did you have?

Zenger-Miller:

So when you set expectations, you begin to establish trust with the group. They know what to expect from you, and you have expectations of them.

Russell Francis:

Right. And if I don't live up to the expectations I said that they should have of me, I expect them to take me to task and tell me what I'm not doing.

Zenger-Miller:

What could you tell me to help me start moving toward being this more facilitative kind of manager?

Russell Francis:

If you want to start on this road, start by talking to the group that you want to walk the road with. Because you are all in it together. It's not a team leader and a team. It really is just a team.

Zenger-Miller:

And what if people aren't all that anxious to walk this particular road?

Russell Francis:

One of the difficulties in starting down this path is that a lot of people don't see the incentive because they're too programmed to coming to work and being told what to do. The idea of coming to work and deciding themselves what to do is very, very new for them, so they'll need a lot of help. It can only be worked out together— you and them.

> *. . . deciding themselves what to do is very, very new for them, so they'll need a lot of help.*

Interview Six

"It Takes a Lot of Talking"

Emily Liggett
Operations Manager
Raychem Corporation

Zenger-Miller:
Why types of teams are you involved with here?

Emily Liggett:
Well we started out with functional teams. Our plan was first to make teams work in operations and, when that was going OK, to move on to the next level, which might be cross-functional teams.

Zenger-Miller:
What's the focus of the cross-functional teams?

Emily Liggett:
It depends. One is involved with strategic planning. Typically, you think of strategic planning as an externally focused, marketing-driven program. But strategic planning is really a cross-functional effort when you get down to it. Another, called the Product Delivery Team, looks at everything it takes to get the product delivered. Again, you'd think it would be a manufacturing issue, but it goes beyond that. It's a sales issue, a credit issue, and a technical issue. Really cross-functional.

Zenger-Miller:
Are these teams very different from your functional teams?

Emily Liggett:
A cross-functional team is like any other team. It has to have a goal and a purpose in life. There have to be inputs and outputs, and there needs to be a feedback route so they can see how that's all working. The team members

> *A cross-functional team is like any other team. It has to have a goal and a purpose in life.*

need to know what their expectations are, who the customers are, their suppliers, internal suppliers, internal customers, and what sort of measurement systems they have to work with. So in many ways, it's no different at all.

Zenger-Miller:
And which of the teams you've described so far do you manage?

Emily Liggett:
It could be any of those. Actually I don't directly manage them. I have people that manage them who work with me.

Zenger-Miller:
So there's a layer between those functional teams and yourself?

Emily Liggett:
That's generally true. Well, actually my role can change. I also belong to the Graveyard High-Performance Working Team. And with this group I participate not as a manager but just as a member of the team. I come in every week on Tuesday at six o'clock and go to their meeting.

Zenger-Miller:
That's a functional team?

Emily Liggett:
Right. And as a team member I do all the regular jobs like taking notes when it's my turn to take notes. I'm just another team member even though I might be working with people who, from a traditional standpoint, are three levels below me. I just become part of it, and that's my style. I like it, they like it, and it keeps me in touch with what's going on. I hear of petty things as well as the major things that go on.

> *. . . I might be working with people who, from a traditional standpoint, are three levels below me.*

Zenger-Miller:
Then you actually perform technical work during your shift?

Emily Liggett:
Absolutely. When we paint the equipment, I paint the equipment. So my role is really not as a manager in that team. I'm just a team member. Whereas, on the cross-functional teams, I can be a member or a leader. I can be a supplier or a customer or a user. All of them.

Zenger-Miller:
I'm assuming that one of the major things that you want to do is create a bond between you and everyone here. Maybe that's not the primary goal, but that's certainly one outcome of your participating on this

team. Are there any other activities you engage in that lead to increased trust or shared commitment?

Emily Liggett:

Well, we have distribution lists like E-mail and voice mail, and we're on all the distribution lists. So when they send out a notice for one thing or another, an upcoming fire drill or a request for a dollar for a baby gift, I know about it and respond when it's appropriate for me to respond. I'm always involved on a day-to-day basis.

Zenger-Miller:

Is there any information that you would rather not share with, say, members of the functional teams, or is it a completely open environment?

Emily Liggett:

Clearly there are sensitive issues that aren't shared. For example, disciplinary actions. The teams deal with their own disciplinary actions, but if I know there's something going on in another team, I don't share that between teams. Anything confidential is kept confidential. If someone is planning to go back to graduate school and they don't want it known *. . . I'll tell the team if I can't share something and why.* right then, I don't share it. Or if there are company issues like cutbacks or programs that might be changed. I'm considered an insider by corporate standards. But I'll tell the team if I can't share something and why. We're open about what can and can't be shared.

Zenger-Miller:

But in terms of operational knowledge—

Emily Liggett:

Oh absolutely. It's all out in the open.

Zenger-Miller:

So it sounds like things people normally don't like talked about are kept confidential, and everything else is pretty open.

Emily Liggett:

Yes. In fact, I just hate it when someone shuts their door because it always looks like they're talking about things they shouldn't be talking about or they're making a personal call at work. I just don't like the message it sends. But there are some times I need to shut the door if I'm on voice mail or talking about disciplinary actions, performance issues, salary issues, things like that. Even so, what I try to do is handle these things from home or do it all at once so my door is shut one time rather than opening and shutting all day.

Zenger-Miller:

What other differences are there now in how you manage groups versus the way it used to be? I mean, everything's open, but there's still got to be some control. And you have to deal with many more points of view.

Emily Liggett:

Yes, there is more input now. I think you can run into team paralysis if you don't make decisions and take action because you can spend so much time reading and communicating that you never get work done. I think that's something we need to deal with better. Another thing is to clearly define when it's an individual decision and when it's a team decision. Not everything is a team decision. You need to define those boundaries.

Zenger-Miller:

Does it take longer to make decisions when you have teams?

Emily Liggett:

Working as a team takes more time than doing it on your own. I spent many years with [a large chemical company] where the managers did make decisions that the employees had not okayed. It worked pretty well. Here, when a manager makes a decision and doesn't consult people, the employees very rightfully say, "Wait a minute, I didn't understand." However, there are times when a manager simply has to act. This spring during our planning process for next year, we had one day to come up with *. . . there are times when a* more money. So the division *manager simply has to act.* manager said, "All right, I know you're not going to like this, but there's no time. So I'm going to say Sales will come up with X dollars, and Operations, with Y dollars. That's the only way to make ends meet, and we'll sort it out later." Everybody said OK. The point is, as long as you tell people this is how we're going to make the decision, then it's OK. The rub comes when you're inconsistent or you don't tell them what the process is going to be for making the decision.

Zenger-Miller:

So it's partly sharing information so they can make their own choices?

Emily Liggett:

Right. You want people to make their own choices, but they need all the facts in order to make those choices.

Zenger-Miller:

And do you give them more latitude for mistakes now that you've given them more independence?

Emily Liggett:

They had that freedom before. I think what's different now is that there's more understanding and less fingerpointing. There's more a spirit of let's understand what happened so we don't keep making the same mistakes. There's more understanding of why something happened. Certainly we're not making the same mistakes over and over.

. . . there's more understanding and less fingerpointing.

Zenger-Miller:

Is that because of the increased communication?

Emily Liggett:

I think so.

Zenger-Miller:

And because people act more independently?

Emily Liggett:

I would say so. There's more willingness to solve the issue because people are empowered to make changes. For example, if you see something in the plant that could be a safety issue, you don't go to the safety engineer and say, "You've got to fix that problem." You fix it yourself. True, they always could have done it before, but they didn't. Or let's say you come to a meeting and you say, "The change machine's always out of change for the vending machines." Now someone will say, "Well, did you E-mail the purchasing people who manage those vendors?" People have a responsibility to fix the problem that they didn't before. You can still be lazy, but at least you don't get to gripe about it.

You can still be lazy, but at least you don't get to gripe about it.

Zenger-Miller:

I know we've already touched on access to information, but do you have an example of where information may not have been shared before and now is?

Emily Liggett:

In Operations there's clearly a lot more information. I think it was always available, but now people are either reading it or understanding it. Now, because goals are so much clearer and because the teams are working on projects to meet these goals, and because people have been trained on SPC so they understand what variability is and things like that, the information makes sense to them. I don't know if people have more information, but it's clearly more focused, more useful information. You know, you can dump too much information on a team and bury them in stuff they don't really need to know. In the past, we sent a lot of "data" but no "information."

Zenger-Miller:
You say goals are clearer and better understood. Is that because of differences in the ways goals are set?

Emily Liggett:
That's part of it. Goals are typically set by the team. Well, actually they go both ways. Sometimes the company says, "This is what we're going to do," and then the team needs to come up with projects to support those goals. And sometimes we come up with the goals ourselves. In either case, people understand why they're working toward those goals. They certainly monitor the goals more, especially those they set themselves.

Zenger-Miller:
How did you get people to work as a team? Was that difficult to do?

Emily Liggett:
No. They have absolutely embraced the team. It would be hard to go back to the old way.

Zenger-Miller:
How about the transition?

Emily Liggett:
People knew for months that this is where we were heading. It was well planned out. In some cases, the group had to wait maybe six months to formally kick off their teams and start their weekly meetings. So there was a lot of anticipation, a lot of eagerness to do that.

Zenger-Miller:
And now that you've switched over, are there things you rely on teams for that you didn't before?

Emily Liggett:
Oh, absolutely. They schedule equipment, do their own reviews, things that classic supervisors or production people used to do. They're taking on more and more of the overall responsibility.

Zenger-Miller:
What about the cross-functional teams?

Emily Liggett:

They're either doing things that weren't done before, or they're doing the same things better. In the case of new product introductions, their plans are better thought out. They're more right on, more complete. All in all, we do more things with fewer people. We do them better. We do less re-work. There's less waste. We're simply more efficient and more profitable.

We're simply more efficient and more profitable.

Zenger-Miller:

And how about the teams? How do they perceive this?

Emily Liggett:

I think they look forward to coming to work every day, because they're in greater control of their destiny. They're not waiting for someone to tell them what to do. They truly feel empowered. Also, the politics are gone. All the arbitrating, the babysitting, it's just all gone. They deal with things on their own.

Zenger-Miller:

How did you get that change to happen? Did you just say, "OK, this is what it's going to be," and people accepted it?

Emily Liggett:

A lot of it was training. They had to have the skills because, when people have a problem, the managers can't just take over and solve it for them. As soon as management resolves it, then you've lost all the ground you gained. You've got to keep handing it back to them and be willing to put up with the resistance and unhappiness that's sure to come up. So you have to have the long-term vision that in the end they're going to be better off.

A lot of it was training. They had to have the skills . . .

Zenger-Miller:

So there's lots of turmoil during that time.

Emily Liggett:

Yes. And there are still interpersonal things that come up. People that don't want to work together and so on. You simply have to say, "You don't have to like this person, but you've got to work with him. So deal with it."

Zenger-Miller:

Do you envision handing even more responsibilities off to these teams, and if so, why are you waiting?

Emily Liggett:

Yes, but they have to have the skills. Otherwise you won't have a win-win situation. One training we've got planned is in cost accounting so they can keep a lot more track of their costs. But until they *understand* cost accounting, it's not a job they can take over. Same with technical writing. You can't ask them to write a report until they've had a course in technical writing. Same with public speaking. So they need to have lots of support to learn all those skills. Right now they have a long list of courses they want to take.

Zenger-Miller:

Are you having to manage the pace of handing off these responsibilities? Or is that not an issue?

Emily Liggett:

Not really. They still have to get their regular job done. Production still has to go out. So if you say, "All right, 10 percent of your time is training" and let them work it out, pretty soon

They still have to get their regular job done.

they see the need to prioritize in what order they want to take which classes.

Zenger-Miller:

How are you going about managing the problems that occur between different groups or teams?

Emily Liggett:

They each have a team coach, and the leaders and coaches get together once a week to talk about issues that involve the whole plant and all teams.

Zenger-Miller:

What's a typical issue?

Emily Liggett:

One came up last week at the fiber plant. To work overtime on the weekend, they have to commit by Thursday noon or however it's set up. Anyway, the person who schedules the overtime canceled the weekend overtime at the last minute because of an equipment breakdown. The problem was, the people scheduled for overtime had already changed their weekend plans and were counting on the extra money, so there were a lot of very disgruntled guys come Monday morning. The guy hadn't communicated well to the teams. So that was a big deal yesterday in the meeting. People really discussed it with him.

Zenger-Miller:

Have you had trouble dealing with all these changes?

Emily Liggett:

No, it's been a nice change. There's a lot of talking and communicating. I mean, any time you've got a major change in an organization, you've got certain people that are OK with the changes and people that aren't, so you have to spend a lot of time just talking. Sometimes it's saying the same thing over and over to the same people because they didn't hear it the first time or they want to make sure it's really true. It takes a lot of talking.

Zenger-Miller:

Now that the idea of teams has taken hold at your facility, do you think it will spread?

Emily Liggett:

I think the whole total quality issue is forcing it. I mean, just the notion of writing down a procedure, documenting what you do, is a radical idea. For so long, people kept what they did in their heads on purpose because they wanted to be able to gallop in on a horse and fix the problem when no one else could. But if you want to create a total quality environ-

. . . you need to stop rewarding people for galloping in . . .

ment, you need to stop rewarding people for galloping in and start rewarding them for acting like team members.

Interview Seven

"That's When You Become a Facilitator"

Ramiro Mendoza
Group Leader
Subaru-Isuzu Automotive, Inc.

Zenger-Miller:

What are the main differences between leading teams and leading in a more traditional organization.

Ramiro Mendoza:

Well, for one thing, with everybody able to give their input, you have more ideas coming at you. Somebody's always thinking of some different way to do their job. It's not always a better way, but you still want to listen. You got to be careful not to discourage anybody from contributing because then they won't be as willing to volunteer the next time you're

> *Somebody's always thinking of some different way to do their job.*

looking for ideas. A team is similar to a battery, you know. If you let one cell go dead, then it's much harder to get the car started.

Zenger-Miller:

What is it that you like about your job? Is there anything you do on a regular basis that you really enjoy?

Ramiro Mendoza:

What I like the most, I think, is the freedom to get right beside an associate and work with them, especially when they're having a problem, whether it's in body fit or some other area. I like working with them to find out what their problem is so I can better relate back to our supplier, which is the shop right before us that's supplying our material. It makes it easier to fix that problem for the associate working on the line.

Zenger-Miller:

Is that different from most manufacturing groups?

Ramiro Mendoza:

In most of the groups I've ever worked in, the supervisor's not allowed to get next to somebody and actually get his hands dirty by working with them.

Zenger-Miller:

Do you see yourself as somebody who brings information to your team from somewhere else? Is that part of your role too?

Ramiro Mendoza:

Yes, I give them information. For example, I might pass along quality reports about problems that are showing up in a certain area. When I do this, they're usually able to explain why we're having that problem. If I were to look at the quality data and simply assume that I knew what the problem was, I might go down on the floor and issue an order like, "I need you to put more material in that area." If I simply did that without first asking any questions, I'd probably have a lot of unhappy people. Whereas if you go out and work with them, you may find that the real problem is with material that's coming from one of our suppliers or whatever. You just don't know the whole problem until you get out there and actually experience it first-hand.

Zenger-Miller:

So you're relaying information, and you're coming to them for creative ideas. Do you ever do this in meetings?

Ramiro Mendoza:

Yes. I do it in morning team meetings to basically give information about what happened the previous day, what happened on the previous shift, problems that they were seeing, problems that they didn't know how to deal with. Maybe one of our associates on another shift had the same problem before and knows how to deal with it, so we transfer that information to the opposite shift.

Zenger-Miller:

Do you facilitate or lead those meetings?

Ramiro Mendoza:

Generally, the team leader will conduct those meetings. I'll sit in on meetings where I'm giving information to the team leader, and I'll also sit in to make sure that the information I'm giving to him is being disseminated to the associates.

Zenger-Miller:

What do you do about people who don't seem to want to get involved? How do you handle them?

Ramiro Mendoza:

I coach the people that aren't really interested in being involved. Those are the ones that you want to bring into the fold and say, "I need your ideas." And that's where the real challenge of coaching comes along. You already have people that know what they need to do. But you've got to bring this other one, who really isn't sure about anything, into the group. When that person molds in with the team, it's an accomplishment for me. That's when I'm standing there beaming. And I think I have a right to because our whole group is working the way it's supposed to.

Zenger-Miller:

How does your role change as the team grows into the job?

Ramiro Mendoza:

At first, you're kind of helping them to walk. Then once they start grasping hold of that and have fallen a few times, pretty soon they're trotting, and then all of a sudden they're running. Sometimes the ideas start flying at you so fast you know you'll have to spend more time weeding through them. A lot of times it's a matter of trial and error. But as long as you're willing to try what they want to do, that's all they're really look-

> *. . . pretty soon they're trotting, and then all of a sudden they're running.*

ing for. Then, if they find out for themselves their idea doesn't work, that's better than you saying up front, "No, I don't think that's a good idea." When you let them learn by trying out their own ideas, that's when you become a facilitator.

Zenger-Miller:

And I guess that's where the satisfaction is. You're bringing people along, not just the ones that are easy to deal with, but the ones that aren't. And you're building a team that can handle a lot of responsibility.

Ramiro Mendoza:

Right. It goes all the way from doing their own clean-up to ordering the equipment and supplies they use on the floor. They basically take over all the duties that need to be done. At that point my role as a facilitator is to give them what they need to get their job done. That might be getting the information they need to order parts. Or it might be going to another shop to find out whether something needs to be manufactured the way it is, then bringing this information back to them and letting them run with it from there.

Zenger-Miller:

So it sounds like your job is not static. It seems to change as the conditions change and as the teams grow.

Ramiro Mendoza:

It's ever-changing. That's what keeps my job interesting from beginning to end. I feel like I'm going to be learning all of my life, and as long as I can make other people feel that way also, then they're going to continue to learn.

I feel like I'm going to be learning all of my life . . .

Zenger-Miller:

What do you see happening to the team members? How do they change as a result of getting involved and becoming more contributing members of the organization?

Ramiro Mendoza:

What I see is that I've got younger associates and older associates, and no matter how old they are, I actually see people grow up more. I mean, giving their input not only affects them here at work, it also affects them outside the factory. I think teams have made me more of an adult than before I came here. It's made me aware of people's feelings a lot more. I continue to grow from it, and I also see that in the associates as well. I see them changing from people who maybe didn't want to give their input or who didn't really care about anything else other than just coming to work and doing their job and going home. I see them changing to people who are more considerate of those they work with. And that's all because everybody's more involved in what's going on in their area on a daily basis.

Zenger-Miller:

Have you made any mistakes along the way.

Ramiro Mendoza:

Oh, yeah. I've made mistakes where I went out to the floor and said, "This is the way you're going to do that," and didn't know what all the ramifications were or what was causing that problem. And they've gotten genuinely upset with me. I've had to back down and say, "I've made a mistake." It doesn't hurt to tell them

It doesn't hurt to tell them you've made a mistake.

you've made a mistake. It only brings them closer to you. Instead of being the traditional guy that sits in the chair and you can't approach him, it brings you more on an even keel.

Zenger-Miller:

It sounds like the human part, relating to people as people, is important for you.

Ramiro Mendoza:

Yes. Everybody thinks a little differently than the next person, so the more people you have in your group, the more you have different attitudes, different backgrounds, and so on. That makes it really difficult at times because you're trying to keep people from having conflicts and yet keep the ideas flowing and keep people happy. So sometimes you're an instructor and other times you're like a truant officer. You've got to tell somebody, "You can't do that." And sometimes you have to be their best friend. You listen to things that are bothering them, maybe not only at work but outside of work also. It just keeps the job interesting. I can't express how much working with those people and being able to just walk up and work beside them and talk to them keeps my job interesting.

Zenger-Miller:

As the teams become more responsible, do you see a continuing need for your role and what you do?

Ramiro Mendoza:

Sure, because my role will always be changing. If you like being flexible, this is the perfect job, because, as the teams grow, you're also going to have to change. You have to keep moving with it just to keep them rolling in the right direction.

If you like being flexible, this is the perfect job . . .

Interview Eight

·"A Lot Less Turfism"

Sharon Chinn
Employee Relations Specialist
Meridian Insurance

Zenger-Miller:
What's the hardest thing for leaders in a team environment?

Sharon Chinn:
Probably the hardest thing in terms of cultural change is letting go.

Zenger-Miller:
Could you elaborate on that idea?

Sharon Chinn:
It's allowing people to learn what they need to know and then letting them do it their way even though you think you may know how to do it faster and better. That's very hard to do because you're still accountable for the results.

Zenger-Miller:
As a manager, how do you help people to take those first steps?

Sharon Chinn:
You do it by giving them opportunities they may not have volunteered for. You say something like, "Look, this issue has come up, and it's something you know a lot about. Why don't you work on this team?" So they do, and they see their contribution is really of value because what comes out of the team is actually implemented, or their input is at least considered. Things like that.

> *... they see their contribution is really of value because what comes out of the team is actually implemented.*

231

Zenger-Miller:

What I hear you saying is that you're setting realistic expectations for the team.

Sharon Chinn:

Exactly.

Zenger-Miller:

Has the amount or type of information communicated to employees changed?

Sharon Chinn:

Very much so. In fact, it starts with the president who now has quarterly meetings with employees all over the corporation. She goes out to the employee groups and talks about the business so they can better understand what's going on. She tells what's happening with us. All of it. And that philosophy carries over to the divisions. For example, as divisions become trained in quality and start instituting it, they share their experiences company-wide including all the difficulties and pitfalls they've gone through. Sometimes the sharing is even more direct. Our division has already gone through the initial phase, so they'll volunteer to help a division that's just getting started. In the past we would never tell war stories or even admit to decisions that didn't work out well. So, of course, we wouldn't talk about why something didn't work. We're a lot more open, now.

Zenger-Miller:

Have you had any problems getting people to work as a team?

Sharon Chinn:

You know, that's not a big problem because we've always had project teams, task forces, and so on. Working in teams is not unusual here.

. . . we've always had project teams, task forces, and so on. Working in teams is not unusual here.

Zenger-Miller:

But there are differences.

Sharon Chinn:

Absolutely. Most of the teams that are formed now are working on process improvement, and they go about it in an organized way rather than flying by the seat of their pants. They use the tools they've learned to expand their thinking, gather data, organize, and come up with a conclusion. They also come up with solid solutions which are more factually-based, and these solutions have more of a long-term impact. To give you an example, we consolidated one of our big divisions. We had parts of it scattered in different states and regional offices, and we combined some of those processes here in our home office. Many people on the team indicated that they had worked on numerous teams but had never had that kind of well-organized, systematic approach that worked out so well.

Zenger-Miller:

What do you rely on your people to do as teams?

Sharon Chinn:

We look for them to find the opportunities for improvement—and, once they've identified them, to do the analysis and make recommendations. For instance, in one of our major operations, teams analyzed processes and implemented process improvements that resulted in significant reductions in cycle time. This had a direct impact on customer satisfaction and the achievement of corporate objectives.

Zenger-Miller:

Did you rely on teams this way before?

Sharon Chinn:

No. Generally, the managers in the division would get together and talk about what they needed. We had lots of project teams and task forces that involved management-level people. But given clear expectations and parameters, the employees bring so much more to this because they have the line experience.

> *. . . employees bring so much more to this because they have the line experience.*

Zenger-Miller:

What is all this gaining you in the organization?

Sharon Chinn:

Hopefully, long-term customer loyalty, greater market share, and employees who feel valued and who have a sense of ownership. It's really a survival issue to us. We see quality improvement and customer focus as the only way to gain and maintain profitability. But making it happen takes a long time because people have to internalize everything they're doing.

Zenger-Miller:

What are the teams now doing that management used to do?

Sharon Chinn:

They're making a lot more decisions. They're involved in evaluating new hires in some cases. Certainly they're involved in looking at anything that has to do with work flow and work process.

Zenger-Miller:

What needed to happen in order to hand over responsibilities to teams?

Sharon Chinn:

First, the senior management level had to say that this is what we will do. Then we had to start trusting our people and giving them whatever training they needed to prepare them for problem solving, once again making sure that the teams clearly understood the expectations and parameters. Now we have to continually back away and trust they can do it. That's the biggest cultural hurdle. It's very, very hard to let go. It's probably even harder at the executive level because they're so results-oriented. There's such a focus on quarterly results. It's tough for middle management too. These people have struggled for power and control by operating the old way. So for some people, it's a complete cultural change.

> *That's the biggest cultural hurdle. It's very, very hard to let go.*

Zenger-Miller:

How is your role being redefined in all this change?

Sharon Chinn:

It will continue to expand into a kind of clearing house for all the team activities, training activities, and monitoring and measurement activities—to make sure that all those systems are integrated and coordinated. Also, I'll be involved with keeping momentum and enthusiasm going, removing obstacles, and facilitating team activities, especially when they need help to understand the corporate perspective.

Zenger-Miller:

Do you see the relationships between managers changing as you explore new ways to move work across boundaries?

Sharon Chinn:

I see a lot less turfism, more people looking at the big picture rather than just their piece of it, and more people working toward the overall goal. I see more peer interaction, peer partnerships, and things like being willing to release people from their immediate area because they're needed on some other activity relating to process improvement. A lot less factionalism and more peer partnerships.

> *I see a lot less turfism, more people looking at the whole picture . . .*

Zenger-Miller:

Has there been a change in the way your own boss delegates work to you?

Sharon Chinn:

Yes, absolutely. Before, if a director came to her asking how some planning was being implemented, I'd provide her with what she needed. Now she says to the director, "Sharon really has done quite a bit of study on this. You really need to talk with her."

Zenger-Miller:

Sounds like she's convinced that empowering others is the way to go.

Sharon Chinn:

Her position is, there is no option. This is the only way we're going to be competitive. The by-product of that will be profitability, and the by-product of that will be competitive survival. So this is it, gang. It really may be the first time that something has been viewed as having no other option. Certainly the magnitude is greater than any other program we've seen here. But because we have seen other programs, there's still some skepticism around about the long-term commitment. This skepticism should be expected for some time because the process may or may not produce instant quantifiable results. But as improvements start to impact results favorably and consistently, skepticism will lessen.

> *. . . there is no option. This is the only way we're going to be competitive.*

"Am I Going Too Fast?"

Gus Boetzkes
Manager, Clinical Engineering
University of Alberta Hopsitals

Zenger-Miller:

How would you describe what's been happening here recently? What's different now?

Gus Boetzkes:

I'd say that over the last three or four years people's roles have been really expanding. Plus there's a lot more cross-functional communication and a greater feeling of responsibility. Another thing, managers are less authoritarian because they know the best decisions come from the people who are closest to the action. I'd say those are the key differences.

Zenger-Miller:

What new things are people doing that they didn't do in the old days?

Gus Boetzkes:

Before, issues were seen as residing within a single department or division, and they had to be addressed within those artificial confines. That's no longer the case. People feel quite at ease now disregarding those vertical lines and forming cross-functional teams to address issues and problems. That's really new.

People feel quite at ease now disregarding those vertical lines and forming cross-functional teams . . .

Zenger-Miller:

Have you led any of these cross-functional teams?

Gus Boetzkes:

No. Mainly I participate in them. I represent the area, or I represent the division, or I come in as an expert in a particular thing. These teams can be facilitated by almost anyone. Sometimes it's the vice president, and sometimes it's one of the team members.

Zenger-Miller:

So process improvement occupies much of your time now?

Gus Boetzkes:

It does. But I also have a role in the training program because a lot of training is required in the transition. Maybe 15 percent of my time I do trainings, and maybe another 20 percent I work on cross-functional activities. The rest of my time is devoted to the department.

Zenger-Miller:

I'm sure you were very busy five years ago, but now you also have to do training and work on the cross-functional teams. How do you find the time?

Gus Boetzkes:

It's just something we've all had to do. We're in a competitive business, and we weren't operating as efficiently as we might, so managers have had to look at how we do things and try and find ways to improve. In doing this, it's forced them to let go of some of the decision-making.

Zenger-Miller:

What was the process of letting go like for you? Was it a matter of saying, "OK, you do it," or was there an orderly transfer of authority?

Gus Boetzkes:

It's never completely orderly. Often, when issues arise, you may automatically find yourself using the old tools. Or if you do try a new approach, sometimes you have happy results and sometimes not so happy. You may even wonder if you're really going in the right direction. But, by and large, it does help if there's already a movement toward teams within the organization. People can identify with the process a lot more easily if they see it happening everywhere around them.

> *. . . when issues arise, you may automatically find yourself using the old tools.*

Zenger-Miller:

You mentioned tools that you need in order to let go of that power in a reasonably orderly way. What are some of those tools you'd use to empower the people that work for you?

Gus Boetzkes:

Well, let's say someone comes to you with a problem. Your immediate reaction is to take ownership of the problem and gather information, analyze it, make a decision, and implement the decision. Except now you say, "Do I really need to do this?" So a new tool might be to get the group together and facilitate a problem-solving session. Whereas before, the ownership of the problem was clearly mine.

Zenger-Miller:

So before, people looked to you to take charge?

Gus Boetzkes:

Exactly. I had slogans like, "My door is always open." And that was my invitation for people to pass over problems to me. I don't use that slogan necessarily. The door is always open, yes. But not for that. I'm there as a facilitator to bounce ideas off of. I'll still lead a group through a session if they want me to, but in our department others also lead sessions. I'm primarily there as a coach or facilitator.

Zenger-Miller:

But with your experience, wouldn't it be much quicker if you just said, "Look, I know how to solve this. Here's what to do." I mean, what's the pay-off?

Gus Boetzkes:

It does take more time to involve people in a problem-solving session, but I've discovered that the kind of information you deal with and the decisions that are made are far better and more comprehensive. That's because, first of all, the information comes from the people who are closest to the action, and secondly, once they develop their own solution, they're more committed to implementing it.

Zenger-Miller:

What support do you get from the organization that allows you to move more easily in this direction? What helps you play this role more effectively?

Gus Boetzkes:

It helps that the concept is widely publicized, widely talked about throughout the whole organization, so people understand pretty readily what I'm trying to do. Now this doesn't mean that I don't periodically have to explain what's happening. It always helps to explain what you're trying to do and solicit their help, and even ask for their feedback on whether or not you're successful.

It always helps to explain what you're trying to do and solicit their help . . .

Zenger-Miller:

But I can't imagine that you don't have some resistance from team members to taking on more responsibilities. For example, somebody might say, "Hey, you're not delegating. You're just asking me to do all your work." How do you handle that?

Gus Boetzkes:

As a matter of fact I do get that response often enough, and it makes me stop because we're talking about a transition, and everybody doesn't go through it at the same speed. Some people take to it like a duck to water because they naturally want the extra responsibility. Others feel uncomfortable in any system other than the old one. So what do I do? I guess I constantly ask myself, "Am I going too fast?" I'm con-

If there are too many complaints, then I probably am going too fast.

stantly checking to see whether I'm going at the right speed. If there are too many complaints, then I probably am going too fast. So I do take the feedback seriously. But mainly I use it to find out whether I'm going at the right pace for them.

Zenger-Miller:

Being a manager always involves stress—in the old days and now—because there's always something to worry about. What are the things that you worry about nowadays?

Gus Boetzkes:

Well I know that I'm going into territory that's new for me. I also know that, when people are given more responsibility and get used to it, there's no turning back. So I worry what the future has in store and whether I'll remain the right kind of leader. I worry whether I'm the right kind of leader now. My role will continue to change as people accept more and more responsibility and really become more independent. But what will my role be like then? I worry about that. Will I lose touch with people as they become independent? Right now I guess I have to confess that I used to enjoy being depended upon. I suppose everybody has a secret wish that, if they left the organization, their old group would just fall apart. So I would want to know that my role was meaningful to the organization even though it may seem to some to be less tangible.

Zenger-Miller:

You said earlier, and you're saying now, that you're still valuable and maybe even more valuable and qualified than you were in the old environment. How would you describe your value to the organization these days?

Gus Boetzkes:

I think that I now have a broader skill set. Although I still have technical expertise, I've developed skills as a facilitator and as a coach. Also, I used to only be clear about my department's activities. Whereas now I have a better understanding of the corporate vision, the corporate values. I monitor the whole organization more than ever before.

Zenger-Miller:

And what about the members of your team? How have they changed?

Gus Boetzkes:

They're getting a bigger sense of what's happening around them. And that's pretty essential because, in order to be effective in what they do, they need to understand how they interact with the whole hospital. It's not enough to simply ask someone, "What do I do next?" That was the old system where they simply followed directions. Now they also need to understand the *impact* of what they're doing. They need to make priority decisions like, "What do I do *first*? How does this effect other members of the team? What information do I have to pass on to other members of the team or to my boss?"

> *It's not enough to simply ask someone, "What do I do next?"*

Zenger-Miller:

So it sounds like everybody is playing a bigger role, and that even with the struggle to master a lot of new information and skills, the benefits are really beginning to show up.

Gus Boetzkes:

It really looks that way.

Interview Ten

"The Protector, the Guide, the Teacher of Values"

RoseAnn Stevenson
Manager, Organization and Management Development
The Boeing Company

Zenger-Miller:
What kind of teams do you have at Boeing?

RoseAnn Stevenson:
We have functional work teams which we're moving toward total involvement. We also have temporary, voluntary problem-solving teams.

Zenger-Miller:
I assume those are also cross-functional?

RoseAnn Stevenson:
Right.

Zenger-Miller:
Any other types?

RoseAnn Stevenson:
A third type is what we call special purpose teams, formed to develop brand new systems—for example, for recognition. Or for recreation and socialization.

Zenger-Miller:
Like what to do for the company picnic?

RoseAnn Stevenson:
Right. Or things like—should we put a basketball court in the back? We have several teams like this to set up new systems or programs or processes. Their job is simply to come up with new ideas and plan their implementation.

Zenger-Miller:
So they're not necessarily geared to making process improvements or solving existing problems. They're more geared to "let's make something different happen."

RoseAnn Stevenson:
Yes. They don't use the cause-and-effect diagrams and the other tools you'd use in a process problem-solving team.

Zenger-Miller:
Let's talk about the functional work teams. How are they managed?

RoseAnn Stevenson:
Since we're only a year into our Start-Up Phase, they're still managed, in effect, by first-line supervisors. We call them team leaders. Generally, they're people who've been transferred to share their expertise—the teacher, the problem solver, the mentor. This individual functions as the center of the team for six to nine months, until people start to know how to do the tasks.

Zenger-Miller:
Then they go back to Seattle?

RoseAnn Stevenson:
No. In the next step, what we call Steady State 1, the team leader begins to share authority. They're still really the team leader, but instead of sitting at the head of the table, they become more of a group member where they join everyone around the circle. So they're still there, but as an information provider, a helper, an example setter.

Zenger-Miller:
As the transition continues, do they tend to loosen their control?

RoseAnn Stevenson:
Yes. They'll begin to share the authority with the group but not let go yet. It's almost like, in child development at age three or four, you can't really let the kid go down the street by himself. But he's pretty independent anyway.

Zenger-Miller:
And are you at that stage yet?

RoseAnn Stevenson:
We will be probably by the end of this year. We didn't just move directly from our Start-Up to this Steady State 1 because we've been adding three or four hundred people, 18 or 20 at a time. You can't move down this

We're following a real systematic process to look at the readiness of the team . . .

path too quickly when you have so many new people. We're following a real systematic process to look at the readiness of the team, so the team leader can begin letting go. Then, after maybe another year, they'll know how to make their parts, understand the processes, and fix problems. But the team leader will still be attached to that team as a resource and information provider. The leader will also manage the boundaries between other functions—in other words, a cross-functional coordinator.

Zenger-Miller:

So in another year, these first-line supervisors are going to get a promotion in terms of responsibilities.

RoseAnn Stevenson:

Their job will change significantly. They'll no longer be the traditional planner, organizer, decision-maker. Their role will be more of a developer of people—the coach, the encourager, the mentor, the supporter. In essence, they're moving from task to relationship, so they'll systematically let go of the tasks and provide a higher level of coaching.

> *In essence, they're moving from task to relationship . . .*

Zenger-Miller:

How will these people handle the diverse viewpoints now that more people have a voice in problem solving and decision-making?

RoseAnn Stevenson:

They'll know more about managing conflict. We've seen that already. As we remove fear from the workplace, people feel willing to speak up, and you automatically increase the level of confidence.

> *As we remove fear from the workplace, people feel willing to speak up . . .*

Zenger-Miller:

How about the diversity of opinions with teams? Do you see this as an emerging problem? And if so, what are you planning to do about it?

RoseAnn Stevenson:

I think it's probably more of a problem now.

Zenger-Miller:

Really? Why is that?

RoseAnn Stevenson:

Well, let's look at the model I like to use—"forming, storming, norming, performing." The forming stage is pretty much accomplished now. The next stage, storming, deals directly with that diversity of opinion, diversity of values, diversity of culture. That's where the teams begin to challenge one another. Power issues come up as well as competition around who's going to do what and who's going to have what role on the team. I think of this as the crisis stage.

Zenger-Miller:

You're approaching that point?

RoseAnn Stevenson:

We're right in the middle of it.

Zenger-Miller:

How are you handling it? You mentioned training—managing conflict, coaching, mentoring skills. Is there anything else?

RoseAnn Stevenson:

The team leaders often use me as an intervention consultant. If the team seems to be stuck in that stage and can't seem to resolve it, the team leaders typically request that I come in and look at the situation and suggest an appropriate next step.

Zenger-Miller:

What are the team leaders doing to help the teams resolve their own issues?

RoseAnn Stevenson:

When Johnny's having trouble with Susan, instead of the team leader going in and resolving it, he's saying, "Johnny, I want you to go sit down with Susan and figure out an agreement that you can both live with."

Zenger-Miller:

So instead of solving the problem, he says, "You go back and solve it." Sounds like raising my kids.

RoseAnn Stevenson:

Kind of like that. I mean, if you have children, you understand this whole development process. At first you need to be the protector, the guide, and the teacher of values. Then, as the child becomes more experienced through the elementary school, you need to back away a little, but you're still right there. Then, as they move to the teenage years, the confusion and crises come up. Typically, the toughest time for a parent, as well as the team leader, comes when this person or this

> *. . . if you have children, you understand this whole development process.*

team is ready to be more independent. Sometimes, and I speak from experience here, the toughest time is when the kid is ready before the parent is willing to let go.

Zenger-Miller:

So the team might be ready before the leader is?

RoseAnn Stevenson:

Exactly. The team may be ready for the leader to miss a few meetings, but the leader's not. Just like when the child is 17 or 18, they're ready to make their own decisions, but the parent isn't.

> *The team may be ready for the leader to miss a few meetings, but the leader's not.*

Zenger-Miller:

So how are decisions made while you're going through this transition?

RoseAnn Stevenson:

Let's continue the analogy. When the child is in elementary school, my guess is that most of the decisions are made by the parent. It's usually not up to the kids what class they're going to take after school or whether they can do this or that. And that's about where we are now with the teams. We're beginning to let go as we move out of Start-Up and into Steady State 1. At this particular point, I would say 75 percent of the decisions are made by the team leaders. By the end of this year in five months, I would say that will be closer to 65 percent. And soon after, it will be more like 35 percent.

Zenger-Miller:

So it's gradual.

RoseAnn Stevenson:

Right. By the end of this year they'll be sitting down as a team to decide things like whether to work overtime. And the team leader won't be saying too much.

Zenger-Miller:

What's all this gonna buy for you? What's the payoff of empowering these functional teams?

RoseAnn Stevenson:

Well, we do much of our measurements in terms of quality and flow time, so our expectation is that we'll be doing up to 99.9 percent of these measurements through the teams.

> *. . . we'll be doing up to 99.9 percent of these measurements through the teams.*

Zenger-Miller:

So the teams will improve quality?

RoseAnn Stevenson:

They will definitely improve quality. We're moving to first level self-inspection, so instead of the team leader or an inspector coming around, everybody will be given the skills to inspect their own work. They'll actually have a stamp, what we call a bug, and they'll stamp their work.

Zenger-Miller:

Are you managing expectations about how much authority the teams will have?

RoseAnn Stevenson:

We're trying. That's probably the toughest thing in this whole process, managing expectations. The expectations range everywhere from "I'm going to run the company" to "Gee, somebody asked my opinion—that's real nice." Generally, our associates want us to move significantly faster than we think the business will allow. Again, it's the parent model. My 12-year-old thinks she's 18. I would say our teams are very much like those kids who want to push ahead faster into adulthood or push into the *privileges* of adulthood—like driving the car or wearing makeup or going out on dates.

> *. . . expectations range everywhere from "I'm going to run the company" to "Gee, somebody asked my opinion— that's real nice."*

Zenger-Miller:

But the team leaders and everybody else say the skill level isn't there yet.

RoseAnn Stevenson:

The skill level for performing the task is beginning to develop. But to have the whole team establish priorities in making parts when they haven't really made all the parts yet, or they haven't experienced how long it takes to make them, or they don't know the troubles you can have with a particular part—that doesn't make sense.

Zenger-Miller:

It sounds like the cross-training isn't finished yet.

RoseAnn Stevenson:

And it won't be for three years. Our goal is to have 50 percent of our people cross-trained in at least one area by the end of this year. But if there are five processes involved in making one of our products, it's going to take three to five years to be completely cross-trained.

Zenger-Miller:
There's no way to speed it up?

RoseAnn Stevenson:
You can't because then you'd have work teams with nobody really knowing what to do.

Zenger-Miller:
You mean it takes a lot of time doing the job before they're really proficient?

RoseAnn Stevenson:
Right.

Zenger-Miller:
Can you step back a bit and say how you're managing problems between different teams? Is that something that comes up?

RoseAnn Stevenson:
Yes. The most common way to handle that is to let the people go talk it out with one another.

Zenger-Miller:
So it's just handled informally.

RoseAnn Stevenson:
Yeah. If engineering is having difficulty with manufacturing, usually those people sit down and talk it out without the team leaders. If they see they can't resolve it, then they ask for help.

. . . people sit down and talk it out without the team leaders.

Zenger-Miller:
And what about work processes going across team boundaries. Are there issues there?

RoseAnn Stevenson:
We really stress the customer-supplier relationship and that your customers have the right and responsibility to go back to you if what you turn out doesn't meet their expectations.

Zenger-Miller:
Have the team leaders' relationships with their bosses changed at all as their responsibilities change?

RoseAnn Stevenson:
I would say that there's more willingness from the team leaders to voice their opinion and challenge their bosses' thinking. I'm not talking

about confronting them but
challenging their thinking and
questioning. And there's per-   *Our team leaders don't just*
haps more two-way communi-   *fall in line and comply . . .*
cation compared to a traditional
organization. Our team leaders
don't just fall in line and comply as they might in a traditional hierarchy.

Zenger-Miller:

Has the organization changed its relationship with the outside at all,
and is that going to change as you become more team oriented? I
know some places have team members actually talking to outside
customers.

RoseAnn Stevenson:

We do some of that now. For example, if we want somebody to go out
and talk about what we do here, we don't necessarily send out a
supervisor. We may send somebody who's simply interested in doing
it.

Zenger-Miller:

How about the amount of time they spend with suppliers? Is that
changing?

RoseAnn Stevenson:

Yes, they spend more time with suppliers and customers. For example,
our customers came over to Spokane and we had a town hall meeting
of all the associates, and we got a chance to hear directly from our
customers about what they thought of our parts.

Zenger-Miller:

So that's very direct feedback.

RoseAnn Stevenson:

Very, very direct feedback.

Zenger-Miller:

How close do your people stay to suppliers?

RoseAnn Stevenson:

At the two major sites we actually had our own associates living and
working there to make sure that the suppliers are producing raw materials that meet our needs.

Zenger-Miller:

Impressive. Well, is there anything I left out that you wanted to add?

RoseAnn Stevenson:

Just that many companies who want to install this process think they can do it in a year or two. I'd say four to five years is more realistic for a start-up plant.

> *. . . companies who want to install this process think they can do it in a year or two.*

Zenger-Miller:

Your message then is that it really takes longer than people think.

RoseAnn Stevenson:

Much longer than these people who want to come right in and fix the world would like to believe. But the time and effort is well worth it.

"Like Quitting Smoking"

Stephen Merrill
Section Manager
Spectra Physics

Zenger-Miller:

Was there anything that was difficult to master in taking on your new role?

Stephen Merrill:

The hardest thing for me in a team environment has been taking on a new role with my subordinates. That's because the very hardest thing is to give up power—positional power. I'm still struggling with that today. You look at a project and you say to yourself, "I'm an engineer by trade. I've been in the trenches doing these jobs, and I know the answers. Another guy comes along, and he certainly doesn't know the answers I know. How do I let that guy go out and find the answers without sinking?" That's the tough thing. You just want to tell him the answer and be done with it. I've struggled a long time with this.

Zenger-Miller:

Is there anything that makes it easier?

Stephen Merrill:

I had a boss once who used to say, "Every time somebody comes to you with a situation, the first thing you need to ask yourself is, 'Do I care?' If it's not a life-or-death matter, then don't even get involved. Let the person do it their way." I still ask myself that question.

> *. . . the first thing you need to ask yourself is, 'Do I care?'*

Zenger-Miller:

And people are satisfied with that?

Stephen Merrill:

Sometimes when I've gone laissez-faire and let people do what they want to do, they fail or they take a long time doing it. And because I'm very open, people have come back and just chewed me out and said, "You knew that answer. How come you didn't tell me that?" Other times I've been too tight with some people. They come back and say, "You're not giving me enough breathing room. Give me the whole project. Don't give me a task. Give me everything. Help me do it, but don't tell me how to do it." I find it's just a very tough balance because it's trusting your career, your family, the fate of the company to somebody else. Once you can do it, you can make the transition. Some people do it intuitively, and some, like myself, do it less intuitively. I've got to work at it.

Stephen Merrill:

You said that one of the hardest things to give up is power. Very few people are willing to give up something unless they're going to get something back. What do you get in exchange?

Zenger-Miller:

I guess the reason I've continued to struggle with this is that every time I do something by myself, making my own decisions without properly listening to input, I get a result that's less than satisfactory. When I get other people involved, painful as it is, the result that I get is *so much better*. I'm not talking twice as good, quality-wise, or twice as fast. I'm talking *10 times* better—almost an order-of-magnitude better result by getting people involved.

Zenger-Miller:

Anything else you get in exchange for your positional power?

Stephen Merrill:

I've learned a whole lot more about manufacturing. I've seen things done that I would never have gotten to see—simple things like how to lay out a manufacturing line. I have seen more answers to more problems than you could ever read in a hundred books just by letting people do it on their own. I've seen people who aren't normally doing conceptual work come up with these tremendous ideas which you might then read about in an article in the *Harvard Business Review* three years later. Just some great results.

> *I have seen more answers to more problems than you could ever read in a hundred books . . .*

Zenger-Miller:

And the source of that is your ability and willingness to share power and leadership with them.

Stephen Merrill:

It's part of it. But that alone isn't sufficient. It's not just a matter of me giving up control. You've got to foster the right environment. Remember you've also got a lot of other people who know the answers—production supervisors, R&D engineers. It's having them adopt the same attitude I have. Because if they go off and operate in their own normal way, you don't get the same kinds of results. My role has changed from directing projects to facilitating team success. Now when I say "facilitating," I'm not talking about leading teams.

On the current project, I'm not the team leader. We have a core team of real worker bees, and they have their own leader. I'm there as a sponsor of that team. I'm there to make that team

I'm running the program without ever doing it.

work. My role is to watch the interaction in the team, work with leadership problems, and to follow up—like checking whether they have scribes in the meeting and whether they're taking notes and doing meeting agendas right. It's a whole different role. I'm running the program without ever doing it.

Zenger-Miller:

How do you go about getting the right people on a team?

Stephen Merrill:

You have to call it based on your experience of the people involved. Some people don't work on some teams, and some people don't work on any team. It's really a hard call, but you've got to do it and face it. If a team is dysfunctional, it stays that way until you fix it. You may have to coach a certain person and bring them around or remove the person and restructure the team. If you don't, your team is never successful. That's a real tough management call, but it's a different situation than, "Can you do your job technically?"

Zenger-Miller:

Every leader has worries no matter what the environment. What are your major concerns these days in this highly developed team environment?

Stephen Merrill:

The concerns I have today relate more to my peers—the lower-to-middle management group and the management above me. Managers don't realize that, once you commit specific members to a team, it's important not to change that makeup without real cause. There's a natural tendency when you're going through pressures to respond by reorganizing. It's one of the great management responses. But if you pull people out of the team and put them in different roles, it really disrupts the team. I'm as guilty as anybody in this regard. It's easy to forget you're doing business a different way, so you slip back into the old way of doing business, and you just rip up your teams. We're still not all focused on how important and powerful teams are and how essential it is to maintain a climate that supports them. That's probably my biggest concern.

Zenger-Miller:

Given the current development of this environment, what's the best use of your time?

Stephen Merrill:

The best use of my time right now is getting support for these teams. I'm there when they have an issue that needs to be elevated to management to give them the support they need in terms of people, money, whatever it is. But support also goes beyond that. I also support them through coaching. I help them be better team players individually. And not only do I coach people who work directly for me, I've also had people come to me from marketing and R&D and ask me for input and direction. So I spend my time making the teams work doing whatever I need to do.

> *. . . people come to me from marketing and R&D and ask me for input and direction.*

Zenger-Miller:

What advice do you have for somebody, a traditional manager or supervisor, who needs to transition to this new leadership role?

Stephen Merrill:

You've got to want to make the transition. There's something in your life that's got to make you want this because, if you don't want it, it's going to be like quitting smoking. You'll make a lot of efforts, but you'll never get there.

Zenger-Miller:

Is there anything that can help you motivate yourself?

Stephen Merrill:

The very best thing that could ever happen in your life is to find a sponsor, a mentor, somebody that knows how to do it. You've got to first understand what it's all about and have a good mental picture of what you want to do. So it helps to visit with other people and see how they do it and talk to people in your situation one-on-one. Talk to people who think they're successful, and you'll hear a lot of useful things. That's a big thing.

Zenger-Miller:

And if you don't have a mentor, what then?

Stephen Merrill:

My advice is just go do it. Just try. I find you generally can't lose, but you've got to remember that patience is important. Patience with people. Patience with yourself.

"A Process That They Own"

Sharon Faltemier
Operations Manager
Raychem Corporation

Zenger-Miller:

How has your management style evolved over the years?

Sharon Faltemier:

That's difficult to answer because I really don't think my general management style has changed over the last 10 years. I have been able to modify it so it can be more effective. When I started at Procter & Gamble in 1980, works teams were just evolving there, so my whole career has been focused around managing in a team environment.

> *. . . I really don't think my general management style has changed over the last 10 years.*

Zenger-Miller:

In building a team environment, where do you start? How do you get people motivated?

Sharon Faltemier:

To begin with, people need to understand the need for change—why it's important and how it'll improve things. If they start to understand this and if they can see how it fits with their own needs, it's much easier to effect a change in their behavior.

Zenger-Miller:

How do you determine who should make decisions here?

Sharon Faltemier:

First, you have to identify the decisions and then decide who the most appropriate people are to make those decisions. If you're looking at manufacturing flow, you want the manufacturing work teams to make most of the day-to-day decisions. If you're looking at the needs of the outside customer, then maybe it should be a cross-functional business team centered around the customer. All the teams need to be focused around a process that they own.

Zenger-Miller:

What level of independence do you give to people?

Sharon Faltemier:

Our people have a lot of independence in how they manage their businesses. They don't come upstairs and say, "Can I do this" or "Can I do that." They clearly understand the areas in which they can go off and make decisions.

> *They clearly understand the areas in which they can go off and make decisions.*

Zenger-Miller:

Is there more freedom to make mistakes because the people at the top aren't directly overseeing anymore?

Sharon Faltemier:

Oh, absolutely. Let me give you an example. The scheduling for one of our manufacturing operations was always done by a production control manager. At some point, we said we wanted the teams to handle scheduling because they're in a position to make better day-to-day decisions. We knew there were going to be mistakes, and we did in fact have some mis-shipments. We could have said, "Forget it. We can't allow teams to make scheduling decisions. They don't understand the customers' needs." Instead, we said, "Let's learn from this. What information do they need to make good decisions? What criteria should they use?" Instead of going back to the old way, we talked about how it could be corrected. And we did it together.

Zenger-Miller:

OK, so the teams need information. What kind of information do you make available?

Sharon Faltemier:

Let's see. Team members know our financial information, they know our market share, they know about our competitors. They have access to any costing information they need. We don't go telling them, "Our product costs this much a foot to make," but they have access to that information if they need it. We don't have many filters on the information systems.

Zenger-Miller:

Do you find any resistance among managers to sharing information?

Sharon Faltemier:

When we first started out, it was more difficult. But a year into the program we started to see results, and then people became more willing, particularly some of our old-time manufacturing engineers.

Zenger-Miller:

Can you explain a little more about the types of teams you have here?

Sharon Faltemier:

We call the manufacturing teams the functional, high-performance teams. The sales order office is more of a white-collar administrative-type team. We also have cross-functional project teams that could be created around a new product or market opportunity.

Zenger-Miller:

They're temporary?

Sharon Faltemier:

Generally so. Then you have the cross-functional high-performance business teams. They're focused around a business segment. For example, we do spec work and non-spec work, and each of those two types of customers has different needs.

Zenger-Miller:

Are there differences in how you control these groups?

Zenger-Miller:

There are different degrees of control depending on their leadership, the clarity of their goals, their skill level, and their overall development as a team. The teams do self-assessments, so that helps the team understand where they're at and also serves to guide me.

There are different degrees of control depending on their leadership . . .

Zenger-Miller:

So you increase or decrease the level of autonomy based on leadership, skill development, and so on?

Sharon Faltemier:

Right, although there are some areas we will not compromise on—for example, safety glasses, hearing protection, and safety shoes.

Zenger-Miller:

Any other areas where team responsibility is limited?

Sharon Faltemier:

When firing an individual, the team can make recommendations around discipline and even carry out the disciplinary action, but when it gets down to the actual termination, there are some real legal standards that we need to control. Some of the teams want the individual gone immediately, and they don't understand why you have to follow procedures.

Zenger-Miller:

Are there differences in how the teams solve problems?

Sharon Faltemier:

Right now? Yeah, it really does depend on their level of team development. But I would say most of the teams are now able to handle even their most difficult issues by themselves.

> *. . . most of the teams are now able to handle even their most difficult issues . . .*

Zenger-Miller:

What about improvement ideas? Are they handled differently now?

Sharon Faltemier:

One big difference is that people will tell you whenever they have an idea because they know they can go off and work it. Whereas before, they'd bring it upstairs and never hear anything back about it.

Zenger-Miller:

So has that increased the number of ideas they'll put forth?

Sharon Faltemier:

Absolutely. The teams have come up with some wonderful ideas. For example, we sent one of our operators to a wire supplier. Whereas before, we never sent people off to see suppliers. He was concerned that the reels were always sent in different weights, which created slowdowns. So he was back there and said, "Why are you giving us different reel weights," and they said, "Does it matter?" No one had even told the supplier why matched weights were important. So now he's getting matched weights. I mean, that was a major cost savings.

Zenger-Miller:

But only obvious to the person who's using it.

Sharon Faltemier:

That's right.

Zenger-Miller:

Are there special things you've done to get people to work as a team?

Sharon Faltemier:

There's a lot of training—team building, problem-solving skills, interpersonal skills.

Zenger-Miller:

I know all this has led to real gains in productivity. Are there other benefits that you haven't talked about?

Sharon Faltemier:

It's also contributed to the bottom-line profits.

Zenger-Miller:

How about the general job satisfaction?

Sharon Faltemier:

Most people say they're much more satisfied with their job, although it's hard to measure how satisfied. We have had attrition—probably 10 percent terminations after the training. We didn't hire people, you know, to be part of these teams. We've also had two people go to another division because they didn't want to learn these new skills or pick up these responsibilities.

. . . people say they're much more satisfied with their job, although it's hard to measure . . .

Zenger-Miller:

How are you managing the problems that can occur between different teams?

Sharon Faltemier:

The representatives from the teams meet on a weekly basis. They address a variety of problems, such as any perceived inconsistencies in policies between one team and another. Like one team was feeling that they had to do all the rework in the plant.

Zenger-Miller:

So the teams are charged with working out their problems with one another?

Sharon Faltemier:

Yes. It's just like with individuals. People should not come into my office and even bring up a problem if they haven't first addressed it with the individual or with the team. In the past they used to be up here all the time. Now, if an individual has a problem with someone and they don't know how to discuss it with that person, I'll help facilitate the discussion the first time. But after that, they have to carry the ball.

Zenger-Miller:

So you coach on interpersonal skills.

Sharon Faltemier:

That's right. I just don't let them hang. But I wouldn't come up with the solution or the answer or fix it for them. It's the same with team issues. If there's a rework issue between one team and that other team, the people from those teams need to get together and discuss it, try to work it out, before I get involved.

I just don't let them hang. But I wouldn't come up with the solution . . .

Zenger-Miller:

Tell me, has the relationship with your boss changed?

Sharon Faltemier:

Well, he's added to my workload. He's put me in charge of coordinating some of these cross-functional programs.

Zenger-Miller:

What about the relationships between managers. Have they changed in working across boundaries?

Sharon Faltemier:

Definitely.

Zenger-Miller:

How so?

Sharon Faltemier:

We no longer make certain kinds of decisions in operations that we may have made in the past. For example, I may be faced with scrapping a hundred thousand dollars worth of product. Before, I would have been completely responsible. Now I can go to the other functional managers to see if there's anything we can do because they also have ownership of the manufacturing process in those areas where they can help out. Or we can look at the product development process. In the past, manufacturing was never in-

Before, I would have been completely responsible. Now I can go to the other functional managers . . .

volved in the development of new products, so we'd never run capability studies on new products. Now the development manager will say, "Well, manufacturing, is this what you want? Do you feel confident that your processes can meet these specs?" It's what a lot of businesses are going through.

Zenger-Miller:

I know that you're a driver of change in this organization. It's obvious because of all you've done. Do you ever get criticized for moving too quickly?

Sharon Faltemier:

I've been told that I'm sometimes too aggressive, that I move too quickly. But I believe that when people start to see the benefits, even the nonbelievers will come along. Some managers feel they need 60 to 70 percent of the people on board to start the change process. I'll start change with only 30 percent buy-in as long as I've got a critical leadership group there. I may even go with less than 30 percent. If I have 10 percent and they're key leaders and they're there, we'll move on it.

Interview Thirteen

"How Can It Make You Feel Bad?"

Thelma Inkson
Nurse Manager
University of Alberta Hospitals

Zenger-Miller:

What are the things that have changed generally since the early days when you became a manager?

Thelma Inkson:

When I first became a manager, the hospital was starting to transition from the bureaucratic structure into a team structure where everyone has a say. It was a very difficult concept for people to accept. The staff took a long time because they didn't really believe that I was going to listen to them. The didn't believe that they really had a say.

Zenger-Miller:

Did they test you in the beginning to see whether you meant what you said?

Thelma Inkson:

They still are testing me—not necessarily me, but the system. Because the minute anything goes wrong or they feel that there has been a decision made that they didn't have input into, there is still that level of mistrust that says, "I thought we were supposed to work as teams. How come this decision was made without our input?" It takes a while for people to realize that even in a new team structure, a new environment, a new culture, there still has to be decision-making at different levels. That's where we're all struggling right now, deciding what decisions should be made at what levels.

Zenger-Miller:

Let's look at what you do on a daily basis—what you did early on and how you spend your time today. How has that changed?

Thelma Inkson:

What has changed the most is me and how I approach issues. When I first started I had to make sure that the patient care was high quality, make sure that the budget was met. If I wanted any changes, I would research it and go to the staff and say, "This is what we are going to do." Now when I work with my staff, everything is their unit, and they are responsible for it. When issues come up, they will make those decisions knowing that there won't be any repercussion. It might be the wrong decision, but that's OK. We'll change it.

> *. . . everything is their unit, and they are responsible for it.*

Zenger-Miller:

Could you give us an example showing how things have changed?

Thelma Inkson:

Before, people might come to me and say, "We have a problem with the material carts. Material management has put all this material in the wrong place. Why don't they do something?" Now they know that when they come to me with something like that, they need to be prepared to fix it. It is not my responsibility. Before, I would contact material management, and we would work it through and fix things. Recently, two staff nurses completely took over responsibility for redoing all the carts—working directly with material management, not with me as a go-between—and things are great. The rest of the staff know that it was staff nurses who did it, so it is that much more acceptable than if I had done it.

Zenger-Miller:

I imagine you need to be sensitive to what the staff are capable of taking on. Are there clues that people are ready for a new challenge?

Thelma Inkson:

Somehow you just know that. The people you give responsibility to are keen, ready to take it on. They realize that you're going to be there for them. Those people who are ready will carry it through, and it is very rewarding for them.

Zenger-Miller:

Do you have any misgivings about giving new responsibilities to those people?

Thelma Inkson:

Although people say to you, "You're giving up all your control, anything that you are responsible for," I find it very self-satisfying to watch these people grow. These are people I have worked with for a long time, and in the past two and a half years I have seen more personal growth in a lot of them than I had seen in a number of years before that. Which is very rewarding for both them and me.

Zenger-Miller:

I'll bet it's gratifying to see people blossom when maybe they didn't even know what they could do.

Thelma Inkson:

Then they're not afraid to question. They questioned before but in a different way—behind your back when you weren't around. What I'm finding is that more and more issues don't become issues because they are never allowed to get to that point. When people are concerned about something, we talk about it. If we feel that something needs to be done, we will do that. But it's taken a long time to convince them that we can actually work through these problems.

> *They questioned before but in a different way—behind your back . . .*

Zenger-Miller:

Sounds like you've built some real trust between you and the staff.

Thelma Inkson:

If there is a key word, it is trust. If you don't have their trust, you don't get anywhere.

Zenger-Miller:

What would you advise a new team leader to do to develop trust with a group?

Thelma Inkson:

I guess you do these things rather unconsciously so it is hard to pick them out of a hat. You need to respect people. When I come in, I try to be positive and friendly to the staff and treat them very equally. It becomes a role model. What I see now are staff nurses that maybe don't really like each other very much. But at least they have a working relationship. I would suggest that you have to be alert to everything that your staff says to you. You have to listen. And that's where you can perceive that these people are ready for something more. Then you can say to them, "Why don't you take this on because I see that you are really interested. I can help you by doing this and this."

Zenger-Miller:

What about the people who don't seem to want anything more than what they're doing now?

Thelma Inkson:

I still expect them to take responsibility for their own actions. And with that responsibility comes the necessity to communicate and give input. That is working for the people who don't want to take on the extra jobs.

Zenger-Miller:

You've been involved with teams for several years now. What were the hardest things for you to learn during this period?

Thelma Inkson:

That you have to be a risk taker. You have to believe in the people you work with. If you're not willing to take a risk, you're never going to hand over the control to the people it belongs to at the front line. I also had to learn not to take it personally when things went wrong because it is not a failure. It is just another opportunity to continue to improve. I've also learned that you get more respect when you listen to people

If you're not willing to take a risk, you're never going to hand over the control . . .

and respect them for their knowledge at their level. But the hardest part is convincing people that it is really going to work. And it has worked. We have been very successful.

Zenger-Miller:

I imagine this transition was especially tricky in a hospital, an institution I think of as very authoritarian.

Thelma Inkson:

That's true. It takes a long time to realize that the world is changing and our institution is changing and that change is a way of life. Now we make changes every day and have become quite comfortable with change. We made some very critical changes within the burn unit. But at the time it was a nightmare because we had gone from using a very nice, neat, clean dressing on our patients to using silver nitrate—I'm not sure if you know that silver nitrate turns everything black. Now the staff are starting to cope with change better, rather than this scenario of, "We've done it that way for so long, why do we have to change?" You don't get that anymore.

Zenger-Miller:

Has there been a greater concern about the wishes of the customer, or the patient, as a result of moving to teams?

Thelma Inkson:

We work as a burn team, which is multidisciplinary, so we have always met once a week to look at our patients and discuss what was needed for them from every angle. But I do see that we are really changing because we are doing what is better for the patients. And what the patients *want*. For example, we have started to use patient-controlled pain medication. They control it. And this was quite interesting because the nurses initially felt like they were losing control—exactly what we managers were feeling. It took the nurses some time to realize that this is much better for patients. The nurses think it is wonderful now.

> *. . . nurses initially felt like they were losing control— exactly what we managers were feeling.*

Zenger-Miller:

Did you make changes affecting your other customers as well?

Thelma Inkson:

We looked seriously at the visiting policy within our unit—by asking patients what they wanted, asking families what they wanted, asking nurses what they wanted, and then developing a policy that serves everybody's needs. We are in the process of developing an outpatient clinic, and one of the staff nurses actually prepared a patient satisfaction survey with the quality improvement group—to find out where these patients had had outpatient care before, what they felt was wrong with the service, and how could we improve it. We also have family conferences now on every burn patient. That has been very positive for the staff because they feel much more informed and they get to know the families much better.

Zenger-Miller:

You've mentioned "losing control" a couple of times now—and I think I know what you mean, that a manager might be losing control. I wonder if you could talk about what happens to control as you move to a team environment.

Thelma Inkson:

I definitely remember when things were controlled. Communication was controlled. Scheduling was controlled to the point of people being really unhappy. And when you control communication, people don't know what's going on so they can't respond, and they feel like they are really not a part of anything. They come to work and go home. What I refer to as "losing control" is just moving the control to where it belongs. I have never felt that things are "out of control." The staff recognize that someone familiar with the whole situation still has to be coordinating. Almost every member of my staff makes sure that I know what is going on. I don't feel I have lost that perspective because of giving them more control over what they do.

Zenger-Miller:

Some managers sometimes think that, by empowering a team, they will "disempower" themselves, so to speak. Is that a concern of yours?

Thelma Inkson:

I disagree that you are less empowered because you're giving power to somebody else. I think it gives you *more* power. When I empower the people that work for me, I don't feel like my job is going to be deleted because I have given it away. I feel more empowered because—this is difficult to explain—you have more control because you've given control. I'm not sure that makes sense,

> *. . . you have more control because you've given control.*

but it is the way that I perceive things. The people who work for you will recognize that you can be trusted, that you are not going to take advantage of them, that you support them, that you recognize when mistakes are made but will help them through it. That gives you *more* control, and it makes the people who work for you feel so much better. How can it make you feel bad?

Zenger-Miller:

Thelma, is there any final advice you have for someone about to begin a transition to teams? Anything you could say to get this person rolling?

Thelma Inkson:

You need to recognize that it is a slow process. You don't walk in one morning and say, "OK, now you're all empowered." You yourself have to be prepared. You need to take the responsibility to read some of the literature, to understand the terminology. I recommend any training programs that the organization offers. When they first brought in some of the programs here, I was no different than anybody else. I thought,

> *You don't walk in one morning and say, "OK, now you're all empowered."*

"Oh, really, I don't have time to go to this thing. Why are they insisting that I go?" But they are important, and they do give you a different perspective. Take part in those programs. Start slowly. Don't expect things to happen overnight. And, as I said before, develop trust by respecting the people that you work with.

"A Higher Level of Industrial Intimacy"

John Hofmeister
Vice President, Human Resources
Allied Signal Aerospace

Zenger-Miller:

Can you talk a little about the kinds of teams you have at Allied Signal?

John Hofmeister:

Sure. We have teams we call task forces that are project-oriented. We have teams of managers who are working cross-functionally. We have teams of professional employees. I don't want to give the impression that our teams are all scientifically managed and all very well organized as part of a master team. It's a looser affiliation, a looser approach which takes advantage of what I call "teaming" as opposed to team design. The fact that it's successful generates more teaming.

Zenger-Miller:

How prevalent is "teaming" at Allied Signal?

John Hofmeister:

We're following a team approach to plant operations in most manufacturing facilities in the U.S. and in our Canadian facilities. However, depending on the location, the teams may be at a different stage of development.

Zenger-Miller:

How does the stage of a team's development affect the leadership role?

John Hofmeister:

In the beginning, there is an awful lot of cheerleading, facilitating, and monitoring and heavy doses of influential leadership. And an awful lot of teaching of process skills. It's not control-oriented but very hands-on, working closely with many kinds of involvement. As time goes on, the cheerleading becomes more remote with checkpoints established. The fundamental difference is that trust grows to the point where

. . . trust grows to the point where the work that has to be done is being done.

the work that has to be done is being done. The greatest thing that builds is trust—the level of trust, the quality of trust.

Zenger-Miller:

What are the main things you see affecting the growth of trust?

John Hofmeister:

The big things are culture, values, beliefs, and the sophistication or development of the employees. Take, for example, our Eaton, New Jersey plant. The plant is over 50 years old, and it's been through organizational hell—brutal changes that resulted in significant downsizing. There's a different kind of trust in dealing with employees who have been through these experiences than with employees at a newer facility like Tucson, Arizona.

Zenger-Miller:

Are there any universals that apply to leading teams in your experience?

John Hofmeister:

It really depends on the development of the team. For example, in a team's early days, a facilitator can help the problem-solving process. That's because, early on, the process needs to be controlled. But as a team evolves and becomes more cooperative, more trusting, more interactive, and more dynamic, a facilitator who exercises that same level of control will actually end up creating problems. Even the process itself doesn't move consistently forward. The group may be reconstituted, or maybe there's a downturn in the business, or maybe a key member retires. When that happens, there often has to be a retrenchment where the group moves backward to an earlier, more controlled stage. So there's no one thing that's going to work in all these different situations.

Zenger-Miller:

How do you manage the many viewpoints you find in a team environment?

John Hofmeister:

You do it by building understanding—easy to say but very hard to make happen. That's why I use the term "sophistication level of the employee." I'm not saying education level. Developing sophistication is a process of developing the thinking of people regardless of educa-

tion. This would contribute to
their ability to be more tolerant
of the person next to them, to
understand the impact of individual personality, attitudes,
and behaviors on the team.
We're achieving a higher level

*There's more compassion,
more sensitivity, more
tolerance, and more sharing.*

of industrial intimacy, which leads to a better understanding between
individuals and groups. There's more compassion, more sensitivity,
more tolerance, and more sharing.

Zenger-Miller:

Can tell us a little about how decisions are made?

John Hofmeister:

Wherever possible, we move toward consensus because people feel
more involved and empowered, and they take greater ownership of

the decision. But when something happens and the groups
can't agree, then the person in
charge makes the call. Generally, there's an understanding
that command and control is acceptable when consensus has

*. . . command and control is
acceptable when consensus has
not been achieved . . .*

not been achieved or cannot be achieved. The balance is to make sure
that command and control are not overused.

Zenger-Miller:

Would you say that, in general, team members exercise more autonomy over their work?

John Hofmeister:

Depends what you mean by autonomy. If you mean individualism, I
don't think individualism can succeed. I don't think groups could
tolerate that. In an earlier period, individual workers were paid by the
piece. Anyone with that attitude today would have a negative impact
on the team as a whole. That's not to say there isn't some room for
autonomy and independence, but it's on the basis of greater *interdependence*. Yes, there is more autonomy, but there's much more intimacy and sharing.

Zenger-Miller:

How about *information* sharing? That seems to be a constant in every
successful team environment.

John Hofmeister:

We're no exception. There's been a dramatic change, although I
think we're a long way away from sharing as much information as

we could. What we do share right now is anything that's pertinent to the effective operation of the facility—financials, forecasts, and technical information about quality. As far as personnel information goes, we won't share anything that logically should be kept private. But we will share any information about the resolutions of employee complaints, the rationale for promotions, and the reasons behind individual rewards—even if the downside is the possibility that some people will be jealous.

Zenger-Miller:

What do you do if people do become jealous? How do you deal with it when it comes up?

John Hofmeister:

You simply say, "Look, it's their turn because their contribution was meaningful and worth recognition. But we also encourage you to make your own meaningful contributions so we can recognize you too."

Zenger-Miller:

How do you go about getting people to function more effectively as a team?

John Hofmeister:

I think that people in organizational settings are social beings. It's only a matter of tapping into their wealth as individuals and reaching a shared understanding about how much wealth is present in a group of people. Then, once compatibility is established and people are sharing feelings and experiences, the teaming becomes a natural process.

Zenger-Miller:

Anything else?

John Hofmeister:

A leader or a facilitator with process skills is just invaluable. Identifying potential problems or issues is important, identifying the gaps between the players—different beliefs, different value sets, or different other factors. But the fact that we're all basically social beings makes the teaming process very natural.

Zenger-Miller:

In general, what do you rely on the teams to do?

John Hofmeister:

You rely on them to keep others informed—and by others I mean peers, superiors, and subordinates. You want them to communicate any information that's necessary to make business decisions or to get work done. You rely on them for feedback and updated information so you can monitor and adjust what's happening. And I think you rely on them to take responsibility for what they have to do and to maintain a certain level of goodwill.

Zenger-Miller:

How different is all that from what you relied on employees to do in the past?

John Hofmeister:

I think we relied on them for all that before but in a different way. All of those factors were individualized between supervisor and employee. And while some people just naturally shared information with their peers, there simply wasn't the same overall level of sharing or teaming.

Zenger-Miller:

So that overall level is important.

John Hofmeister:

Oh, absolutely. I believe that, depending on the size of the organization, a group of empowered people operating in a team fashion will outproduce other people who are operating in a hierarchical, controlling environment. This means that the more teaming you have, the more people will achieve their individual level of optimum contribution.

> *. . . the more teaming you have, the more people will achieve their individual level of optimum contribution.*

Zenger-Miller:

How long do you think it takes an organization to build a functioning team environment? Is it a matter of several years or what?

John Hofmeister:

To reach the highest level possible, I think we're talking several generations. If you look at the history of our Phoenix facilities, for example, we've had essentially three generations of employees throughout the years, and they're making great progress. But the people we hire and train and develop over the next 15 years will achieve a much higher level of team orientation. And it's probably the group after that who will operate with the most synergy. I'd say you're looking at 15 to 25 years to achieve the ultimate objective—a totally optimized workplace.

> *. . . you're looking at 15 to 25 years to achieve the ultimate objective . . .*

Zenger-Miller:

So even though progress is gradual, you see major benefits in switching over to teams.

John Hofmeister:

Oh, yes. The result is a more effective, more efficient organization. More inspired, empowered employees. Improvements in the workplace ambiance. A lot fewer employee grievances. And a more simplified organizational life, which has enabled us to spend more of our work time focusing on customers and the competition and internal problems and solutions.

Zenger-Miller:

Has this also resulted in a shift in responsibilities?

John Hofmeister:

Most definitely. In the case of the management task force, they're debating scenarios and analyzing options which were previously undertaken by a single manager or a smaller group of managers. In the case of production employees, they're monitoring quality, productivity, or employee performance, which was a job previously done by managers. In the case of teams of professionals, they're making decisions on product design, direction, and timing previously made by managers. So the point is, more people are more empowered to do more work than before.

Zenger-Miller:

Would you say all this is fairly tightly choreographed?

John Hofmeister:

Not really. It's not happening in a deliberately organized, orchestrated fashion. We're working on it *ad hoc* and building a culture for teaming throughout the organization. I would say it's working because we continue to perform at or above our financial targets. We're achieving certain levels of empowerment and employee involvement that are very satisfying to our overall strategy, and more than ever before our employees are committed to our business goals.

> *It's not happening in a deliberately organized, orchestrated fashion.*

Zenger-Miller:

How do you handle the inevitable conflicts that come up between the various teams?

John Hofmeister:

There is no one single way. Generally, someone will recognize a problem and conduct some kind of intervention. It depends on the team and on the level of the person who's taking the action. In one case in our engine business, we just spent time on a work force intervention to facilitate a problem resolution. That kind of thing is happening all over the organization, not just at the factory team level.

Zenger-Miller:

Do you ever find there's competition between the teams?

John Hofmeister:

Sure. You often see it between shifts of teams that do the same kind of work.

Zenger-Miller:

Does that get in the way of the teams being effective?

John Hofmeister:

If the competition is problematic and dysfunctional, you have to conduct some form of intervention. If, on the other hand, the competition leads to improved performance by both teams, you encourage it in a helpful manner, for example, by sharing information. That's the primary way to help people understand what others are doing.

Zenger-Miller:

I would imagine that sometimes you have problems created by issues beyond the boundaries of individual teams. Is that true? And if so, how do you handle them?

John Hofmeister:

How blurry the boundaries get depends on what stage you're at in the change process. You won't have precise answers all the time, and that's OK. It's basically learning to live in the kind of ambiguity that's critical to the change process. Mostly, you handle these situations by infor-

You won't have precise answers all the time, and that's OK.

mation sharing. The facilitators work cooperatively to share information, and even the plant managers go to the meetings to discuss what's working and what's not.

Zenger-Miller:

Any final remarks you'd like to add?

John Hofmeister:

I guess to sum it up, I'd say that life in an organization is constantly changing, and what we're doing today won't be good enough tomorrow. So anything we can do to facilitate change and to help people to grow and maximize their contribution will lead to the greater success of the organization. I'm very enthusiastic and confident about teams. I

. . . what we're doing today won't be good enough tomorrow.

feel they give people the chance to optimize their performance, and that leads to greater performance by the organization as a whole.

"Real Good at Delegating"

Karen Olson-Vermillion
Group leader
Subaru-Isuzu Automotive, Inc.

Zenger-Miller:

In the beginning, what was the biggest obstacle for you in learning to lead teams?

Karen Olson-Vermillion:

I like tight control. I like things done my way. I'm real organized. So it was a little difficult for me because, in giving control to someone else. I'm aware they may not do it exactly the way I would have done it. That's been the hardest thing for me to adjust to.

I like tight control. I like things done my way. I'm real organized.

Zenger-Miller:

Have you been able to adjust?

Karen Olson-Vermillion:

I think so. In fact, now I love it. I wouldn't want to go back to the old style. I've gotten real good at delegating, and I have a tendency to delegate more and more to the point where sometimes people go, "Wait a second, isn't that a little bit more than I'm supposed to be doing?"

Zenger-Miller:

What do you do in a situation like that? I imagine that an associate who isn't used to this might say, "Hey, that's not my job. It's your job. Why are you giving it to me?" Do you ever get any of that?

Karen Olson-Vermillion:

Sure, that's real common. But people here had a lot of training before they went out on the floor, and they've gotten some understanding of what "team concept" means. So I tell them, "Guys, you know, you've got to handle the whole thing. If I give you a little bit of responsibility, you've got to follow up and come back at me. You can't just pick and choose what you want to do." I know that sometimes they'd like to move back into their old role, just like managers would like to do that from time to time. But overall, I think that everybody believes this works a lot better.

Zenger-Miller:

What specifically is your role?

Karen Olson-Vermillion:

I'm actually a group leader. I delegate to both my team leaders and my associates.

Zenger-Miller:

And what does that entail on a day-to-day basis?

Karen Olson-Vermillion:

My role is largely that of a communicator. I attend a lot of meetings and pass on information to my team leaders and to my teams. I also get their feedback and pass that back up the chain of command. So instead of spending time doing some specific type of work, I delegate those things and use my time more efficiently.

Zenger-Miller:

But it's one thing to say, "Do this or do that." Is there anything more to it than that?

Karen Olson-Vermillion:

There is. It takes a lot longer when you also have to teach people what needs to be done, especially since I do more one-on-ones with my people. I teach them the way I would do it and what kind of end result I'm looking for. But I also let them know there are a lot of different avenues to get there. They can take whatever avenue they want as long as the end result is what I need.

Zenger-Miller:

Do you find this job any more stressful than before? I mean, any time you're in a leadership position, there's going to be pressure. What's it like now as opposed to what it was in the old role?

Karen Olson-Vermillion:

Before, the manager or the group leader was totally responsible, and it was easy to just say, "You do this, you do that." Now you need to work with the people and say, "OK, I'm delegating this to you."

It's a little bit more work because you don't just tell them
what to do. You let them decide
how they want to do it, and then
you've got to follow up and
make sure it's getting done. So
there's a lot more follow-up, I
think, than in the old way.

*It's a little bit more work
because you don't just tell
them what to do.*

Zenger-Miller:

I understand that one part of your role is to talk to your teams about
the industry and maybe explain how the organization fits into the
larger picture. Is this part of the information you pass along?

Karen Olson-Vermillion:

Yes. I try to keep up on the news from a couple of different plants to see
where we are competitively. Also, when we see articles in *Automotive
News, Automotive Industry*, and some of the other trade journals, we
pass that information on to our people. There's a lot of people in the
office that watch for information that would be of interest to everybody
in the industry.

Zenger-Miller:

What effect does it have to share all this information with your people?

Karen Olson-Vermillion:

They have a lot more buy-in, because they're part of the decision-
making. For instance, let's take the warehouse move going on right
now. We have three associates working on it full-time, eight hours a
day. I only spend an hour of my day with them, and they're making
a large number of the decisions. They're talking to all the other associates to find out what they want, so even though I might want this thing
put here, the majority of the associates doing the work may say, "We
want it over there." And that's what we go with. So they buy into a
much bigger part of the organization than they did in the old days.

Zenger-Miller:

Do you think this makes the organization more competitive?

Karen Olson-Vermillion:

Oh, definitely. From what I see
here as opposed to other places
I've worked at, when people
take more of an interest and
have more pride in what they
do, we all accomplish more.

*. . . people take more of an
interest and have more pride
in what they do . . .*

"Only One Train"

Ronald Deane
Manufacturing Training Specialist
Spectra Physics

Zenger-Miller:

Ron, how long have you worked for Spectra Physics?

Ronald Deane:

Just about 13 years now.

Zenger-Miller:

What's the biggest change you've seen over that period?

Ronald Deane:

I used to spend a lot of time down in the trenches managing the everyday details—are the shipments going to get out, who's at what work station, what is the quality level? That's changed tremendously for me. The skills I need now are much different. Then they were technically oriented, how to get the build out. Now they're facilitating skills, how to develop people. For me it was a big change. It's a cultural change. It's not just slapping a new program in place. You have to change a lot of things you're personally doing. You have to give up some power or not so much power as control. You have to work with people and get your job done through them.

Zenger-Miller:

Were you worried at the beginning of this whole process about what would happen once you got to this point?

Ronald Deane:

That's one of the things we didn't do well. We prepared the work force well, but we didn't prepare the supervisory level very well at all. My biggest concern was, "What value do I have

> *. . . we didn't prepare the supervisory level very well at all.*

to the company if I'm not doing the daily traditional management work? What value do I have down the road if the tasks that I am doing today are being done by someone else?''

Zenger-Miller:

How would you describe your value to the company now?

Ronald Deane:

Now my biggest value is in building teams, helping people to participate, so my scope is much broader. I develop people, coach them, help them gain new skills so they're more productive. The biggest thing, and the nicest, is seeing so many quiet individuals step forward and make real contributions to the business. So my role is more valuable now than it was before. I can contribute to the bottom line of the company a great deal more than I could then.

Zenger-Miller:

What was toughest thing for you in making this transition?

Ronald Deane:

For me it was to just let the people do their jobs and make the daily decisions. I wasn't confident at that point in letting them make all the decisions that they really needed to run the business. But more and more, as I saw they were making high-grade decisions and really participating in the business, my confidence grew.

Zenger-Miller:

What was the key for you, the thing that allowed you to succeed?

Ronald Deane:

I had to learn a lot of new skills because to a great extent I was the old style supervisor. I had a lot of struggles with that personally.

Zenger-Miller:

Was the struggling pretty common here—with your peers, for example?

Ronald Deane:

Oh, yes. Some of my peers are not here any longer because they couldn't make the change. I was very surprised at who those people were because I thought that they would be the very ones who would be the champions. What I learned, and this was a big help for me, was it wasn't so much a natural thing. If I developed my skills, I could do it.

Some of my peers are not here any longer . . .

Zenger-Miller:

Is there any particular skill you find really important?

Ronald Deane:

Facilitating and coaching skills are the two biggest—the ability to help them move through the decision-making process instead of telling them how to do the job.

Zenger-Miller:

Are there times when you have to reassert your own authority? Or do you mostly let them learn from their own mistakes?

Ronald Deane:

You have to let them make mistakes from time to time, fall on their face a little bit. But there are times when you do have to step in—if the business is at certain risk levels. So we set boundaries for the teams and let them know that they can make decisions within those boundaries. Then, as they grow and mature, we increase the boundaries so they can make larger decisions in a greater span of influence.

Zenger-Miller:

One of the things I keep hearing about today is the need to "get people involved in the business." What have you done specifically to make that happen?

Ronald Deane:

That's one of the keys for us—to help people understand that they have a real important role. For example, we brought the president of the company over, and he brown-bagged it with the teams. We've just had a lot of information passed on from him, from the marketing group, from the R & D group. We spend a lot of time making people more knowledgeable about the business, helping them understand what we are trying to do and their part in it. Team members lead visitor tours and explain what we do at Spectra Physics and talk about the business themselves. All that has had a real important impact because it brings the business much closer to the floor.

> *. . . we brought the president of the company over, and he brown-bagged it with the teams.*

Zenger-Miller:

What advice would you have for a traditional manager about to make this transition?

Ronald Deane:

I think the issue is really change. Change itself. You first of all have to accept the fact that the change is going to occur. Your job is not going to remain static. And if it does then you'll fall behind. There is only one train. You've got to make that commitment to be on that train. The other issue is you have to realize that you make that transition by developing skills. There are lots of skills you need—facilitating, coaching, people development—all kinds of areas where you need to grow.

Zenger-Miller:

Any final thought for someone like yourself of three or four years ago?

Ronald Deane:

The issue is the need to make a commitment. You need to pay the price because the people who won't will probably fall away. It is certainly worth it to the business and to those who remain. Participation goes right to the bottom line of the company.

You need to pay the price because the people who won't will probably fall away.

Index

Action steps and follow-up, team decisions, 70
Alignment, and team environment, 164–67
American Express, 52, 135, 154
American Institute for Managing Diversity, 119
Amex Life Assurance, 16, 17, 27, 30, 48, 54, 59, 74, 87, 101, 102, 112, 120, 137, 153, 155, 158, 166, 169
Anders, Barb, 52, 135, 154

Balancing internal technical and social systems, 129–30
Baldwin, Randy, 102
Balloon approach to decision making, 58–59
Basic principles of management
focus on issue, behavior, or problem, 43–45
initiating improvements, 48–49
lead by example, 49–50
maintaining constructive relationships, 47–48
maintaining others' self-confidence and self-esteem, 45–47
and team differences, 111–12
Bermudez, Norma, 155, 169
Black & Decker, 54, 130, 135, 136
Boeing, 169
Boetzkes, Gus, 27, 89, 123, 166, 236–240
Boyle, Mike, 73, 112, 169
Bridging gaps between departments, 8–9
Broad view of work, and process improvement, 148–52

Campbell, Alan, 18, 36, 76, 125, 126, 172, 173, 196–201
Candor, and team differences, 113
Carnevale, Anthony, 120
Celebrating accomplishments and learning from mistakes, 99–100
Center for Effective Organization, 7
Change
and balancing internal technical and social systems, 129–30

and closed-system view of world, 126–27
and developing others' potential, 134–35
directing in a team environment, 135–36
and forward thinking, 123–26
and information analysis, 132–33
making case, for, 133–34
and monitoring environment, 131–32
and open-system view of world, 127–28
and participative leadership, 125
traditional leadership reaction to, 124–25
working with others to bring about, 134–35
Change implementation, participative leadership, 125
Chinn, Sharon, 32, 102, 123, 143, 231–235
Citibank, 16
Closed-system view of world, 126–27
Coaching teams, 79, 81–82
Commitment to team decision, need for, 69–70
Conflict
containment of, traditional leadership, 109
dealing with, 108–9
and team differences, 114–19
Conflict resolution, participative leadership, 109
Conover, Jean, 16, 112
Consensus decision, teams and, 61–63, 67–70
Constructive relationship maintenance, 47–48
Cross-functional teams, 12–13
Customer-driven organization, 7, 13, 14
Customer-oriented approach, 144–45
Customer satisfaction
as primary aim, 6–7
and process improvement, 136, 148–52

Deane, Ron, 15, 19, 37, 73, 174, 279–282
Decision making; see also Team decision making
balloon approach to, 58–59
input for, participative leadership, 54
yo-yo approach to, 58

For more information about Zenger-Miller's training systems and services and its Achieve International Division's strategic consulting services, contact:

Zenger-Miller, Inc.
1735 Technology Drive, 6th Floor
San Jose, CA 95110-1313
Tel. (408) 452-1244
Fax (408) 452-1155

— Offices throughout North America and worldwide —
(represented in Canada by The Achieve Group)

A Division of Zenger-Miller, Inc.

Please indicate areas of interest:

Skills Training for:
__ Team Leaders
__ Management Development
__ Front-Line Employees
__ Executives
__ Quality and/or Team Implementations

Strategic Consulting and Planning Services for:
__ Service/Quality
__ Self-Directed Work Teams
__ Organization Change

Name _____

Title _____

Organization _____

Address _____

_____

Telephone (____)_____

There are _____ employees in my organization
and _____ employees at my site.

Type of Business _____

BUSINESS REPLY MAIL

FIRST CLASS MAIL   PERMIT NO. 592   SAN JOSE CA

POSTAGE WILL BE PAID BY ADDRESSEE

ZENGER-MILLER
6TH FLOOR
1735 TECHNOLOGY DRIVE
SAN JOSE CA 95110-9971